A+ taste of home RECIPES

from SCHOOLS Across America

taste of home
B O O K S

taste of home Readers Digest

A TASTE OF HOME/READER'S DIGEST BOOK

© 2011 Reiman Media Group, LLC
5400 S. 60th St., Greendale WI 53129
All rights reserved.

Taste of Home and Reader's Digest are registered trademarks of The Reader's Digest Association, Inc.

Editor-in-Chief: Catherine Cassidy
Vice President, Executive Editor/Books:
Heidi Reuter Lloyd
Creative Director: Howard Greenberg
North American Chief Marketing Officer:
Lisa Karpinski
Food Director: Diane Werner, RD
Senior Editor/Retail Books: Faithann Stoner
Editors: Janet Briggs, Sara Lancaster
Associate Creative Director: Edwin Robles Jr.

Content Production Manager: Julie Wagner
Layout Designers: Catherine Fletcher,
Kathy Crawford, Monica Bergwall
Copy Chief: Deb Warlaumont Mulvey
Proofreaders: Victoria Soukup Jensen,
Julie Schnittka, Barbara Schuetz
Recipe Asset System Manager: Coleen Martin
Recipe Testing & Editing: Taste of Home Test Kitchen
Food Photography: Taste of Home Photo Studio
Administrative Assistant: Barb Czysz

The Reader's Digest Association, Inc.
President and Chief Executive Officer:
Tom Williams
**Executive Vice President, RDA, & President,
North America:** Dan Lagani
President/Publisher, Trade Publishing:
Harold Clarke
Associate Publisher: Rosanne McManus
Vice President, Sales & Marketing: Stacey Ashton

For other Taste of Home books and products, visit us at **tasteofhome.com.**

For more Reader's Digest products and information, visit **rd.com** (in the United States) or **rd.ca** (in Canada).

International Standard Book Number (10):
0-89821-912-4
International Standard Book Number (13):
978-0-89821-912-8
Library of Congress Control Number: 2011927345

Cover Photography
Photographer: Rob Hagen
Food Stylist: Ronne Day
Set Stylist: Dee Dee Jacq

Pictured on front cover, clockwise from bottom:
Chocolate Ganache Peanut Butter Cupcakes, pg. 183;
Quinoa and Black Bean Salad, pg. 59; and
Chicken Marsala Lasagna, pg. 106.

Pictured on back cover, from top to bottom:
Thai Chicken Lettuce Wraps, pg. 162; Baked Greek Ratatouille, pg. 37; and Tuscan Burgers with Pesto Mayo, pg. 141.

Additional Photo Credits:
All photos except for food pg. 4-5
— Larissa Rhodes/Final Hour Films LLC

Melissa Williams/THS Faculty Photo
pg. 203 — Fun Photo/David A. Pickett

Printed in China.
1 3 5 7 9 10 8 6 4 2

contents

Introduction 4

APPETIZERS & SIDES

Appetizers & Snacks.. 7

Soups, Salads & Sides 37

MAIN DISHES

Entrees 93

Healthy Entrees 147

DESSERTS & TREATS

Desserts 167

Bake Sale Treats 199

TASTE OF HOME GRAND-PRIZE WINNERS

Grand-Prize Winners 223

Indexes.. 250

PG. 22

PG. 98

PG. 213

THE RESULTS ARE IN!

Books Are Fun℠ *presents the* taste of home. TEACHERS RECIPE CONTEST

Teachers earn top grades when it comes to good food! With all of those bake sales, potlucks and special events in the teachers lounge, schools are an ideal place to collect fabulous recipes.

That's why **Taste of Home** and **Books Are Fun** joined together to sponsor a huge recipe contest for teachers, school staff and volunteers. In fact, it was our biggest contest ever, with $70,000 in prizes provided by **Books Are Fun**. More than 14,000 **contest entries** poured in from coast to coast!

After sorting, testing, tasting and reviewing the recipes, we compiled the absolute best into this cookbook, including the top three recipes from the cooks who took home the cash. A drum roll from the school pep band, please...

The $20,000 **Grand-Prize Winner** is **Ronda Schabes**. Her divine **Chocolate Ganache Peanut Butter Cupcakes** won over our judges. This rich chocolate cupcake with a surprise peanut butter center is covered with a silky chocolate ganache and then topped with a smooth peanut butter frosting that just melts in your mouth. A matching check for $20,000 was given to Sunset Lake Elementary in **Vicksburg, Michigan**, where Ronda is on staff.

Debbie Shannon won second place and a cash prize of $10,000 for her delectable **Chicken Marsala Lasagna**. Bring your appetite when you sample this hearty entree.

Lasagna noodles are layered with a fantastic portobello mushroom-wine sauce that has bits of ham and chicken and a three-cheese spinach mixture...absolutely *delizioso*. Debbie is a teacher at **Rossville Elementary** in **Rossville, Georgia.** Her school received a matching $10,000 check.

The $5,000 third-place prize was awarded to **Yvonne Compton** and her striking **Quinoa and Black Bean Salad**. Yvonne crowned quick-cooking, good-for-you quinoa with a festive mixture of orange peppers, red onion, black beans, corn, cherry tomatoes and avocado. A lime vinaigrette gives the dazzling dish a wonderful flavor. **Elkton Charter School** in **Elkton, Oregon,** where Yvonne is a teacher, received a $5,000 check.

This book is organized into **three sections—Appetizers & More, Main Dishes** and **Desserts & Treats.** Plus, there is a special bonus section... **Grand-Prize Winners from Taste of Home** national recipe contests. You'll find recipes for appetizers, bake sales, potlucks, lunchtime, weeknight dinners and much more.

You can be assured that these dishes will work since they were all **tested by the cooking professionals** at **Taste of Home**, the world's #1 food and entertaining magazine. Each recipe has clear, concise directions and uses ingredients that are available in most supermarkets.

Imagine the smiles on the faces of your family members when they taste one of the scrumptious winners in this cookbook. Don't delay. Cook up a winning recipe tonight. You'll be happy you did.

Willow Street, Pennsylvania

You might say teaching is in Ellen Finger's blood. "According to my grandmother's calculations, I'm the 10th teacher in the family during her lifetime," she says. For the past three years, Ellen has been the academic support teacher at Pequea Elementary. "My favorite thing to do in the classroom is story-telling," she says. "It is an incredibly interesting way to teach the students without them knowing it!"

TEACHER'S CAVIAR

I love the fresh flavors, colors and convenience of this dish. It adds fun to a workday lunch without adding inches to the waistline or putting a dent in the food budget. This can be served immediately or chilled in the morning and eaten at lunch time! I think it's delicious with baked tortilla chips or spooned over grilled chicken.

Ellen Finger, Lancaster, Pennsylvania

2 cans (15 ounces each) black beans, rinsed and drained

2 medium tomatoes, seeded and chopped

1-1/2 cups frozen corn, thawed

1 medium ripe avocado, peeled and cubed

1 can (8 ounces) unsweetened pineapple chunks, drained and quartered

1 medium sweet orange pepper, chopped

6 green onions, thinly sliced

1/2 cup minced fresh cilantro

1/3 cup lime juice

2 tablespoons olive oil

2 tablespoons honey

1/2 teaspoon salt

1/8 teaspoon cayenne pepper

Baked tortilla chip scoops

1. In a large bowl, combine the first eight ingredients.
2. In a small bowl, whisk the lime juice, oil, honey, salt and cayenne. Pour over bean mixture; toss to coat. Serve with baked chips.

YIELD: 8 CUPS.

NUTRITIONAL FACTS: 1/4 cup (calculated without chips) equals 56 calories, 2 g fat (trace saturated fat), 0 cholesterol, 90 mg sodium, 9 g carbohydrate, 2 g fiber, 2 g protein. DIABETIC EXCHANGE: 1/2 starch.

FETA CHEESE BALLS

Dill and garlic go well with the tang of feta in this cheese ball...in fact, I think it tastes like a million bucks. It's super easy to do, and since the recipe makes two, it's ideal for gatherings.

Teacher, St. Philip Neri School, Metairie, Louisiana

Kelly Yeager, Hahnville, Louisiana

2 packages (8 ounces each) cream cheese, softened
3 tablespoons olive oil
1 cup (4 ounces) crumbled feta cheese
5 green onions, chopped
3 garlic cloves, minced
1 tablespoon dill weed
2 teaspoons dried oregano
3/4 teaspoon coarsely ground pepper
Bagel chips

1. In a large bowl, beat cream cheese and oil until smooth. Stir in the feta cheese, onions, garlic, dill, oregano and pepper. Cover and refrigerate for at least 1 hour.

2. Shape cheese mixture into two balls. Wrap in plastic wrap; refrigerate for at least 1 hour. Serve with bagel chips.

YIELD: 2 CHEESE BALLS (1-1/4 CUPS EACH).

NUTRITION FACTS: 2 tablespoons (calculated without chips) equals 114 calories, 11 g fat (6 g saturated fat), 28 mg cholesterol, 122 mg sodium, 1 g carbohydrate, trace fiber, 3 g protein.

Teacher, Hough Street School

Barrington, Illinois

Terry Skibiski has been teaching for 30 years and currently teaches fourth grade. Terry says he likes to bring his love of cooking into the classroom whenever he can. "Once, when we were frying wontons for Chinese New Year, another teacher thought she smelled smoke and told the principal. The principal calmly responded, 'That must be Terry cooking again.' Since then, the incident has been fondly remembered as our Chinese Fire Drill," Terry recalls.

CANADIAN MEATBALLS

Whenever we have a brunch at school, I always make these meatballs. Everyone looks forward to sampling them. The recipe yields about five dozen, so they are ideal for potlucks.

Terry Skibiski, Barrington, Illinois

2 eggs, lightly beaten

1/2 cup evaporated milk

1 cup dry bread crumbs

1 cup (4 ounces) shredded cheddar cheese

2/3 cup finely chopped onion

1 pound bulk pork sausage

1 pound bulk spicy pork sausage

MAPLE SAUCE:

2 tablespoons cornstarch

1 cup chili sauce

1 cup maple syrup

2 tablespoons Worcestershire sauce

2 teaspoons maple flavoring

1. In a large bowl, combine the eggs, milk, bread crumbs, cheese and onion. Crumble sausages over mixture and mix well. With wet hands, shape into 1-in. balls.

2. Place meatballs on a greased rack in a shallow baking pan. Bake, uncovered, at 400° for 15-20 minutes or until no longer pink. Drain on paper towels.

3. Meanwhile, in a large skillet, whisk the sauce ingredients until smooth. Bring to a boil. Cook and stir for 1-2 minutes or until thickened. Add meatballs; stir to coat.

YIELD: 5 DOZEN.

NUTRITION FACTS: 1 meatball with about 1 teaspoon sauce equals 70 calories, 4 g fat (2 g saturated fat), 15 mg cholesterol, 158 mg sodium, 7 g carbohydrate, trace fiber, 2 g protein.

Staff, Grant Bowler
Elementary School

Logandale, Nevada

Nancy Leavitt is proud to be a staff member of Grand Bowler Elementary. The best part of her job, she says, is seeing the students' progress throughout the school year. A close second would be the annual May Day dance, a school tradition that dates back 100 years!

FRUIT SALSA WITH CINNAMON TORTILLA CHIPS

If you are serious about getting your fruit servings in, this is a fun way to do it. The bright red fruit salsa is addictive, and best eaten the day it is made.

Nancy Leavitt, Logandale, Nevada

1 pound fresh strawberries, finely chopped

2 medium apples, peeled and finely chopped

1 package (12 ounces) frozen unsweetened raspberries, thawed and well drained

2 medium kiwifruit, peeled and finely chopped

3 tablespoons peach or apricot preserves

2 tablespoons sugar

1 tablespoon brown sugar

CINNAMON TORTILLA CHIPS:

Oil for deep-fat frying

10 flour tortillas (10 inches)

1/2 cup sugar

2 teaspoons ground cinnamon

1. In a large bowl, combine the first seven ingredients; cover and chill for 20 minutes or until serving.

2. In an electric skillet or deep-fat fryer, heat oil to 375°. Cut each tortilla in half; cut each half into 10 strips. Fry strips, a few at a time, until light golden brown on both sides. Drain on paper towels.

3. Combine sugar and cinnamon; sprinkle over strips and toss to coat. Serve with salsa.

YIELD: 6 CUPS SALSA AND ABOUT 16 DOZEN TORTILLA CHIPS.

NUTRITION FACTS: 1/4 cup salsa with 8 chips equals 166 calories, 4 g fat (1 g saturated fat), 0 cholesterol, 165 mg sodium, 28 g carbohydrate, 4 g fiber, 3 g protein.

GOAT CHEESE SPREAD IN ROASTED PEPPER CUPS

I had a similar dish at a restaurant in Seattle. When I returned home, I just had to try my hand at making it. This is the fantastic result. I've taken it to work for parties, where my boss once commented, "It's so good, it must be illegal."

Teacher, Delta High School, Richland, Washington

Jenny Rodriquez, Pasco, Washington

4 medium sweet red peppers
3 tablespoons olive oil, divided
1 medium onion, finely chopped
4 garlic cloves, minced
1 package (8 ounces) cream cheese, softened
8 ounces fresh goat cheese, softened
1 cup grated Parmesan cheese
2 to 3 medium tomatoes, seeded and finely chopped
2 tablespoons minced fresh cilantro
1 tablespoon minced fresh parsley
1/2 teaspoon hot pepper sauce
1/8 teaspoon salt
1/8 teaspoon pepper

HERBED GARLIC TOASTS:

1/2 cup butter, softened
1 tablespoon minced fresh parsley
2 garlic cloves, minced
24 slices French bread baguette (1/4 inch thick)

1. Remove tops and seeds from peppers; rub with 1 tablespoon oil. Place in an ungreased 8-in. square baking dish. Bake, uncovered, at 350° for 15-20 minutes. Remove from oven; turn peppers upside down in baking dish to drain.

2. In a small skillet, saute onion in remaining oil until tender. Add garlic; cook 1 minute longer. Transfer to a large bowl. Stir in the cheeses, tomatoes, cilantro, parsley, pepper sauce, salt and pepper. Spoon into pepper cups; return to baking dish.

3. Bake, uncovered, at 350° for 25-30 minutes or until heated through.

4. Meanwhile, in a small bowl, combine the butter, parsley and garlic; spread over the baguette slices. Place on an ungreased baking sheet. Bake at 350° for 10-12 minutes or until lightly browned. Serve with cheese spread.

YIELD: 8 SERVINGS.

NUTRITION FACTS: 1/2 cup spread with 3 toasts equals 445 calories, 35 g fat (19 g saturated fat), 89 mg cholesterol, 583 mg sodium, 23 g carbohydrate, 3 g fiber, 12 g protein.

Teacher, East Alton-Wood
River High School

Wood River, Illinois

Kelly Gardner's love for teaching extends beyond the walls of East Alton-Wood River High School. When Kelly isn't teaching her students the ins and outs of the English language or great American literature, she teaches weekend cooking classes, maintains a food blog (barbaricgulp.com) and writes for a monthly food magazine.

CARAMELIZED ONION DIP

Once you taste this fabulous dip, you'll discover how much better it is than the store-bought variety. While it takes a little longer to make, I promise you'll never go back.

Kelly Gardner, Alton, Illinois

2 large onions, finely chopped

2 tablespoons olive oil

3/4 cup sour cream

3/4 cup plain Greek yogurt

3 teaspoons onion powder

1/2 teaspoon salt

Potato chips, corn chips and/or assorted fresh vegetables

1. In a large skillet, saute onions in oil until softened. Reduce heat to medium-low; cook, stirring occasionally, for 30 minutes or until deep golden brown. Cool completely.

2. In a small bowl, combine the sour cream, yogurt, onion powder and salt; stir in two-thirds cooked onions. Transfer to a serving bowl; top with remaining onions. Serve with chips and vegetables.

YIELD: 2 CUPS.

NUTRITION FACTS: 1/4 cup (calculated without chips and vegetables) equals 117 calories, 9 g fat (4 g saturated fat), 21 mg cholesterol, 170 mg sodium, 6 g carbohydrate, 1 g fiber, 2 g protein.

Staff, Northwestern
Lehigh School District

New Tripoli, Pennsylvania

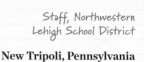

Tammy Rex has been an instructional assistant for eight years in the Northwestern Lehigh School District. She describes working in an elementary school as an adventure. "The kids do and say things that make life interesting every day," she comments. But what she enjoys most is knowing she is helping students succeed in challenging subject areas.

BACON AND FONTINA STUFFED MUSHROOMS

What's better than lots of bacon and cheese in a mushroom cap? You'll be saying "yum"—and so will your guests.

Tammy Rex, New Tripoli, Pennsylvania

24 large fresh mushrooms

4 ounces cream cheese, softened

1 cup (4 ounces) shredded fontina cheese

8 bacon strips, cooked and crumbled

4 green onions, chopped

1/4 cup chopped oil-packed sun-dried tomatoes

3 tablespoons minced fresh parsley

1 tablespoon olive oil

1. Remove stems from mushrooms and set caps aside; discard stems or save for another use. In a small bowl, combine the cream cheese, fontina cheese, bacon, onions, sun-dried tomatoes and parsley. Fill each mushroom cap with about 1 tablespoon of filling.

2. Place on a greased baking sheet. Drizzle with oil. Bake, uncovered, at 425° for 8-10 minutes or until mushrooms are tender.

YIELD: 2 DOZEN.

NUTRITION FACTS: 1 stuffed mushroom equals 60 calories, 5 g fat (2 g saturated fat), 13 mg cholesterol, 105 mg sodium, 2 g carbohydrate, trace fiber, 3 g protein.

CHESAPEAKE CRAB DIP

Our school is a Maryland Green School. As such, many of our students work to improve the health of our local treasure: the Chesapeake Bay. Crab stars in this rich, creamy dip that reminds me of the importance of a healthy Bay.

Teacher, Triadelphia Ridge Elementary School
Ellicott City, Maryland

Carol Brzezinski, Marriottsville, Maryland

1 package (8 ounces) cream cheese, softened

1 cup (8 ounces) sour cream

1 tablespoon lemon juice

1 teaspoon ground mustard

1 teaspoon seafood seasoning

1/8 teaspoon garlic salt

3 cans (6 ounces each) lump crabmeat, drained

1/2 cup shredded cheddar cheese

1/8 teaspoon paprika

Assorted crackers

1. In a large bowl, combine the cream cheese, sour cream, lemon juice, mustard, seafood seasoning and garlic salt. Fold in crab. Transfer to a greased 9-in. pie plate. Sprinkle with cheese and paprika.

2. Bake at 325° for 20-25 minutes or until bubbly. Serve warm with crackers.

YIELD: 2-1/4 CUPS.

NUTRITION FACTS: 3 tablespoons dip (calculated without the crackers) equals 166 calories, 12 g fat (8 g saturated fat), 77 mg cholesterol, 307 mg sodium, 2 g carbohydrate, trace fiber, 12 g protein.

Teacher
Northwood High School

Pittsboro, North Carolina

Jackie Milliken teaches foods and nutrition and advises Northwood's Family, Career and Community Leaders of America organization. "There's nothing like a student telling you that you have made a positive impact in their lives," she says. "To know I'm influencing students to make healthier choices and positive decisions makes my job exciting and rewarding."

BACON-SAUSAGE QUICHE TARTS

As a teacher, you attend many meetings and various special celebrations with rest of the staff. The other teachers are very fond of this treat and often request that I bring it to our functions.

Jackie Milliken, Pittsboro, North Carolina

2 cans (12 ounces each) refrigerated buttermilk biscuits

6 uncooked breakfast sausage links, chopped

2 tablespoons chopped onion

2 tablespoons chopped fresh mushrooms

2 tablespoons chopped green pepper

1 package (8 ounces) cream cheese, softened

2 tablespoons heavy whipping cream

3 eggs

1-1/2 cups (6 ounces) finely shredded cheddar cheese, divided

5 bacon strips, cooked and crumbled

1. Split each biscuit into two layers; press each into an ungreased miniature muffin cup.

2. In a large skillet, cook the sausage, onion, mushrooms and pepper over medium heat until meat is no longer pink and the vegetables are tender; drain.

3. In a large bowl, beat cream cheese and cream until smooth. Beat in eggs. Fold in 3/4 cup cheddar cheese and the sausage mixture. Spoon 1 tablespoon into each cup. Sprinkle with bacon and remaining cheese. Bake at 375° for 10-15 minutes or until golden brown. Serve warm.

YIELD: 40 APPETIZERS.

NUTRITION FACTS: 1 tart equals 97 calories, 5 g fat (3 g saturated fat), 30 mg cholesterol, 245 mg sodium, 9 g carbohydrate, trace fiber, 4 g protein.

Teacher, Kahoa Elementary

Lincoln, Nebraska

As an elementary music teacher and choir director, Jerri Gradert gets to share her love for creative expression with students through music. Outside of the classroom, she enjoys getting creative in the kitchen by preparing and improvising recipes.

GINGERED CRAN-ORANGE SALSA OVER CREAM CHEESE

Fresh cranberries make an unusual but sensational salsa. I especially like it in the fall when the fruit is readily available. The brilliant red color attracts partygoers.

Jerri Gradert, Lincoln, Nebraska

1 package (8 ounces) cream cheese, softened

1-1/2 cups fresh cranberries, rinsed and patted dry

1 cup fresh cilantro leaves

6 tablespoons sugar

1-1/2 teaspoons chopped seeded jalapeno pepper

3/4 teaspoon minced fresh gingerroot

1/4 cup chopped pecans

3 tablespoons thinly sliced green onions, divided

1 tablespoon orange juice

Assorted crackers or baked pita chips

1. Place cream cheese on a rimmed serving plate.

2. In a food processor, combine the cranberries, cilantro, sugar, jalapeno and ginger; cover and pulse until finely chopped. Stir in the pecans, 2 tablespoons green onions and orange juice. Spoon over cream cheese; sprinkle with remaining green onion. Serve with crackers.

YIELD: 8 SERVINGS.

EDITOR'S NOTES: We recommend wearing disposable gloves when cutting hot peppers. Avoid touching your face.

NUTRITION FACTS: 2-1/2 tablespoons salsa with 2 tablespoons cream cheese (calculated without crackers) equals 171 calories, 13 g fat (6 g saturated fat), 31 mg cholesterol, 86 mg sodium, 13 g carbohydrate, 1 g fiber, 3 g protein.

MANGO SALSA

Fresh mango adds eye-catching color and an interesting twist to this healthy and vibrant fruit salsa.

Teacher, Martin Murphy Middle School, San Jose, California

Mala Udayamurthy, San Jose, California

2 medium mangoes, peeled and finely chopped

1/4 cup finely chopped red onion

1/4 cup finely chopped green pepper

1/4 cup finely chopped sweet red pepper

1 jalapeno pepper, chopped

3 tablespoons minced fresh cilantro

2 tablespoons cider vinegar

1 tablespoon sugar

1 tablespoon olive oil

1/2 teaspoon salt

1/2 teaspoon pepper

Assorted crackers or baked potato chips

1. In a large bowl, combine the first 11 ingredients. Chill until serving. Serve with crackers or chips.

YIELD: 2-1/4 CUPS.

EDITOR'S NOTES: We recommend wearing disposable gloves when cutting hot peppers. Avoid touching your face.

NUTRITION FACTS: 1/4 cup (calculated without crackers or baked potato chips) equals 54 calories, 2 g fat (trace saturated fat), 0 cholesterol, 133 mg sodium, 10 g carbohydrate, 1 g fiber, trace protein. DIABETIC EXCHANGE: 1 starch.

Teacher, Chinn Elementary

Kansas City, Missouri

Cara Langer has been teaching first grade for 10 years. She says working with children at such a young age is incredibly rewarding because she gets to lay the groundwork for them to become lifelong learners.

HOT BACON CHEDDAR SPREAD

This is one of my go-to recipes whenever I have people over. The warm and luscious dip is always quite popular.

Cara Langer, Overland Park, Kansas

1 package (8 ounces) cream cheese, softened

1/2 cup mayonnaise

1/4 teaspoon dried thyme

1/8 teaspoon pepper

1 cup (4 ounces) shredded sharp cheddar cheese

3 green onions, chopped

8 bacon strips, cooked and crumbled, divided

1/2 cup crushed butter-flavored crackers

Assorted crackers

1. In a large bowl, combine the cream cheese, mayonnaise, thyme and pepper. Stir in the cheese, green onions and half the bacon. Transfer to a greased 3-cup baking dish.

2. Bake, uncovered, at 350° for 13-15 minutes or until bubbly. Top with crushed crackers and remaining bacon. Serve with assorted crackers.

YIELD: 3 CUPS.

NUTRITION FACTS: 2 tablespoons (calculated without crackers) equals 105 calories, 10 g fat (4 g saturated fat), 19 mg cholesterol, 146 mg sodium, 2 g carbohydrate, trace fiber, 3 g protein.

Staff, Andrew G. Curtin Middle School

Williamsport, Pennsylvania

As a personal instructional support aide, Linda Ross works with primary grade school children who have autism. She loves being able to work one-on-one with the students and help them succeed in the classroom. "The best part for me is the smiles on their faces and the sparkle in their eyes when they learn and understand new things."

HUEVOS DIABLOS

You'll think these eggs really do have a bit of devil's heat in them. For a milder version, remove the ribs and seeds from the jalapeno. My brother-in-law, Tom, is the official deviled egg-maker in our family. I created this recipe for him so that he could step outside of the box occasionally.

Linda Ross, Williamsport, Pennsylvania

12 hard-cooked eggs

6 tablespoons minced fresh cilantro, divided

6 tablespoons mayonnaise

2 green onions, thinly sliced

1/4 cup sour cream

1 jalapeno pepper, seeded and minced

1-1/2 teaspoons grated lime peel

1 teaspoon ground cumin

1/4 teaspoon salt

1/8 teaspoon pepper

1. Cut eggs in half lengthwise. Remove yolks; set whites aside.

2. In a small bowl, mash yolks. Add 3 tablespoons cilantro, mayonnaise, onions, sour cream, jalapeno, lime peel, cumin, salt and pepper; mix well.

3. Stuff or pipe into egg whites. Refrigerate until serving. Garnish with remaining cilantro.

YIELD: 2 DOZEN.

NUTRITION FACTS: 1 stuffed egg half equals 70 calories, 6 g fat (1 g saturated fat), 109 mg cholesterol, 76 mg sodium, 1 g carbohydrate, trace fiber, 3 g protein.

JALAPENO POPPER DIP

Here's a fantastic way to deliver all that blazing jalapeno popper taste without the work. Whenever I bring this jazzed-up dip to a party, I'm always asked for the recipe. Serve it with corn chips, tortilla chips or butter crackers.

Staff, Webster Elementary School, Collinsville, Illinois

Jennifer Wilke, Collinsville, Illinois

2 packages (8 ounces each) cream cheese, softened

1 cup mayonnaise

1/2 cup shredded cheddar cheese

1 can (4 ounces) chopped green chilies

1 can (4 ounces) diced jalapeno peppers

1/2 cup shredded Parmesan cheese, divided

1/2 cup seasoned bread crumbs

1 tablespoon olive oil

Tortilla chips, corn chips or assorted crackers

1. In a large bowl, beat the cream cheese, mayonnaise, cheddar, chilies, peppers and 1/4 cup Parmesan until blended. Spoon into an ungreased 1-1/2-qt. baking dish.

2. In a small bowl, combine the bread crumbs, oil and remaining Parmesan. Sprinkle over cheese mixture. Bake, uncovered, at 350° for 20-25 min. or until golden brown. Serve with chips or crackers.

YIELD: 16 SERVINGS (1/4 CUP EACH).

NUTRITION FACTS: 1/4 cup (calculated without chips and crackers) equals 245 calories, 24 g fat (9 g saturated fat), 42 mg cholesterol, 322 mg sodium, 4 g carbohydrate, trace fiber, 4 g protein.

Mary Jo Slater has volunteered in numerous capacities at Belpre Elementary School over the past few years. "The best part of being a volunteer for the school is to see the smiles on the students' faces when they get to use gym and playground equipment the school and PTO worked together to purchase."

PUMPKIN MOUSSE DIP

I originally received this recipe from my daughter's Girl Scout leader. The fluffy pumpkin dip is great served with gingersnaps, honey graham sticks or pear or apple wedges.

Mary Jo Slater, Belpre, Ohio

1 cup canned pumpkin

1/2 cup confectioners' sugar

1 package (3 ounces) cream cheese, softened

1/2 teaspoon ground cinnamon

1 carton (8 ounces) frozen whipped topping, thawed

Gingersnap cookies and/or pear slices

1. In a large bowl, beat the pumpkin, sugar, cream cheese and cinnamon until smooth. Fold in whipped topping. Refrigerate until serving. Serve with gingersnaps and pear slices.

YIELD: 16 SERVINGS (1/4 CUP EACH).

NUTRITION FACTS: 1/4 cup (calculated without cookies and pears) equals 78 calories, 4 g fat (4 g saturated fat), 6 mg cholesterol, 16 mg sodium, 8 g carbohydrate, 1 g fiber, 1 g protein.

Teacher
Walter Johnson Middle School

Morganton, North Carolina

Donna Lindecamp teaches foreign language (French and Spanish) at Walter Johnson Middle School. In that role, she has the opportunity to teach every student in the school. "I am not limited to just one grade level. I get to see them all," she says

MEDITERRANEAN ARTICHOKE AND RED PEPPER ROLL-UPS

I crave these roll-ups. Not only are they easy to make, they are quite tasty, too. In fact, one roll-up packs in so much flavor, I sometimes enjoy them as is, without the sauce.

Donna Lindecamp, Morganton, North Carolina

1 can (14 ounces) water-packed artichoke hearts, rinsed, drained and finely chopped

4 ounces cream cheese, softened

1/3 cup grated Parmesan cheese

1/4 cup crumbled feta cheese

2 green onions, thinly sliced

3 tablespoons prepared pesto

8 flour tortillas (8 inches), warmed

1 jar (7-1/2 ounces) roasted sweet red peppers, drained and cut into strips

SAUCE:

1 cup (8 ounces) sour cream

1 tablespoon minced chives

1. In a small bowl, combine the artichokes, cream cheese, Parmesan cheese, feta cheese, green onions and pesto until blended. Spread 1/4 cup mixture over each tortilla; top with red peppers and roll up tightly.

2. Place 1 in. apart on a greased baking sheet. Bake at 350° for 12-15 minutes or until heated through. Cut into thirds. Meanwhile, in a small bowl, combine sour cream and chives. Serve with roll-ups.

YIELD: 2 DOZEN.

NUTRITION FACTS: 1 appetizer with 1 teaspoon sauce equals 112 calories, 6 g fat (3 g saturated fat), 14 mg cholesterol, 217 mg sodium, 11 g carbohydrate, trace fiber, 4 g protein.

MACADAMIA-COCONUT CANDY CLUSTERS

These special treats are super easy to make. They are perfect for bake sales, teacher gifts or candy platters. They're also a nice change from milk or dark chocolate clusters.

Volunteer, Lone Oak Elementary, Paducah, Kentucky

Lori Bondurant, Paducah, Kentucky

1 package (10 to 12 ounces) white baking chips
2 teaspoons shortening
1 cup flaked coconut, toasted
1/2 cup crisp rice cereal
1/2 cup chopped macadamia nuts, toasted

1. In a microwave, melt baking chips and shortening; stir until smooth. Add the coconut, cereal and nuts.
2. Drop by teaspoonfuls onto waxed paper; let stand until set. Store in an airtight container at room temperature.

YIELD: 3-1/2 DOZEN.

NUTRITIONAL FACTS: 1 piece equals 62 calories, 4 g fat (2 g saturated fat), 1 mg cholesterol, 19 mg sodium, 6 g carbohydrate, trace fiber, 1 g protein.

Staff
Stow–Munroe Falls High School

Stow, Ohio

Heidi Der is a psychologist at Stow-Munroe Falls High School. The high school is home to several college tech prep initiatives in business, aviation, pre-engineering and culinary arts. In her role, Heidi enjoys helping those students with disabilities map their futures for life after high school. "It is exciting to see where their interests and skills will take them as they enter adulthood," she says.

PEAR-BLUE CHEESE TARTLETS

Here, I've combined some of my favorite ingredients into a sensational bite-size package.

Heidi Der, Stow, Ohio

2 large pears, peeled and finely chopped

2 tablespoons butter

2 tablespoons honey

Dash salt

1/4 cup Mascarpone cheese

1/4 cup crumbled blue cheese

2 packages (1.9 ounces each) frozen miniature phyllo tart shells

1/4 cup finely chopped walnuts

1. In a small skillet, saute pears in butter for 2-3 minutes or until tender. Stir in honey and salt; cook for 4-5 minutes or until pears are lightly browned. Remove from the heat; cool slightly. Stir in cheeses.

2. Fill each tart shell with 1-1/2 teaspoons filling. Place on ungreased baking sheets. Sprinkle with walnuts. Bake at 350° for 6-8 minutes or until golden brown. Serve warm.

YIELD: 2-1/2 DOZEN.

NUTRITION FACTS: 1 tartlet equals 66 calories, 4 g fat (2 g saturated fat), 8 mg cholesterol, 37 mg sodium, 6 g carbohydrate, 1 g fiber, 1 g protein.

Teacher
Pioneer Elementary School

Royal Center, Indiana

Lisa Shaw currently teaches fourth grade at Pioneer Elementary. She says she loves the variety in her job. "Every day is different. You never know what the kids in your class are going to say next," she says. "It keeps life light and entertaining."

MOVIE THEATER PRETZEL RODS

My kids and all of their friends clamor for these large, chewy pretzel rods. They are fantastic fresh from the oven.

Lisa Shaw, Burnettsville, Indiana

1 package (1/4 ounce) active dry yeast

1-1/2 cups warm water (110° to 115°)

2 tablespoons sugar

2 tablespoons butter, melted

1-1/2 teaspoons salt

4 to 4-1/2 cups all-purpose flour

8 cups water

1/2 cup baking soda

1 egg yolk

1 tablespoon cold water

Coarse salt, optional

Cheese sauce for dipping, optional

1. In a large bowl, dissolve yeast in warm water. Add the sugar, butter, salt and 2 cups flour. Beat until smooth. Stir in enough remaining flour to form a soft dough (dough will be sticky).

2. Turn dough onto a floured surface; knead until smooth and elastic, about 6-8 minutes. Place in a greased bowl, turning once to grease top. Cover and let rise in a warm place until doubled, about 1 hour.

3. In a large saucepan, bring 8 cups water and baking soda to a boil. Punch dough down; divide into 32 portions. Roll each into a 5-in. log. Add to boiling water, a few at a time, for 30 seconds. Remove with a slotted spoon; drain on paper towels. Place on greased baking sheets. Lightly beat egg yolk and cold water; brush over pretzels. Sprinkle with coarse salt if desired. Bake 425° for 9-11 minutes or until golden brown. Remove from pans to wire racks. Serve warm with cheese sauce if desired.

YIELD: 32 PRETZEL RODS.

NUTRITION FACTS: 1 pretzel (calculated without coarse salt or cheese sauce) equals 68 calories, 1 g fat (1 g saturated fat), 8 mg cholesterol, 1,060 mg sodium, 13 g carbohydrate, trace fiber, 2 g protein.

SHRIMP SALAD COCKTAILS

Try serving this upscale appetizer in elegant stemmed glasses. For an extra-special touch that will wow your guests, garnish each with an extra shrimp.

Staff, Hope School, McClure, Ohio

Sue Sonnenberg, Napoleon, Ohio

2 cups mayonnaise

1/4 cup ketchup

1/4 cup lemon juice

1 tablespoon Worcestershire sauce

2 pounds peeled and deveined cooked large shrimp

2 celery ribs, finely chopped

3 tablespoons minced fresh tarragon or 3 teaspoons dried tarragon

1/4 teaspoon salt

1/4 teaspoon pepper

2 cups shredded romaine

2 cups seedless red and/or green grapes, halved

6 plum tomatoes, seeded and finely chopped

1/2 cup chopped peeled mango or papaya

Minced chives or parsley

1. In a small bowl, combine the mayonnaise, ketchup, lemon juice and Worcestershire sauce. In a large bowl, combine the shrimp, celery, tarragon, salt and pepper. Add 1 cup dressing; toss to coat.

2. Spoon 1 tablespoon dressing into eight cocktail glasses. Layer each with 1/4 cup lettuce, 1/2 cup shrimp mixture, 1/4 cup grapes, 1/3 cup tomatoes and 1 tablespoon mango. Top with the remaining dressing; sprinkle with the chives. Serve immediately.

YIELD: 8 SERVINGS.

NUTRITION FACTS: 1 serving equals 580 calories, 46 g fat (6 g saturated fat), 192 mg cholesterol, 670 mg sodium, 16 g carbohydrate, 2 g fiber, 24 g protein.

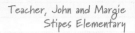

*Carolyn (Susie)
Borougerdi is the Read
Right Interventionist for
third through fifth grade
at John and Margie
Stipes Elementary. Seeing
her students "go from
nonreaders to readers" makes
everyday worthwhile.*

MOZZARELLA APPETIZER TARTLETS

These cheesy little cups are so easy to make but look impressive. Whenever I serve them, I can't seem to keep up with the demand—everyone always wants more!

Carolyn Borougerdi, Irving, Texas

1/4 cup olive oil

2 tablespoons Italian seasoning, divided

1 package (8 ounces) cream cheese, softened

1 teaspoon minced garlic

12 slices white bread, crusts removed

1 plum tomato, seeded and chopped

12 ounces fresh mozzarella cheese, cut into 12 slices

1. In a small bowl, combine the oil and 1 tablespoon Italian seasoning; set aside. In another small bowl, combine the cream cheese, garlic and remaining Italian seasoning; set aside.

2. Flatten the bread with a rolling pin. Brush one side with oil mixture; place oil side down in muffin cups. Spoon cream cheese mixture into each; top with chopped tomato and a cheese slice.

3. Bake at 350° for 10-15 minutes or until cheese is melted. Serve warm.

YIELD: 1 DOZEN.

NUTRITION FACTS: 1 tartlet equals 257 calories, 18 g fat (9 g saturated fat), 43 mg cholesterol, 268 mg sodium, 15 g carbohydrate, 1 g fiber, 9 g protein.

Teacher
George W. Julian Elementary

Indianapolis, Indiana

Katie Klee is a CADRE (Career Advancement and Development for Recruits and Experienced Teachers) teacher with Indianapolis Public Schools. Katie's work is filled with variety. "I am placed at multiple schools around the district and teach kindergarten through 12th grade classes for teachers who are attending professional development meetings," she says.

PHYLLO-WRAPPED BRIE WITH SUN-DRIED TOMATOES

My mom and I would always make this together because it's fast and easy. Using flaky phyllo dough is a different and tasty way to wrap up Brie.

Katie Klee, Noblesville, Indiana

2 tablespoons butter, melted

1 tablespoon oil from oil-packed sun-dried tomatoes

4 sheets phyllo dough

1 tablespoon chopped oil-packed sun-dried tomatoes

1 round (8 ounces) Brie cheese, rind removed

Assorted crackers

1. In a small bowl, combine butter and oil. Lightly brush one sheet of phyllo dough with some of the butter mixture; place another sheet of phyllo on top and brush with butter mixture. Repeat twice.

2. Cut layered phyllo into a 9-in. square; discard trimmings. Spread chopped tomatoes in the center of the square. Place Brie over tomatoes.

3. Brush corners of phyllo with 1 teaspoon butter mixture. Fold pastry over the cheese and pinch edges to seal. Place seam side down on a greased baking sheet. Brush with remaining butter mixture.

4. Bake at 350° for 18-22 minutes or until golden brown. Let stand for 10 minutes before serving with crackers.

YIELD: 8 SERVINGS.

NUTRITION FACTS: 1 serving (calculated without crackers) equals 167 calories, 13 g fat (7 g saturated fat), 36 mg cholesterol, 246 mg sodium, 7 g carbohydrate, trace fiber, 7 g protein.

PORK CANAPES

People will relish these festive and pretty appetizers. They're relatively simple to prepare but are sure to steal the show.

Teacher, Augusta Christian Schools, Martinez, Georgia

Ranee Bullard, Evans, Georgia

1-1/2 teaspoons garlic powder

1 teaspoon dried rosemary, crushed

1 teaspoon dried thyme

3/4 teaspoon pepper

1/2 teaspoon salt

2 pork tenderloins (3/4 pound each)

36 slices French bread baguette (1/2 inch thick)

1/4 cup olive oil

3/4 cup garlic-herb cheese spread

3 tablespoons seedless raspberry or strawberry jam

36 fresh thyme sprigs

1. In a small bowl, combine the first five ingredients; rub over meat. Place pork on a rack in a shallow roasting pan. Bake, uncovered, at 425° for 20-25 minutes or until a meat thermometer reads 160°. Let stand for 10 minutes. Cut each tenderloin into 1/4-in. slices.

2. Brush bread slices with olive oil. Place on an ungreased baking sheet. Bake at 425° for 1-2 minutes or until lightly browned. Spread each with cheese spread; top with meat, 1/4 teaspoon jam and a thyme sprig.

YIELD: 3 DOZEN.

NUTRITION FACTS: 1 appetizer equals 112 calories, 6 g fat (2 g saturated fat), 16 mg cholesterol, 143 mg sodium, 10 g carbohydrate, 1 g fiber, 5 g protein.

Kirkland, Washington

As the main secretary to the principal and staff liaison to district offices, Melody Kieffer jokes that her job is "juggling 18 balls at once to keep the school running smoothly." Despite the required multitasking, Melody enjoys working with the staff and students to ensure the school is efficient and fun.

LAYERED CURRIED CHEESE SPREAD

Pretty and tasty, this layered dip has become my signature appetizer. We make it for almost every party and family occasion we attend.

Melody Kieffer, Kirkland, Washington

1 carton (8 ounces) whipped cream cheese

3/4 cup shredded sharp cheddar cheese

1 teaspoon curry powder

1 bottle (9 ounces) mango chutney

1/2 cup flaked coconut

1/3 cup chopped pecans, toasted

2 green onions, chopped

1/4 cup dried currants

Assorted crackers

1. Place the cream cheese, cheddar cheese and curry powder in a small food processor; cover and pulse until blended.

2. Spread onto a 10-in. round serving platter. Spoon chutney over top; sprinkle with coconut, pecans, green onions and dried currants. Chill until serving. Serve with crackers.

YIELD: 4 CUPS.

NUTRITION FACTS: 1/4 cup (calculated without crackers) equals 155 calories, 9 g fat (5 g saturated fat), 23 mg cholesterol, 240 mg sodium, 16 g carbohydrate, 1 g fiber, 2 g protein.

Staff, Lake Havasu High School

Lake Havasu City, Arizona

Pat Mowery, an assistant for the Student Transition Center at Lake Havasu High School, has been in the special education field for 29 years. "What I really like most about my job is being able to take my students into the community and provide job training for them," she says. When she isn't working, Pat enjoys baking with her two granddaughters.

SMOKY CHIPOTLE ORANGE DIP

Letting the dip sit for two hours really allows the flavors blend together. Not only is it good with chips, but fruit slices would also benefit from the smoky kick. People ask for the recipe as soon as they taste it.

Pat Mowery, Lake Havasu City, Arizona

1/2 cup sour cream

1/2 cup mayonnaise

1/2 cup orange marmalade

1 tablespoon adobo sauce

3/4 teaspoon ground cumin

Tortilla chips

1. In a small bowl, combine the first five ingredients. Cover and refrigerate for at least 2 hours. Serve with chips.

YIELD: 1-1/4 CUPS.

NUTRITION FACTS: 1/4 cup (calculated without chips) equals 303 calories, 23 g fat (5 g saturated fat), 24 mg cholesterol, 206 mg sodium, 23 g carbohydrate, trace fiber, 1 g protein.

TURTLE CHIPS

Salty and sweet, crunchy and chewy...there are so many flavor and texture sensations in one delectable bite! Kids and adults will be reaching for this irresistible snack.

Teacher, Lacy Elementary School, Hopkinsville, Kentucky

Leigh Ann Stewart, Hopkinsville, Kentucky

1 package (11 ounces) ridged potato chips

1 package (14 ounces) caramels

1/3 cup heavy whipping cream

1 package (11-1/2 ounces) milk chocolate chips

2 tablespoons shortening

1 cup finely chopped pecans

1. Arrange whole potato chips in a single layer on a large platter. In a large saucepan, combine caramels and cream. Cook and stir over medium-low heat until caramels are melted. Drizzle over chips.

2. In a microwave, melt chocolate and shortening; stir until smooth. Drizzle over caramel mixture; sprinkle with pecans. Serve immediately.

YIELD: 16 SERVINGS (1/2 CUP EACH).

NUTRITION FACTS: 1/2 cup equals 396 calories, 24 g fat (7 g saturated fat), 13 mg cholesterol, 223 mg sodium, 43 g carbohydrate, 2 g fiber, 5 g protein.

Staff, Alexander Central School Elementary

Alexander, New York

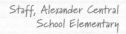

Deborah Helser credits her mom for teaching her everything she knows about baking and cooking. When she isn't in the kitchen, you will likely find Deborah in the classroom at Alexander Central School Elementary. She treasures her dedicated team of coworkers as well as the cute things her students say each day.

BUFFALO WING CHEESE MOLD

I took a baked version of a hot wing dip and turned it into a cheese ball appetizer for summertime parties. My family thinks this variation is ideal for warm-weather snacking.

Deborah Helser, Attica, New York

2 packages (8 ounces each) cream cheese, softened

2 celery ribs, finely chopped

2 cups (8 ounces) crumbled blue cheese

1 cup (4 ounces) shredded Monterey Jack cheese

1-1/2 cups finely chopped cooked chicken breasts

3 tablespoons buffalo wing sauce

1 French bread baguette (16 ounces)

1/4 cup olive oil

1/2 cup shredded carrots, optional

1. In a large bowl, combine the cream cheese, celery, blue and Monterey Jack cheeses. In a small bowl, combine chicken and wing sauce.

2. Line a 1-qt. bowl with plastic wrap, overlapping the sides of the bowl. Spread 1-1/2 cups of cream cheese mixture over the bottom and up the sides of the prepared bowl. Layer with chicken mixture and remaining cream cheese mixture. Bring plastic wrap over the cheese; press down gently. Refrigerate for at least 4 hours or until firm.

3. Just before serving, cut baguette into 1/4-in. slices. Place on an ungreased baking sheet; brush with oil. Bake at 375° for 10-12 minutes or until lightly browned.

4. Remove mold from the refrigerator and invert onto a serving plate. Remove bowl and plastic wrap. Garnish with carrots if desired. Serve with toasted baguette slices.

YIELD: 24 SERVINGS.

NUTRITION FACTS: 1 serving equals 234 calories, 15 g fat (8 g saturated fat), 40 mg cholesterol, 392 mg sodium, 15 g carbohydrate, 1 g fiber, 9 g protein.

Teacher
East Calloway Elementary

Murray, Kentucky

During her career as an educator, Lisa Armstrong has taught both third and fourth grades as well as reading and language arts, math and science. In fact, she says a highlight in her career was receiving a Science and Math Improvement Grant from the Toshiba America Foundation in New York City to purchase a weather station for the school.

JALAPENO HUMMUS

Hummus is an easy, tasty and nutritious snack or appetizer. Friends are often surprised at the uncommonly good taste. The addition of jalapeno gives it a slight kick. Serve the tempting treat with crackers, raw vegetables or tortilla chips.

Lisa Armstrong, Murray, Kentucky

- 2 cans (15 ounces each) garbanzo beans or chickpeas, rinsed and drained
- 2/3 cup roasted tahini
- 1/2 cup water
- 1/3 cup lemon juice
- 1/4 cup olive oil
- 2 tablespoons minced garlic
- 2 tablespoons pickled jalapeno slices, chopped
- 1 tablespoon juice from pickled jalapeno slices
- 1/2 to 1 teaspoon crushed red pepper flakes
- 1/2 teaspoon salt
- 1/2 teaspoon pepper
- 1/8 teaspoon paprika
- Assorted fresh vegetables

1. Place first 11 ingredients in a food processor; cover and process until well blended. Garnish with paprika. Serve with assorted vegetables.

YIELD: 4 CUPS.

NUTRITION FACTS: 1/4 cup (calculated without vegetables) equals 153 calories, 11 g fat (1 g saturated fat), 0 cholesterol, 182 mg sodium, 11 g carbohydrate, 3 g fiber, 4 g protein. DIABETIC EXCHANGES: 2 fat, 1 starch.

SPANAKOPITA PINWHEELS

I'm obsessed with spanakopita. This is a quick and easy version, which I have used for teacher get-togethers and family events. I think it's simply wonderful with a glass of white wine.

Teacher, Lake Region Middle School, Naples, Maine

Ryan Palmer, Windham, Maine

- 1 medium onion, finely chopped
- 2 tablespoons olive oil
- 1 teaspoon dried oregano
- 1 garlic clove, minced
- 2 packages (10 ounces each) frozen chopped spinach, thawed and squeezed dry
- 2 cups (8 ounces) crumbled feta cheese
- 2 eggs, lightly beaten
- 1 package (17.3 ounces) frozen puff pastry, thawed

1. In a small skillet, saute onion in oil until tender. Add the oregano and garlic; cook 1 minute longer. Add spinach; cook 3 minutes longer or until liquid is evaporated. Transfer to a large bowl; cool.

2. Add feta cheese and eggs to spinach mixture; mix well. Unfold puff pastry. Spread each sheet with half the spinach mixture to within 1/2 in. of edges. Roll up jelly-roll style. Cut each into twelve 3/4-in. slices. Place cut side down on greased baking sheets.

3. Bake at 400° for 18-22 minutes or until golden brown. Serve warm.

YIELD: 2 DOZEN.

NUTRITION FACTS: 1 appetizer equals 197 calories, 13 g fat (5 g saturated fat), 39 mg cholesterol, 392 mg sodium, 14 g carbohydrate, 3 g fiber, 7 g protein.

LIME-IN-THE-COCONUT ALMOND BARK

I love the combination of flavors in this tropical treat! It takes mere minutes to make. If you need something for a school or church bake sale this will get you out of the kitchen in a flash.

Staff, Talala Elementary School, Park Forest, Illinois

Julie Beckwith, Crete, Illinois

1 package (10 to 12 ounces) white baking chips

4 teaspoons shortening

2 to 4 drops green food coloring, optional

1/2 cup flaked coconut, toasted

1/2 cup chopped almonds, toasted

4 teaspoons grated lime peel

1. Line a 9-in. square baking pan with foil and set aside. In a microwave, melt chips and shortening; stir until smooth. Stir in food coloring if desired. Stir in the coconut, almonds and lime peel. Spread into prepared pan. Chill for 10-15 minutes or until firm.

2. Break into small pieces. Store in an airtight container at room temperature.

YIELD: ABOUT 1 POUND.

NUTRITION FACTS: 1 ounce equals 143 calories, 10 g fat (5 g saturated fat), 2 mg cholesterol, 24 mg sodium, 13 g carbohydrate, 1 g fiber, 2 g protein.

Administrator
McPherson County Schools

Tryon, Nebraska

Joe Sherwood has been
the Superintendent of
Schools in McPherson
County, Nebraska, for the
past three years. "I most
enjoy collaborating with
the board of education,
staff and parents to lead
school improvement," he says.
"Watching students grow
toward their full potential
is truly rewarding."

BAKED GREEK RATATOUILLE

When I lived in Florida, I went to dinner at a friend's home. His Greek wife served a beautiful and delicious side dish that used eggplant and shared the recipe with me. While I've made her version many times with great success, I was inspired by the movie "Ratatouille" to modify the dish. This was the wonderful result.

Joe Sherwood, Tryon, Nebraska

1 small eggplant

2 small zucchini

2 small yellow summer squash

4 plum tomatoes

1 large sweet onion

1/2 cup butter, melted

1/2 cup minced fresh parsley

3 garlic cloves, minced

1/2 teaspoon salt

1/2 teaspoon each dried thyme, oregano, tarragon and basil

1/2 teaspoon dried rosemary, crushed

1/2 teaspoon pepper

1 cup (4 ounces) shredded part-skim mozzarella cheese

1. Cut vegetables into 1/4-in. thick slices; layer in a greased 13-in. x 9-in. baking dish.

2. In a small bowl, combine the butter, parsley, garlic and seasonings; pour over the vegetables. Cover and refrigerate overnight.

3. Remove from the refrigerator 30 minutes before baking. Bake, uncovered, at 375° for 35 minutes. Sprinkle with cheese. Bake 10-15 minutes longer or until cheese is melted. Serve with a slotted spoon.

YIELD: 13 SERVINGS (3/4 CUP EACH).

NUTRITION FACTS: 3/4 cup equals 120 calories, 9 g fat (5 g saturated fat), 24 mg cholesterol, 190 mg sodium, 8 g carbohydrate, 3 g fiber, 4 g protein.

Staff, Ridgeview Elementary

Yucaipa, California

Jan Ruiz is a special education instructional aide at Ridgeview Elementary where her main duties are to assist the teacher in instructing and implementing curriculum for students who are learning disabled. She says the best part of her job is when she can see a student has finally grasped a concept. "It's always followed by a huge smile; that's worth a million bucks."

BLUEBERRY SPINACH SALAD

I came up with this recipe while trying to use up blueberries that I didn't want to go to waste. The combination of flavors and textures is delightful.

Jan Ruiz, Yucaipa, California

1/2 cup olive oil

1/4 cup white balsamic vinegar

2 teaspoons Dijon mustard

1 teaspoon sugar

1/4 teaspoon salt

1 package (10 ounces) fresh spinach, trimmed

1 cup (4 ounces) crumbled feta cheese

1 cup fresh blueberries

1/2 cup pine nuts, toasted

1. Place the first five ingredients in a jar with a tight-fitting lid; shake well. Refrigerate until serving.

2. In a large bowl, combine the spinach, cheese, blueberries and nuts. Just before serving, shake dressing and drizzle over salad; toss to coat.

YIELD: 8 SERVINGS.

NUTRITION FACTS: 1-1/4 cups equals 229 calories, 20 g fat (4 g saturated fat), 8 mg cholesterol, 269 mg sodium, 8 g carbohydrate, 2 g fiber, 6 g protein.

Natalie Knowlton has been the family and consumer science teacher at Treasure Mountain Junior High for two years. "My favorite part of teaching at Treasure is our involvement with our sister school in Uganda, Africa," she says. "To raise money for the school, we held a hunger banquet where my Food and Nutrition classes prepared dinner for nearly 300 guests."

GRILLED SWEET POTATO WEDGES

I love when an entire meal can be cooked outside on the grill and I don't need to heat up the kitchen. These tasty fries not only meet that requirement, but they are healthy, too.

Natalie Knowlton, Kamas, Utah

4 large sweet potatoes, peeled and cut into 1/2-inch wedges

1/2 teaspoon garlic salt

1/4 teaspoon pepper

DIPPING SAUCE:

1/2 cup reduced-fat mayonnaise

1/2 cup fat-free plain yogurt

1 teaspoon ground cumin

1/2 teaspoon seasoned salt

1/2 teaspoon paprika

1/2 teaspoon chili powder

1. Place potatoes in a large saucepan and cover with water. Bring to a boil. Reduce the heat; cover and simmer for 4-5 minutes or until crisp-tender. Drain; pat dry with paper towels. Sprinkle potatoes with garlic salt and pepper.

2. Grill, covered, over medium heat for 10-12 minutes or until tender, turning once. In a small bowl, combine mayonnaise, yogurt and seasonings. Serve with sweet potatoes.

YIELD: 8 SERVINGS.

NUTRITION FACTS: 3/4 cup with 2 tablespoons sauce equals 166 calories, 5 g fat (1 g saturated fat), 6 mg cholesterol, 349 mg sodium, 28 g carbohydrate, 3 g fiber, 3 g protein. DIABETIC EXCHANGES: 1-1/2 starch, 1 fat.

Staff, J.F. Kennedy High School

Burien, Washington

During the school year, J.F. Kennedy regularly plans staff social events where food is always a central part. School bookkeeper Madeline Etzkorn is always happy to provide a dish. "Many of my recipes have been complimented, which is why I decided to share some of them with Taste of Home," she says. She asserts that it's her way to give back to the school some of the blessings she has received by being part of such a wonderful school family.

SWISS SWEET ONION CASSEROLE

I think this is a great side dish for barbecued chicken or ribs. Sweet onions are available most of the year, so don't substitute another type of onion...the dish will not be as fantastic.

Madeline Etzkorn, Burien, Washington

1/2 cup uncooked long grain rice

8 cups halved sliced sweet onions

2 tablespoons butter

1 cup (4 ounces) shredded Swiss cheese

1/2 cup half-and-half cream

1/2 teaspoon salt

1/8 teaspoon ground nutmeg

1. Cook rice according to package directions.
2. In a large skillet, saute onions in butter until tender. Remove from the heat; stir in the cooked rice, cheese, cream, salt and nutmeg. Pour into a greased 8-in. square baking dish.
3. Bake, uncovered, at 325° for 1 to 1-1/4 hours or until golden brown.

YIELD: 6 SERVINGS.

NUTRITION FACTS: 2/3 cup equals 285 calories, 12 g fat (8 g saturated fat), 40 mg cholesterol, 300 mg sodium, 34 g carbohydrate, 4 g fiber, 10 g protein.

Teacher, Parley Coburn
Elementary School

Elmira, New York

Tonia Billbe has been
teaching fifth grade
at Parley Coburn
Elementary for 11 years.
Prior to this, she worked
for 10 years at Belle
Sherman Elementary
School in Ithaca, New York,
where she taught special
education. "I love watching
children get excited about
learning new things and gaining
confidence in themselves,"
she says.

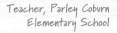

BASIL TOMATO SOUP WITH ORZO

The soup is so scrumptious, it is worth the time it takes to chop the fresh basil. I think the soup is even better the next day, after the flavors have had a chance to blend overnight.

Tonia Billbe, Elmira, New York

- 1 large onion, chopped
- 1/4 cup butter, cubed
- 2 garlic cloves, minced
- 3 cans (28 ounces each) crushed tomatoes
- 1 carton (32 ounces) chicken broth
- 1 cup loosely packed basil leaves, chopped
- 1 tablespoon sugar
- 1/2 teaspoon pepper
- 1-1/4 cups uncooked orzo pasta
- 1 cup heavy whipping cream
- 1/2 cup grated Romano cheese

1. In a Dutch oven, saute onion in butter for 3 minutes. Add garlic; cook 1-2 minutes longer or until onion is tender. Stir in the tomatoes, broth, basil, sugar and pepper. Bring to a boil. Reduce heat; cover and simmer for 15 minutes.

2. Meanwhile, cook the orzo according to package directions; drain. Add orzo and cream to soup; heat through (do not boil). Sprinkle servings with cheese.

YIELD: 16 SERVINGS (4-1/2 QUARTS).

NUTRITION FACTS: 1 cup equals 204 calories, 10 g fat (6 g saturated fat), 33 mg cholesterol, 533 mg sodium, 24 g carbohydrate, 3 g fiber, 7 g protein.

Teacher
Antelope Elementary School

Littlerock, California

Allison Strain has a total of 17 years teaching experience in Minnesota, Hawaii and California. "I have had the opportunity to teach every grade level from kindergarten to sixth, but most of my experience is in kindergarten and second grade," she says. When she isn't busy with her students, you'll likely find Allison sharing a tasty recipe with a coworker. "I enjoy swapping recipes with colleagues at our school's breakfast events and potlucks."

CRANBERRY BROCCOLI SLAW

Perk up any cookout with this fun broccoli slaw. This super easy salad is ready in minutes.

Allison Strain, Lancaster, California

1 package (14 ounces) coleslaw mix

4 cups fresh broccoli florets

1 cup dried cranberries

1/2 cup chopped walnuts

1/2 cup raisins

1/3 cup chopped red onion

6 bacon strips, cooked and crumbled

1 cup reduced-fat mayonnaise

1/4 cup sugar

1 tablespoon cider vinegar

1. In a large bowl, combine the first seven ingredients. In a small bowl, whisk the mayonnaise, sugar and vinegar. Pour over cabbage mixture; toss to coat. Chill until serving.

YIELD: 16 SERVINGS (3/4 CUP EACH).

NUTRITION FACTS: 3/4 cup equals 146 calories, 8 g fat (1 g saturated fat), 8 mg cholesterol, 184 mg sodium, 17 g carbohydrate, 2 g fiber, 2 g protein. DIABETIC EXCHANGES: 1-1/2 fat, 1 starch.

AU GRATIN POTATOES WITH GREEN CHILES

These cheesy potatoes would be quite popular at holiday meals or potlucks. I usually serve them with ham.

Teacher, Sam Case Primary School, Newport, Oregon

Cathy Rau, Newport, Oregon

8 medium Yukon Gold potatoes (about 4 pounds), peeled and cut into 1/4-inch slices

1 small onion, thinly sliced

1 tablespoon butter

1 tablespoon olive oil

1/4 cup all-purpose flour

1 teaspoon salt

1 teaspoon pepper

1 can (14-1/2 ounces) chicken broth

3/4 cup 2% milk

3/4 cup half-and-half cream

2 cans (4 ounces each) chopped green chilies

1 cup (4 ounces) shredded cheddar cheese

1 cup (4 ounces) shredded Swiss cheese

1/2 cup plus 2 tablespoons shredded Parmesan cheese divided

1 teaspoon Dijon mustard

1/2 teaspoon garlic powder

3 to 4 drops hot pepper sauce

Dash ground nutmeg

1. Place potatoes in a Dutch oven; cover with water. Bring to a boil. Cover and cook for 2-3 minutes. Drain and pat dry; set aside.

2. In a large saucepan, saute onion in butter and oil until tender. Stir in the flour, salt and pepper until blended. Gradually stir in the broth, milk and cream. Bring to a boil; cook and stir for 2-3 minutes or until thickened.

3. Stir in the chilies, cheddar cheese, Swiss cheese, 1/2 cup Parmesan cheese, mustard, garlic powder, pepper sauce and nutmeg until cheese is melted.

4. In a greased 13-in. x 9-in. baking dish, arrange half of the potatoes and cheese sauce. Repeat (dish will be full).

5. Cover and bake at 350° for 30 minutes. Uncover; sprinkle with remaining Parmesan cheese. Bake 10-15 minutes longer or until potatoes are tender and top is lightly browned. Let stand for 5 minutes before serving.

YIELD: 13 SERVINGS (3/4 CUP EACH).

NUTRITION FACTS: 3/4 cup equals 242 calories, 10 g fat (6 g saturated fat), 32 mg cholesterol, 576 mg sodium, 27 g carbohydrate, 3 g fiber, 10 g protein.

Volunteer, Sierra Hills School

Meadow Vista, California

Alia Shuttleworth has been a parent volunteer at Sierra Hills School since 2007. In this role, she has been involved in everything from being the classroom "cooking mom" to making the classroom quilt and helping coordinate the Lunchtime Running Club.

ROASTED VEGETABLE PASTA SALAD

I can't make this dish without printing enough copies of the recipe to hand out to girlfriends at my book club and potlucks all year round! I love it because it is a beautiful dish to look at and it's delectable. To top that, it's easy to make.

Alia Shuttleworth, Auburn, California

1/3 cup lemon juice
1/3 cup olive oil
1/2 teaspoon kosher salt
1/2 teaspoon pepper

ROASTED VEGETABLES:
1 small eggplant, peeled and cut into 3/4-inch cubes
1 medium sweet red pepper, cut into 1-inch pieces
1 medium sweet yellow pepper, cut into 1-inch pieces
1 large red onion, cut into 1-inch pieces
6 garlic cloves, peeled and halved
1/2 cup olive oil
1/2 teaspoon kosher salt
1/2 teaspoon pepper

SALAD:
1-1/4 cups uncooked orzo pasta
4 green onions, finely chopped
15 fresh basil leaves, thinly sliced
1/4 cup pine nuts, toasted
12 ounces feta cheese, cut into 3/4-inch cubes

1. In a small bowl, whisk the first four ingredients; set aside.

2. In a large bowl, combine the eggplant, sweet peppers, onion and garlic. Add oil, salt and pepper; toss to coat. Transfer to a 15-in. x 10-in. x 1-in. baking pan. Bake at 425° for 35-40 minutes or until the vegetables are tender. Cool to room temperature.

3. Meanwhile, cook orzo according to package directions; drain.

4. In a large serving bowl, combine roasted vegetables, pasta, green onions, basil and pine nuts. Drizzle with dressing and toss to coat. Add cheese; toss gently.

YIELD: 9 SERVINGS.

NUTRITION FACTS: 3/4 cup equals 388 calories, 27 g fat (8 g saturated fat), 34 mg cholesterol, 637 mg sodium, 29 g carbohydrate, 3 g fiber, 11 g protein.

HOT AND SOUR SOUP

We've tried several recipes for this soup without finding one that tasted similar to the one we enjoyed at a restaurant. So, I made up my own. Regular or hot chili sauce can be used, according to taste.

Volunteer, Mancelona Schools, Mancelona, Michigan

Vera Leitow, Mancelona, Michigan

3/4 pound pork tenderloin, cut into 1-1/2-inch x 1/4-inch strips

1 tablespoon olive oil

1/2 pound sliced fresh mushrooms

6 cups chicken broth

1/4 cup soy sauce

2 tablespoons chili garlic sauce

3/4 teaspoon pepper

1 package (14 ounces) extra-firm tofu, drained and cut into 1/4-inch cubes

1 can (8 ounces) bamboo shoots, drained

1 can (8 ounces) sliced water chestnuts, drained

1/2 cup white vinegar

1/3 cup cornstarch

1/3 cup cold water

2 teaspoons sesame oil

Finely chopped green onions

1. In a Dutch oven, brown pork in oil until no longer pink; remove meat and keep warm. Add mushrooms; saute until tender. Set aside and keep warm.

2. Add the broth, soy sauce, chili garlic sauce and pepper to the pan. Bring to a boil. Reduce the heat; cover and simmer for 10 minutes. Return the meat and mushrooms to the pan. Stir in the tofu, bamboo shoots, water chestnuts and vinegar. Simmer, uncovered, for 10 minutes.

3. In a small bowl, combine cornstarch and water until smooth; gradually stir into soup. Bring to a boil; cook and stir for 2 minutes or until thickened. Remove from the heat; stir in sesame oil. Garnish servings with onions.

YIELD: 6 SERVINGS (ABOUT 2 QUARTS).

NUTRITION FACTS: 1-1/2 cups equals 240 calories, 10 g fat (2 g saturated fat), 37 mg cholesterol, 1,779 mg sodium, 18 g carbohydrate, 2 g fiber, 21 g protein.

Staff, Christ the King School

Terrytown, Louisiana

Sue Shepard has held her position as the administrative assistant for Christ the King Parish Elementary School for 30 years. While her job responsibilities vary, she says her most important duty is taking care of the students by "showing them the love they need and deserve."

SUE'S CREAM OF BAKED POTATO SOUP

With a garnish of shredded cheese and crumbled cooked bacon, this rich, velvety soup feels like something you'd get at a restaurant. Serve it with crusty bread and a crisp salad.

Sue Shepard, Terrytown, Louisiana

3 medium potatoes

6 bacon strips, chopped

1 large onion, chopped

3 garlic cloves, minced

1 can (14-1/2 ounces) chicken broth

1 can (10-3/4 ounces) condensed cream of chicken soup, undiluted

1 can (5 ounces) evaporated milk

1 package (8 ounces) process cheese (Velveeta), cubed

1 cup 2% milk

1/4 cup butter, cubed

1 teaspoon dried basil

1/8 teaspoon pepper

Shredded cheddar cheese

1. Scrub and pierce potatoes. Bake at 400° for 50-60 minutes or until tender.

2. Meanwhile, in a large saucepan, cook the bacon over medium heat until crisp. Remove the bacon to paper towels with a slotted spoon. Drain; reserve 2 tablespoons bacon drippings. Set aside bacon.

3. Saute onion in drippings until tender. Add the garlic; cook 1 minute longer. Stir in the broth, soup and evaporated milk. Bring to a gentle boil. Remove pulp from potatoes; stir into soup mixture. Discard potato shells.

4. Cool slightly. In a blender, process half of the soup until smooth. Return to pan. Add the process cheese, 2% milk, butter, basil and pepper; cook and stir until cheese is melted. Sprinkle servings with cheddar cheese and bacon.

YIELD: 7 SERVINGS.

NUTRITION FACTS: 1 cup (calculated without cheddar) equals 381 calories, 25 g fat (13 g saturated fat), 66 mg cholesterol, 1,191 mg sodium, 25 g carbohydrate, 2 g fiber, 13 g protein.

CILANTRO COUSCOUS SALAD

Since the salad serves 12, I usually make it for potlucks, where it is always appreciated. My 11-year-old daughter likes it so much, she requested it for her birthday party.

Staff, Three Peaks Elementary, Cedar City, Utah

Cindy Gifford, Cedar City, Utah

1 package (10 ounces) couscous

1 medium cucumber, finely chopped

2 medium tomatoes, seeded and finely chopped

2/3 cup minced fresh cilantro

1/3 cup olive oil

1/4 cup lemon juice

3 garlic cloves, minced

1 package (8 ounces) feta cheese, crumbled

1. Prepare couscous according to package directions; let cool to room temperature.

2. In a large serving bowl, combine the cucumber, tomatoes, cilantro and couscous. In a small bowl, whisk the oil, lemon juice and garlic. Drizzle over salad; toss to coat. Add cheese and toss gently to combine. Chill until serving.

YIELD: 12 SERVINGS (2/3 CUP EACH).

NUTRITION FACTS: 2/3 cup equals 196 calories, 10 g fat (4 g saturated fat), 17 mg cholesterol, 215 mg sodium, 21 g carbohydrate, 2 g fiber, 6 g protein.

SPINACH SOUFFLE

You just can't make an easier, more delicious side than this. The cheesy, comforting dish is great with beef, pork and lamb. I especially like serving it for a festive meal.

Staff, Sandburg Elementary, Kirkland, Washington

Bette Duffy, Kenmore, Washington

2 packages (10 ounces each) frozen chopped spinach, thawed and squeezed dry

1 package (8 ounces) cream cheese, cubed

1-1/2 cups (6 ounces) shredded Monterey Jack cheese

4 eggs, lightly beaten

1/4 cup butter, melted

1 garlic clove, minced

1/2 teaspoon salt

1. In a large bowl, combine all ingredients. Transfer to a greased 1-1/2-qt. baking dish. Bake at 350° for 35-40 minutes or until edges are lightly browned.

YIELD: 6 SERVINGS.

NUTRITION FACTS: 1/2 cup equals 375 calories, 33 g fat (20 g saturated fat), 228 mg cholesterol, 630 mg sodium, 5 g carbohydrate, 3 g fiber, 17 g protein.

Staff, Antigo High School

Antigo, Wisconsin

Andrea Gilkenson has been with the Antigo School District as an educational interpreter for the past two years. "My role as an interpreter is to translate between spoken English and American Sign Language for the deaf and hard-of-hearing students," she says. "Helping students to better communicate with the world around them gives me a great sense of fulfillment. I couldn't ask for a better job!"

CHIPOTLE BUTTERNUT SQUASH SOUP

Autumn has always been my favorite time of year, and the combination of butternut squash and apples in this soup reminds me of the season. The spicy chipotle peppers add the right amount of zip. If you prefer less heat, add only one pepper or no peppers at all.

Andrea Gilkenson, Wausau, Wisconsin

- 1 medium butternut squash (3-1/2 to 4 pounds), peeled, seeded and cubed
- 2 medium carrots, chopped
- 1 large onion, chopped
- 2 celery ribs, chopped
- 3 tablespoons butter
- 2 medium tart apples, peeled and cubed
- 3 garlic cloves, minced
- 3 cans (14-1/2 ounces each) chicken broth
- 1 cup unsweetened apple cider or juice
- 1 chipotle pepper in adobo sauce, seeded and chopped
- 1/2 teaspoon salt
- 1/2 cup sour cream

1. In a Dutch oven, saute the squash, carrots, onion and celery in butter for 5 minutes. Add the apples and garlic; cook 3 minutes longer. Stir in the broth, apple cider, chipotle pepper and salt. Bring to a boil. Reduce heat; cover and simmer for 20-25 minutes or until vegetables are tender.

2. Cool slightly. In a blender, process soup in batches until smooth. Return all to pan and heat through. Stir in sour cream (do not boil).

YIELD: 12 SERVINGS (3 QUARTS).

NUTRITION FACTS: 1 cup equals 136 calories, 5 g fat (3 g saturated fat), 16 mg cholesterol, 594 mg sodium, 22 g carbohydrate, 5 g fiber, 2 g protein. DIABETIC EXCHANGES: 1-1/2 starch, 1 fat.

Paw Paw, Michigan

Deanna Hindenach serves as an administrator and teacher at Trinity Lutheran School. "I look at teaching as a calling," she says. "The best part of my day is being in my classroom teaching and building relationships with students."

CURRIED CHICKEN SOUP

My German mother would occasionally cook dishes that were not traditional German recipes. One of my favorites was her chicken soup. I've added my own touches to it, such as chickpeas, coconut milk and fresh cilantro.

Deanna Hindenach, Paw Paw, Michigan

4 teaspoons curry powder

1/2 teaspoon salt

1/2 teaspoon pepper

1/2 teaspoon cayenne pepper

1 pound boneless skinless chicken breasts, cut into 1-inch cubes

3 medium carrots, chopped

1 medium sweet red pepper, chopped

1 small onion, chopped

2 tablespoons olive oil

1 garlic clove, minced

1 can (15 ounces) garbanzo beans or chickpeas, rinsed and drained

1 can (14-1/2 ounces) chicken broth

1 can (14-1/2 ounces) diced tomatoes, drained

1 cup water

1 can (13.66 ounces) coconut milk

3/4 cup minced fresh cilantro

1. In a large resealable plastic bag, combine the curry, salt, pepper and cayenne. Add chicken, a few pieces at a time, and shake to coat.

2. In a large saucepan over medium heat, cook the chicken, carrots, red pepper and onion in oil for 4 minutes. Add garlic; cook 1-2 minutes longer or until chicken is browned and vegetables are tender; drain.

3. Stir in the garbanzo beans, broth, tomatoes and water. Bring to a boil. Reduce heat; cover and simmer for 30 minutes. Stir in coconut milk; heat through. Garnish individual servings with fresh cilantro.

YIELD: 8 SERVINGS.

NUTRITION FACTS: 1-1/4 cups equals 270 calories, 16 g fat (10 g saturated fat), 32 mg cholesterol, 555 mg sodium, 17 g carbohydrate, 5 g fiber, 16 g protein.

SPICY CUCUMBER SALAD

Salting the cucumbers makes them crisp and crunchy for the salad. The soy sauce and sesame oil dressing is a wonderful change from the usual vinegar or mayonnaise-coated cukes. I made this for a faculty picnic one year, and it was a hit.

Teacher, East Alton-Wood River High School, Wood River, Illinois

Kelly Gardner, Alton, Illinois

---

3 medium cucumbers, peeled, halved, seeded and sliced

1/2 teaspoon salt

2 tablespoons rice vinegar

2 tablespoons soy sauce

1 tablespoon sesame oil

1-1/2 teaspoons sugar

1-1/2 teaspoons red curry paste

1. Place cucumbers in a strainer over a plate; sprinkle with salt and toss. Let stand for 30 minutes. Rinse and drain well.

2. Transfer cucumbers to a large bowl. In a small bowl, whisk the vinegar, soy sauce, oil, sugar and curry paste; pour over cucumbers and toss to coat. Chill until serving. Serve with a slotted spoon.

YIELD: 5 SERVINGS.

NUTRITION FACTS: 3/4 cup equals 64 calories, 3 g fat (trace saturated fat), 0 cholesterol, 466 mg sodium, 8 g carbohydrate, 2 g fiber, 3 g protein.

SPICY COUSCOUS & TOMATO SOUP

This vegetarian soup has a wonderful Middle Eastern flavor. It's low in calories and fat, which makes it great for those who are trying to watch their weight.

Parent Teacher Organization Officer
Sallas Mahone Elementary School, Valdosta, Georgia

Rita Combs, Valdosta, Georgia

2 medium sweet yellow peppers, chopped
1 medium red onion, chopped
2-1/2 teaspoons olive oil
3 garlic cloves, minced
6 cups vegetable broth
6 plum tomatoes, chopped
1-1/2 teaspoons ground cumin
1-1/2 teaspoons ground coriander
1/2 teaspoon ground cinnamon
1/2 teaspoon cayenne pepper
1/4 teaspoon pepper
1/2 cup uncooked couscous

1. In a Dutch oven, saute peppers and onion in oil until tender. Add garlic; cook 1 minute longer. Stir in the broth, tomatoes, cumin, coriander, cinnamon, cayenne and pepper. Bring to a boil. Reduce heat; cover and simmer for 20-25 minutes or until flavors are blended.

2. Stir in couscous; cover and cook 4-6 minutes longer or until couscous is tender.

YIELD: 7 SERVINGS.

NUTRITION FACTS: 1 cup equals 106 calories, 2 g fat (trace saturated fat), 0 cholesterol, 812 mg sodium, 19 g carbohydrate, 2 g fiber, 3 g protein. DIABETIC EXCHANGE: 1 starch.

Staff
Black River School District

Sullivan, Ohio

Jill Fox is a cook in the Black River School District. She said she enjoys her job because "lunch is the best part of the students' day!"

THREE POTATO SALAD

We love this creamy salad because it has the colorful and nutritious addition of sweet potatoes. When I bring it to parties, people are always commenting on how good it is and asking for the recipe.

Jill Fox, Wellington, Ohio

3 medium potatoes, peeled and cubed
3 medium red potatoes, cubed
1 large sweet potato, peeled and cubed
6 green onions, chopped
1 celery rib, chopped
1/3 cup chopped green pepper
1/4 cup seeded chopped cucumber
1 cup mayonnaise
2 teaspoons white vinegar
1 teaspoon salt
1 teaspoon dill weed
1/2 teaspoon pepper
8 bacon strips, cooked and crumbled

1. Place potatoes in a Dutch oven; cover with water. Bring to a boil. Reduce heat; cover and cook for 10-15 minutes or until tender. Drain and cool.

2. In a large bowl, combine the potatoes, green onions, celery, green pepper and cucumber. In a small bowl, combine the mayonnaise, vinegar, salt, dill and pepper. Pour over salad and toss to coat. Cover and refrigerate for 4 hours or overnight. Sprinkle with bacon.

YIELD: 10 SERVINGS.

NUTRITION FACTS: 3/4 cup equals 276 calories, 20 g fat (3 g saturated fat), 14 mg cholesterol, 483 mg sodium, 20 g carbohydrate, 2 g fiber, 4 g protein.

Teacher
Brownwood Elementary School

Scottsboro, Alabama

Richi Reynolds has been an educator for 34 years, with 25 of those years spent teaching kindergarten. Brownwood Elementary School is one of four elementary schools in the district. "We have tremendous community involvement," Richi says. "This year, in November, we had an American Heritage Day celebration and had approximately 25 different stations—mule drawn wagons, natural dyes and bead and leather work. The entire school participated. It was a wonderful learning experience for our students."

FIESTA CORN SALAD

This recipe is special because I was able to take a delectable, but somewhat complicated, appetizer and turn it into a salad that's easy to make and transport. Adjust the jalapeno and chipotle amounts to suit your spiciness level.

Richi Reynolds, Scottsboro, Alabama

TAMALE CROUTONS:
3 cups frozen corn, divided
2/3 cup butter, softened
1/3 cup sugar
1/4 teaspoon salt
1 cup masa harina
1/4 cup all-purpose flour

CHIPOTLE RANCH DRESSING:
1/4 cup buttermilk
1/4 cup mayonnaise
1 teaspoon buttermilk ranch salad dressing mix
1 teaspoon minced chipotle peppers in adobo sauce

SALAD:
6 cans (7 ounces each) white or shoepeg corn, drained
2 cups grape tomatoes, chopped
1 can (10 ounces) diced tomatoes and green chilies, well drained
1 small red onion, chopped
1/2 cup chopped peeled jicama
1/4 cup minced fresh cilantro
1/4 cup lime juice
1 jalapeno pepper, seeded and minced
4 medium ripe avocados, peeled and cubed
3/4 cup shredded Mexican cheese blend

1. Place 2 cups corn in food processor; cover and process until finely chopped. Add the butter, sugar and salt; cover and process until blended. Stir in masa harina and flour until a soft dough forms; fold in remaining corn. Using wet hands, press dough into a greased 15-in. x 10-in. x 1-in. baking pan.

2. Bake at 400° for 20 minutes. Score the dough into 1-in. squares. Bake 4-6 minutes longer or until golden brown. Immediately cut along the scored lines; cool in pan on a wire rack.

3. In a small bowl, combine the dressing ingredients. In a large bowl, combine the corn, tomatoes, onion, jicama, cilantro, lime juice and jalapeno. Pour dressing over salad and toss to coat; gently stir in avocados. Sprinkle with cheese and croutons. Serve immediately.

YIELD: 12 SERVINGS (3/4 CUP EACH).

EDITOR'S NOTE: We recommend wearing disposable gloves when cutting hot peppers. Avoid touching your face.

NUTRITION FACTS: 3/4 cup with 1/3 cup croutons and 1 tablespoon cheese equals 449 calories, 26 g fat (10 g saturated fat), 35 mg cholesterol, 638 mg sodium, 53 g carbohydrate, 9 g fiber, 8 g protein.

PECAN RICE PILAF

This is one of my tried-and-true side dishes, which complements most meat and meatless entrees. It is special enough for company and quick enough for weeknights.

Teacher, West McDowell Junior High, Marion, North Carolina

Jacqueline Oglesby, Spruce Pine, North Carolina

1 cup chopped pecans

5 tablespoons butter, divided

1 small onion, chopped

2 cups uncooked long grain rice

1 carton (32 ounces) chicken broth

3 tablespoons minced fresh parsley, divided

1/2 teaspoon salt

1/4 teaspoon dried thyme

1/8 teaspoon pepper

1 cup shredded carrots

1. In a large saucepan, saute pecans in 2 tablespoons butter until toasted; remove from the pan and set aside.

2. In the same pan, saute onion in remaining butter until tender. Add rice; cook and stir for 3-4 minutes or until rice is lightly browned. Stir in the broth, 2 tablespoons parsley, salt, thyme and pepper. Bring to a boil. Reduce heat; cover and simmer for 10 minutes.

3. Add carrots; simmer 3-5 minutes longer or until the rice is tender. Stir in toasted pecans and remaining parsley. Fluff rice with a fork.

YIELD: 9 SERVINGS.

NUTRITION FACTS: 3/4 cup equals 313 calories, 16 g fat (5 g saturated fat), 19 mg cholesterol, 623 mg sodium, 37 g carbohydrate, 2 g fiber, 5 g protein.

GREEK SALAD WITH GREEN GRAPES

Prepared with ingredients traditionally associated with Greece, this healthy and colorful salad offers a delightful combination of tastes. This salad is outstanding with any entree, but especially lamb or pork dishes prepared Mediterranean-style.

Teacher, Foothills Elementary, Colorado Springs, Colorado

Holly Heupel, Colorado Springs, Colorado

1 package (5 ounces) spring mix salad greens

3-1/2 cups torn romaine

1 large cucumber, chopped

1 cup green grapes

1 cup (4 ounces) crumbled feta cheese

1/2 cup cherry tomatoes, halved

1/2 cup chopped walnuts

1 can (3.8 ounces) sliced ripe olives, drained

GREEK YOGURT VINAIGRETTE:

3/4 cup white wine vinegar

2 tablespoons plain Greek yogurt

2 tablespoons honey

2 teaspoons snipped fresh dill

1/8 teaspoon salt

1/8 teaspoon pepper

7 tablespoons olive oil

1. In a large bowl, combine first eight ingredients.

2. In a small bowl, whisk the vinegar, yogurt, honey, dill, salt and pepper. Gradually add the oil in a steady stream until combined. Pour over salad; toss to coat.

YIELD: 9 SERVINGS.

EDITOR'S NOTE: If Greek yogurt is not available in your area, line a strainer with a coffee filter and place over a bowl. Place 1/4 cup plain yogurt in prepared strainer; refrigerate overnight. Discard liquid from bowl; proceed as directed.

NUTRITION FACTS: 1-1/2 cups salad equals 229 calories, 19 g fat (4 g saturated fat), 8 mg cholesterol, 268 mg sodium, 13 g carbohydrate, 2 g fiber, 4 g protein.

DILL AND CHIVE BREAD

Store-bought chive and onion cream cheese is such an effortless way to give plain bread dough a punch. I love how easy and wonderful this flavorful loaf is.

Teacher, Cambridge Elementary School, Cambridge, Illinois

Dawn Higgs, East Moline, Illinois

3/4 cup water (70° to 80°)
1/2 cup spreadable chive and onion cream cheese
2 tablespoons sugar
2 teaspoons dill weed

1-1/4 teaspoons salt
3 cups all-purpose flour
1 package (1/4 ounce) active dry yeast

1. In bread machine pan, place all ingredients in the order suggested by manufacturer. Select basic bread setting. Choose crust color and loaf size if available. Bake according to bread machine directions (check dough after 5 minutes of mixing; add 1 to 2 tablespoons of water or flour if needed).

YIELD: 1 LOAF (1-1/2 POUNDS, 16 SLICES).

NUTRITION FACTS: 1 slice equals 121 calories, 3 g fat (2 g saturated fat), 8 mg cholesterol, 219 mg sodium, 20 g carbohydrate, 1 g fiber, 3 g protein. DIABETIC EXCHANGES: 1 starch, 1/2 fat.

Teacher
Lincoln Elementary School

Winchester, Massachusetts

During the day, budding chef Paul DeBenedictis moonlights as "Mr. D," a fun-loving and dedicated first and second grade teacher. "Working with 6-, 7-, and 8-year-olds is much like cooking," he says. "It involves thinking outside the box, being quick on one's feet, putting out fires,
and maintaining a sense of creativity!" After school, Paul looks for opportunities to share his love of cooking with his wife and brothers.

FRENCH ONION SOUP

In my opinion, the key to a delicious French Onion Soup is a dark, savory broth, which you traditionally get from beef stock. But to make a vegetarian version with the same robust taste using vegetable broth is more difficult. To achieve the earthy tones I'm looking for in this recipe, I use a few nontraditional ingredients.

Paul DeBenedictis, Reading, Massachusetts

3 pounds yellow onions

1 pound sweet onions, thinly sliced

2 tablespoons butter

1 tablespoon olive oil

1 teaspoon dried thyme

1 teaspoon brown sugar

1 teaspoon balsamic vinegar

1 tablespoon all-purpose flour

1 can (14-1/2 ounces) vegetable broth

1 can (12 ounces) dark beer or additional
vegetable broth

1/4 cup white wine or additional vegetable broth

2 tablespoons reduced-sodium soy sauce

1 tablespoon Worcestershire sauce

2 teaspoons brandy

1/2 teaspoon coarsely ground pepper

1/4 teaspoon salt

1/8 teaspoon cayenne pepper

6 slices French bread (1 inch thick)

6 slices Swiss cheese

1. In a Dutch oven, saute onions in butter and oil until tender. Reduce heat to medium-low; cook for 1 hour or until golden brown, stirring occasionally. Stir in the thyme, brown sugar and vinegar.

2. Combine flour and broth until blended. Gradually stir into onion mixture. Stir in beer, wine, soy sauce, Worcestershire sauce, brandy, pepper, salt and cayenne. Bring to a boil. Reduce heat; cover and simmer for 10 minutes.

3. Meanwhile, place bread on a baking sheet. Broil 4 in. from the heat for 2 minutes on each side or until toasted. Top each with a cheese slice; broil for 2-3 minutes or until cheese is melted and lightly browned. Ladle soup into bowls; garnish with cheese-topped toast.

YIELD: 6 SERVINGS.

NUTRITION FACTS: 1 cup with 1 bread slice with cheese equals 377 calories, 14 g fat (8 g saturated fat), 35 mg cholesterol, 875 mg sodium, 45 g carbohydrate, 6 g fiber, 12 g protein.

Teacher, Elkton Charter School

Elkton, Oregon

Yvonne Compton was born and raised in Australia, where she taught for 15 years before moving to the small rural town of Elkton, Indiana (population 180), 20 years ago. Today, she teaches kindergarten. "I love what I do," she says. "My teaching philosophy can be summed up by this poem: 'Every stage of development is complete in itself. A 3-year-old is not an incomplete 5-year-old. The child is not an incomplete adult. Never are we simply on our way! Always we have arrived. Enjoy now!'"

QUINOA AND BLACK BEAN SALAD

This good-for-you dish can be served either cold as a side salad for eight people or warm as an entree for four people. The lime vinaigrette adds a punch of flavor to this wonderful dish.

3rd place

Yvonne Compton, Elkton, Oregon

1 cup vegetable broth

1 cup water

1 cup quinoa, rinsed

1 medium sweet orange pepper, chopped

1 small red onion, chopped

1 garlic clove, minced

1 can (15 ounces) black beans, rinsed and drained

1 cup frozen corn, thawed

2 cups cherry tomatoes, halved

1/4 cup olive oil

2 tablespoons lime juice

1 teaspoon balsamic vinegar

1/2 teaspoon salt

1/4 teaspoon pepper

1/4 teaspoon chili powder

1 medium ripe avocado, peeled and cubed

2 tablespoons minced fresh cilantro

1. In a small saucepan, bring broth and water to a boil. Add quinoa. Reduce heat; cover and simmer for 12-16 minutes or until liquid is absorbed. Remove from the heat; fluff with a fork.

2. In a large nonstick skillet coated with cooking spray, cook the orange pepper, onion and garlic for 2 minutes. Stir in beans and corn; cook 2-3 minutes longer or until onion is tender. Remove from the heat; cool for 5 minutes. Stir in the tomatoes.

3. In a small bowl, whisk the oil, lime juice, vinegar, salt, pepper and chili powder. Pour over tomato mixture; toss to coat.

4. Spoon quinoa onto a serving platter. Top with the tomato mixture, avocado and cilantro.

YIELD: 8 SERVINGS.

EDITOR'S NOTE: Look for quinoa in the cereal, rice or organic food aisle.

NUTRITION FACTS: 1 cup equals 255 calories, 12 g fat (2 g saturated fat), 0 cholesterol, 378 mg sodium, 33 g carbohydrate, 6 g fiber, 7 g protein.

COWBOY BAKED BEANS

Baked beans are a perennial favorite at barbecues and potlucks. My meaty recipe uses a variety of beans and has a great smoky taste.

Administrator, McPherson County Schools, Tryon, Nebraska

Joe Sherwood, Tryon, Nebraska

1 pound ground beef

1 pound bacon, cooked and crumbled

2 cups barbecue sauce

1 can (16 ounces) butter beans, rinsed and drained

1 can (15-3/4 ounces) pork and beans

1 can (15-1/2 ounces) navy beans, rinsed and drained

1 can (15 ounces) black beans, rinsed and drained

2 medium onions, chopped

1/4 cup packed brown sugar

1/4 cup molasses

2 tablespoons balsamic vinegar

2 teaspoons ground mustard

2 teaspoons Worcestershire sauce

1 teaspoon salt

1 teaspoon garlic powder

1 teaspoon pepper

1. In a Dutch oven, cook beef over medium heat until no longer pink; drain. Stir in the remaining ingredients. Transfer to a greased 13-in. x 9-in. baking dish. Bake, uncovered, at 350° for 50-60 minutes or until heated through.

YIELD: 12 SERVINGS (3/4 CUP EACH).

NUTRITION FACTS: 3/4 cup equals 350 calories, 12 g fat (4 g saturated fat), 34 mg cholesterol, 1,232 mg sodium, 43 g carbohydrate, 8 g fiber, 20 g protein.

PORTOBELLO RISOTTO WITH MASCARPONE

Portobello mushrooms add a beefy flavor to this creamy classic. Each serving is topped with soft, buttery Mascarpone cheese to make it extra special.

Staff, Francis F. Wilson Elementary School
Rockville Centre, New York

Carmella Ryan, Rockville Centre, New York

1-1/2 cups water

1 can (14 ounces) reduced-sodium beef broth

1/2 cup chopped shallots

2 garlic cloves, minced

1 tablespoon canola oil

1 cup uncooked arborio rice

1 tablespoon minced fresh thyme or 1 teaspoon
   dried thyme

1/2 teaspoon salt

1/2 teaspoon pepper

1/2 cup white wine or additional reduced-sodium
   beef broth

1 cup sliced baby portobello mushrooms, chopped

1/4 cup grated Parmesan cheese

1/2 cup Mascarpone cheese

1. In a large saucepan, heat water and broth and keep warm.

2. In another large saucepan, saute shallots and garlic in oil for 2-3 minutes or until shallots are tender. Add the rice, thyme, salt and pepper; cook and stir for 2-3 minutes. Reduce heat; stir in wine. Cook and stir until all of the liquid is absorbed.

3. Add the heated broth, 1/2 cup at a time, stirring constantly. Allow the liquid to absorb between additions. Cook just until risotto is creamy and rice is almost tender. (Cooking time is about 20 minutes.)

4. Add mushrooms and Parmesan cheese; stir gently until the cheese is melted. Garnish each serving with a heaping tablespoon of Mascarpone. Serve immediately.

YIELD: 6 SERVINGS.

NUTRITION FACTS: 3/4 cup risotto with a heaping tablespoon Mascarpone cheese equals 350 calories, 21 g fat (10 g saturated fat), 51 mg cholesterol, 393 mg sodium, 31 g carbohydrate, 1 g fiber, 7 g protein.

Staff
El Dorado Adventist School

Placerville, California

Charlotte Thomas is a licensed caterer who runs the hot lunch program for El Dorado Adventist School, where her son is a student. When she isn't serving lunch or acting as president of the school's Parent-Teacher Association, she is busy running her catering business, Fresh Start. This past year, she began teaching a culinary arts class at the school. "I am trying to teach the students that preparing food from scratch is better for you and your budget," she says. "I prep all my food from scratch. No prepackaged food here."

GARLIC ASIAGO BREAD

My friends and family rave about this recipe. It has chunks of cheese and fabulous garlic taste. We have bread sales at our school as a fundraiser, and this is always one of the top sellers.

Charlotte Thomas, Pollock Pines, California

1 package (1/4 ounce) active dry yeast
1-1/4 cups warm water (110° to 115°)
2 tablespoons plus 2 teaspoons olive oil
7 garlic cloves, minced
1 tablespoon sugar
2 teaspoons salt
1-1/2 teaspoons white vinegar
3 to 3-1/4 cups bread flour
1 cup cubed Asiago cheese
EGG WASH:
1 egg
1 tablespoon water

1. In a large bowl, dissolve yeast in warm water. Add the oil, garlic, sugar, salt, vinegar and 2 cups flour. Beat until smooth. Stir in enough remaining flour to form a firm dough. Stir in the cheese.

2. Turn onto a floured surface; knead until smooth and elastic, about 6-8 minutes. Place in a greased bowl, turning once to grease the top. Cover and let rise in a warm place until doubled, about 1 hour.

3. Punch dough down; divide in half. Shape into 5-in.-round loaves. Place on lightly greased baking sheets. Cover and let rise in a warm place until doubled, about 30 minutes.

4. For egg wash, in a small bowl, combine egg and water. Brush over loaves. Bake at 375° for 20-25 minutes or until golden brown. Cool on wire racks.

YIELD: 2 LOAVES (10 WEDGES EACH).

NUTRITION FACTS: 1 wedge equals 107 calories, 4 g fat (1 g saturated fat), 9 mg cholesterol, 254 mg sodium, 15 g carbohydrate, 1 g fiber, 5 g protein. DIABETIC EXCHANGES: 1 starch, 1/2 fat.

CRAB SOUP WITH SHERRY

Everybody loves this rich, comforting soup that's a tradition in the South. It is brimming with crab and has a smooth texture.

Staff, Newington Elementary School, Summerville, South Carolina

Regina Huggins, Summerville, South Carolina

1 pound fresh or frozen crabmeat, thawed

6 tablespoons sherry or chicken broth

1 small onion, grated

1/4 cup butter, cubed

1/4 cup all-purpose flour

1/2 teaspoon salt

2 cups 2% milk

2 chicken bouillon cubes

3 cups half-and-half cream

2 tablespoons minced fresh parsley

1. In a small bowl, combine crabmeat and sherry; set aside.

2. In a large saucepan, saute onion in butter until tender. Stir in flour and salt until blended; gradually add milk and bouillon. Bring to a boil; cook and stir for 2 minutes or until thickened. Stir in the cream and crab mixture; heat through. Sprinkle servings with parsley.

YIELD: 6 SERVINGS.

NUTRITION FACTS: 1 cup equals 382 calories, 23 g fat (14 g saturated fat), 162 mg cholesterol, 936 mg sodium, 14 g carbohydrate, trace fiber, 23 g protein.

CURRIED FRIED RICE WITH PINEAPPLE

This is a special fried rice dish called "khao pad," which is frequently enjoyed in Thai restaurants. It has a bit of heat, a little sweetness and some crunch.

Teacher, AJ Dorsa Elementary School, San Jose, California

Joanna Yuen, San Jose, California

4 tablespoons canola oil, divided

2 eggs, beaten

1 small onion, finely chopped

2 shallots, finely chopped

3 garlic cloves, minced

4 cups cold cooked rice

1 can (8 ounces) unsweetened pineapple chunks, drained

1/2 cup lightly salted cashews

1/2 cup frozen peas

1/3 cup minced fresh cilantro

1/4 cup raisins

3 tablespoons chicken broth

2 tablespoons fish sauce

1-1/2 teaspoons curry powder

1 teaspoon sugar

1/4 teaspoon crushed red pepper flakes

1. In a large skillet or wok, heat 1 tablespoon oil over medium-high heat; add eggs. As eggs set, lift edges, letting uncooked portion flow underneath. When eggs are completely cooked, remove to a plate and keep warm.

2. In the same pan, stir-fry onion and shallots in remaining oil until tender. Add garlic; cook 1 minute longer. Stir in the rice, pineapple, cashews, peas, cilantro, raisins, broth, fish sauce, curry, sugar and pepper flakes; heat through. Chop egg into small pieces; add to rice mixture.

YIELD: 8 SERVINGS.

NUTRITION FACTS: 3/4 cup equals 286 calories, 13 g fat (2 g saturated fat), 53 mg cholesterol, 413 mg sodium, 36 g carbohydrate, 2 g fiber, 7 g protein.

Teacher, Onamia Elementary

Onamia, Minnesota

Teresa Lueck has been teaching fourth and fifth grade students at Onamia Elementary for the past 21 years. "The best part of being a teacher is seeing students develop into caring, responsible young adults," she says. Onamia Elementary is located in a rural area that is big on community. "Adults and children share in a camaraderie of enjoying the abundance that nature has to offer," she says. "Many of us partake in hunting, fishing, wild ricing, maple sugaring, skiing, snow shoeing...the works!"

HALIBUT CHOWDER

have a passion for cooking and entertaining. Several times a
ear, I invite both my retired and current teaching friends to
 dinner party with their spouses. I serve this halibut chowder
t those parties and it is always a big hit.

Teresa Lueck, Onamia, Minnesota

4 celery ribs, chopped

3 medium carrots, chopped

1 large onion, chopped

1/2 cup butter, cubed

1/2 cup all-purpose flour

1/4 teaspoon white pepper

2 cups 2% milk

1 can (14-1/2 ounces) chicken broth

1/4 cup water

1 tablespoon chicken base

3 medium potatoes, peeled and chopped

1 can (15-1/4 ounces) whole kernel corn, drained

3 bay leaves

2 cups half-and-half cream

2 tablespoons lemon juice

1 pound halibut or other whitefish fillets, cut into 1-inch pieces

1 cup salad croutons

3/4 cup grated Parmesan cheese

1/2 cup minced chives

1. In a large saucepan, saute the celery, carrots and onion in butter until tender. Stir in flour and pepper until blended; gradually add the milk, broth, water and chicken base. Bring to a boil; cook and stir for 2 minutes or until thickened.

2. Add the potatoes, corn and bay leaves. Return to a boil. Reduce heat; cover and simmer for 15-20 minutes or until potatoes are tender.

3. Stir in cream and lemon juice; return to a boil. Add halibut. Reduce heat; simmer, uncovered, for 7-11 minutes or until fish flakes easily with a fork. Discard bay leaves.

4. Garnish servings with croutons, cheese and chives.

YIELD: 12 SERVINGS (3 QUARTS).

EDITOR'S NOTE: Look for chicken base near the broth and bouillon.

NUTRITION FACTS: 1 cup equals 316 calories, 16 g fat (9 g saturated fat), 61 mg cholesterol, 671 mg sodium, 25 g carbohydrate, 2 g fiber, 16 g protein.

Teacher, Hillside Elementary

West Valley City, Utah

Jason Johnson has been an educator for eight years, and currently teaches third grade. You might say his classroom is a zoo—there are three classroom pets! "Our class currently has three pets for hands-on science learning: a Chilean rose-hair tarantula, a corn snake and a ball python," he says. "Parents allow their children in my class to babysit the animals during school breaks. Very few parents want to babysit the tarantula, but all the kids want to take it home!"

HARVEST PUMPKIN SOUP

With its dazzling golden orange color, this soup will brighten any day. I especially enjoy it on a cool autumn night.

Jason Johnson, West Valley City, Utah

6 medium carrots, shredded

1 large sweet onion, finely chopped

2 celery ribs, finely chopped

3 tablespoons butter

1 medium apple, peeled and shredded

5 garlic cloves, minced

1 can (29 ounces) solid-pack pumpkin

1 can (14-1/2 ounces) chicken broth

1/4 cup minced fresh parsley

2 teaspoons dried thyme

1 teaspoon salt

1 teaspoon brown sugar

1 teaspoon ground cumin

1/2 teaspoon ground nutmeg

1/2 teaspoon ground ginger

1/4 teaspoon pepper

2 cups 2% milk

1 cup heavy whipping cream

Salted pumpkin seeds or pepitas

1. In a Dutch oven, saute the carrots, onion and celery in butter for 4 minutes. Add apple and garlic; cook 2 minutes longer or until vegetables are tender.

2. Stir in the pumpkin, broth, parsley and seasonings. Bring to a boil. Reduce heat; cover and simmer for 20 minutes. Add milk and cream. Cool slightly. In a blender, process soup in batches until smooth. Return all to pan and heat through. Garnish servings with pumpkin seeds.

YIELD: 10 SERVINGS (2-1/2 QUARTS).

NUTRITION FACTS: 1 cup (calculated without pumpkin seeds) equals 208 calories, 14 g fat (8 g saturated fat), 46 mg cholesterol, 511 mg sodium, 19 g carbohydrate, 6 g fiber, 5 g protein.

BLACK-EYED PEA SPINACH SALAD

Here's a Southern take on a classic spinach salad. It has black-eyed peas and pecans. It is always a hit with my guests.

Teacher, Hubbertville School, Fayette, Alabama

Debbi Ingle, Winfield, Alabama

1/4 cup olive oil

1/4 cup red wine vinegar

4 teaspoons Dijon mustard

1 teaspoon salt

1 teaspoon pepper

2 cans (15-1/2 ounces each) black-eyed peas, rinsed and drained

3 medium tomatoes, seeded and chopped

1/2 cup thinly sliced red onion

1 package (9 ounces) fresh spinach

1/2 cup chopped pecans, toasted

6 bacon strips, cooked and crumbled

1. In a large bowl, whisk the first five ingredients. Stir in the peas, tomatoes and onion. Cover and refrigerate until serving.

2. Place the spinach and vegetable mixture in a large serving bowl; toss gently. Sprinkle with pecans and bacon.

YIELD: 16 SERVINGS (3/4 CUP EACH).

NUTRITION FACTS: 3/4 cup equals 121 calories, 7 g fat (1 g saturated fat), 3 mg cholesterol, 356 mg sodium, 10 g carbohydrate, 2 g fiber, 5 g protein.

GARLIC CHEESE BREADSTICKS

Breadsticks complement so many dishes. Brushed with a delicious buttery topping, they bake to a pretty golden brown and taste wonderful.

Staff, ACES (Area Cooperative for Educational Support) Maryville, Missouri

Ann Volner, Maryville, Missouri

1 package (1/4 ounce) active dry yeast

1-1/2 cups warm water (110° to 115°)

1/2 cup warm 2% milk (110° to 115°)

3 tablespoons sugar

3 tablespoons butter, melted

1-1/2 teaspoons salt

1/2 teaspoon baking soda

4-1/2 to 5-1/2 cups all-purpose flour

TOPPING:

1/2 cup butter, melted

1 cup grated Parmesan cheese

4-1/2 teaspoons Italian seasoning

1 teaspoon garlic powder

1. In a large bowl, dissolve yeast in warm water and milk. Add the sugar, butter, salt, baking soda and 3 cups flour. Beat until smooth. Stir in enough remaining flour to form a firm dough.

2. Turn onto a floured surface; knead until smooth and elastic, about 6-8 minutes. Place in a greased bowl, turning once to grease the top. Cover and let rise in a warm place until doubled, about 1 hour.

3. Turn dough onto a lightly floured surface; cover and let rest for 10 minutes. Divide into 32 pieces. Shape each piece into a 4-1/2-in. rope.

4. Place melted butter in a shallow bowl. Place Parmesan cheese in a separate shallow bowl. Dip ropes in butter then coat with the cheese. Place 3 in. apart on lightly greased baking sheets. Combine Italian seasoning and garlic powder; sprinkle over breadsticks. Cover and let rise until doubled, about 30 minutes.

5. Bake at 375° for 10-15 minutes or until golden brown. Remove to wire racks. Serve warm.

YIELD: 32 BREADSTICKS.

NUTRITION FACTS: 1 breadstick equals 117 calories, 5 g fat (3 g saturated fat), 13 mg cholesterol, 199 mg sodium, 15 g carbohydrate, 1 g fiber, 3 g protein.

Administrator, Bataan Memorial
Elementary School

Port Clinton, Ohio

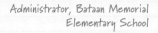

As the principal at Bataan
Memorial Elementary
School, Kendra Van Doren
feels honored that she
gets the opportunity to
influence and interact
with her students on a
daily basis. "There is never a boring day," she says. "And as a K-2
principal, I get a lot
of hugs every day."

ITALIAN SAUSAGE SOUP

This hearty and warming soup makes a comforting dinner. The herbs make the kitchen smell incredible! You can use lower-calorie turkey sausage for the Italian sausage if you like. I also recommend adding 2 teapoons olive oil to the sausage while cooking to prevent sticking.

Kendra Van Doren, Clyde, Ohio

1 pound Italian turkey sausage links, casings removed

1 large onion, chopped

1 medium carrot, chopped

1 celery rib, chopped

2 cartons (32 ounces each) reduced-sodium
  chicken broth

1 can (14-1/2 ounces) diced tomatoes, undrained

1 can (8 ounces) tomato sauce

1 garlic clove, minced

1 teaspoon dried oregano

1/2 teaspoon dried rosemary, crushed

1/2 teaspoon dried basil

1/4 teaspoon dried thyme

1/4 teaspoon fennel seed, crushed

1 bay leaf

3/4 cup uncooked orzo pasta

Grated Parmesan cheese, optional

1. In a Dutch oven coated with cooking spray, cook the sausage, onion, carrot and celery over medium heat until meat is no longer pink; drain.

2. Add the broth, tomatoes, tomato sauce, garlic, seasonings and bay leaf. Bring to a boil. Stir in orzo; cook, uncovered, for 8-10 minutes or until pasta is tender. Discard bay leaf. Sprinkle servings with cheese if desired.

YIELD: 11 SERVINGS (2-3/4 QUARTS).

NUTRITION FACTS: 1 cup equals 144 calories, 4 g fat (1 g saturated fat), 25 mg cholesterol, 811 mg sodium, 16 g carbohydrate, 2 g fiber, 11 g protein.

Teacher
James Island Middle School

Charleston, South Carolina

Angie Pitts is the seventh grade reading and math resource teacher at James Island Middle School. She enjoys watching students accomplish tasks they once struggled with. "I am also fortunate to co-teach with some wonderful teachers," she says.

MEDITERRANEAN CHICKEN SOUP

This is my go-to soup when I'm feeling under the weather. The comforting flavors always make me feel better, although the hearty soup is still a favorite even when I'm feeling great!

Angie Pitts, Charleston, South Carolina

1-1/2 pounds boneless skinless chicken breasts, cut into 3/4-inch cubes

1 tablespoon Greek seasoning

1 teaspoon pepper

1 tablespoon olive oil

4 green onions, thinly sliced

1 garlic clove, minced

1/4 cup white wine or chicken broth

7 cups reduced-sodium chicken broth

1/4 cup chopped sun-dried tomatoes (not packed in oil)

1/4 cup pitted Greek olives, sliced

1 tablespoon capers, drained

1-1/2 teaspoons minced fresh basil or 1/2 teaspoon dried basil

1-1/2 teaspoons minced fresh oregano or 1/2 teaspoon dried oregano

1-1/2 cups uncooked orzo pasta

2 tablespoons lemon juice

1-1/2 teaspoons minced fresh parsley

1. Season chicken with Greek seasoning and pepper. In a Dutch oven, saute chicken in oil until no longer pink; remove and set aside. Add green onions and garlic to the pan; saute for 1 minute. Add wine; stir to loosen browned bits from the pan.

2. Stir in the broth, tomatoes, olives, capers, basil, oregano and chicken. Bring to a boil. Reduce heat; cover and simmer for 15 minutes. Return to a boil. Stir in orzo. Cook 8-10 minutes longer or until pasta is tender. Stir in lemon juice and parsley.

YIELD: 8 SERVINGS (2 QUARTS).

NUTRITION FACTS: 1 cup equals 285 calories, 5 g fat (1 g saturated fat), 47 mg cholesterol, 1,042 mg sodium, 31 g carbohydrate, 1 g fiber, 25 g protein.

GARDEN MASHED POTATOES

This is a great way to dress up mashed potatoes. This colorful dish has lots of veggies and is full of flavor. It will be a tasty complement to many meals.

Teacher, Chadron High School, Chadron, Nebraska

Brenda Budler, Chadron, Nebraska

1 pound medium Yukon Gold potatoes, cubed

1 pound medium red potatoes, cubed

1 pound medium carrots, chopped

4 garlic cloves, peeled and halved

1 jalapeno pepper, seeded and chopped

1/4 cup butter, cubed

1/2 teaspoon salt

1/4 teaspoon pepper

1-1/2 cups frozen white corn, thawed

1/2 cup shredded Monterey Jack cheese

1. Place the potatoes, carrots, garlic and jalapeno in a large saucepan; cover with water. Bring to a boil. Reduce heat; cover and cook for 15-20 minutes or until tender. Drain.

2. Mash vegetables with butter, salt and pepper; stir in corn and cheese.

YIELD: 8 SERVINGS.

EDITOR'S NOTE: We recommend wearing disposable gloves when cutting hot peppers. Avoid touching your face.

NUTRITION FACTS: 3/4 cup equals 211 calories, 8 g fat (5 g saturated fat), 21 mg cholesterol, 275 mg sodium, 30 g carbohydrate, 4 g fiber, 5 g protein.

CRANBERRY AMBROSIA SALAD

My paternal grandmother made this fluffy and fruity salad for Christmas dinner. I'm not sure how many batches she made, as there were nearly fifty aunts, uncles and cousins in our family. I still make the recipe in memory of her, and it's still as good as I remember.

Teacher, Shell Rock Elementary, Shell Rock, Iowa

Janet Hurley, Shell Rock, Iowa

1 pound fresh or frozen cranberries
1 can (20 ounces) crushed pineapple, drained
1 cup sugar
2 cups miniature marshmallows
1 cup heavy whipping cream, whipped
1/2 cup chopped pecans

1. In a food processor, cover and process cranberries until coarsely chopped. Transfer to a large bowl; stir in pineapple and sugar. Cover and refrigerate overnight.

2. Just before serving, fold in the marshmallows, whipped cream and pecans.

YIELD: 9 SERVINGS.

NUTRITION FACTS: 3/4 cup equals 331 calories, 15 g fat (7 g saturated fat), 36 mg cholesterol, 17 mg sodium, 52 g carbohydrate, 3 g fiber, 2 g protein.

Teacher
Dowdell Middle Magnet School

Tampa, Florida

As a lead teacher, Susan Ferrell "leads" and encourages educators to incorporate the magnet theme into their lessons. "As a lead teacher you are the spokesperson for programs offered, tour guide and representative to the community," she says. "The best part of this position is the flexibility to work with different groups of students and to see the impact of our environmental program on students."

EASY GAZPACHO

I really enjoy gazpacho a lot. Sometimes I make this soup on Sunday evening and then take it to school for lunch all week. The crunchy vegetables in the tomato base add a healthy item to my menu.

Susan Ferrell, Tampa, Florida

2 cups Clamato juice
3 plum tomatoes, seeded and finely chopped
1/2 cup finely chopped green pepper
1/2 cup finely chopped seeded cucumber
1/2 cup finely chopped celery
1/4 cup finely chopped onion
2 tablespoons olive oil
2 tablespoons red wine vinegar

2 teaspoons minced fresh parsley
1 teaspoon minced chives
1 garlic clove, minced
1/2 teaspoon pepper
1/2 teaspoon Worcestershire sauce
1/4 teaspoon salt
Salad croutons, optional

1. In a large bowl, combine the Clamato juice, tomatoes, green pepper, cucumber, celery, onion, oil, vinegar, parsley, chives, garlic, pepper, Worcestershire sauce and salt. Cover and refrigerate for at least 4 hours. Serve with croutons if desired.

YIELD: 4 SERVINGS.

NUTRITION FACTS: 1 cup (calculated without croutons) equals 114 calories, 7 g fat (1 g saturated fat), 0 cholesterol, 611 mg sodium, 11 g carbohydrate, 1 g fiber, 1 g protein.

Blaine, Minnesota

Mother and son, Patty Tkach and Josh Perkins, teach at two different schools in the same district. Josh says his mom has been known to send him odd items through inner-school mail. On numerous occasions, he opened a manila envelope at Johnsville Elementary expecting official papers, only to find a loaf of tasty banana bread, socks or a T-shirt. "Only a mom trying to take care of her 36-year-old son," he says. Aside from a shared love of teaching, both enjoy trying new soup recipes.

HERBED TOMATO BISQUE

This creamy tomato soup chases away any chill. It has a hint of sweetness from honey and great herb flavor.

Josh Perkins, Maple Grove, Minnesota
Patty Tkach, Coon Rapids, Minnesota

1 medium onion, finely chopped

1/4 cup butter, cubed

1/4 cup all-purpose flour

1 teaspoon dill weed

1 teaspoon dried oregano

3 cups chicken broth

3 cans (14-1/2 ounces each) diced tomatoes, undrained

1/4 cup minced fresh parsley

2 tablespoons honey

3/4 teaspoon salt

3/4 teaspoon white pepper

1-1/2 cups half-and-half cream

1. In a large saucepan, saute onion in butter until tender. Stir in the flour, dill and oregano until blended; gradually add chicken broth. Bring to a boil; cook and stir for 2 minutes or until thickened.

2. Stir in the tomatoes, parsley, honey, salt and pepper. Return to a boil. Reduce heat; simmer, uncovered, for 15 minutes. Stir in cream; heat through.

YIELD: 8 SERVINGS (2 QUARTS).

NUTRITION FACTS: 1 cup equals 187 calories, 10 g fat (7 g saturated fat), 39 mg cholesterol, 850 mg sodium, 19 g carbohydrate, 3 g fiber, 4 g protein.

CORNUCOPIA SALAD

I first enjoyed this salad at a church potluck. Since then, it has become a Thanksgiving tradition at my house. I've made some adjustments to the original recipe to please my vegetarian friends. But for a complete meal, add three cooked, shredded chicken breasts to the salad mix.

Teacher, Granville Elementary, Prescott Valley, Arizona

Cheryl Peterman, Prescott Valley, Arizona

1/2 cup sliced almonds

3 tablespoons sugar

4 cups torn leaf lettuce

4 cups torn romaine

2 celery ribs, chopped

4 green onions, chopped

1/4 cup dried cranberries

1 can (11 ounces) mandarin oranges, drained

1 medium apple, chopped

VINAIGRETTE:

1/4 cup canola oil

2 tablespoons sugar

2 tablespoons rice vinegar

1 tablespoon minced fresh parsley

1/2 teaspoon salt

1/4 teaspoon pepper

1/2 cup crumbled blue cheese, optional

1. In a small heavy skillet over medium-low heat, stir almonds and sugar until sugar is melted and almonds are coated. Cool on waxed paper. Break apart and set aside.

2. In a large bowl, combine the lettuce, romaine, celery, onions and cranberries. Add oranges and apple.

3. In a small bowl, whisk the oil, sugar, vinegar, parsley, salt and pepper. Drizzle over salad; toss to coat. Sprinkle with almonds and blue cheese if desired.

YIELD: 8 SERVINGS.

NUTRITION FACTS: 1-1/4 cups (calculated without cheese) equals 186 calories, 10 g fat (1 g saturated fat), 0 cholesterol, 170 mg sodium, 24 g carbohydrate, 3 g fiber, 2 g protein.

CRUNCHY APPLE SALAD

Whenever our staff celebrates a birthday or a special occasion, "Mary's Apple Salad" is always at the top of the wish list! The ingredients can be prepared the day before and put together in a flash for our teachers' 20-minute lunchtime.

Teacher, Malcolm B. Chancey Elementary, Louisville, Kentucky

Mary Robertson, Louisville, Kentucky

2 packages (5 ounces each) spring mix salad greens
2 large apples, chopped
2 cups bagel chips, coarsely crushed
1-1/2 cups honey-roasted peanuts
1 cup (4 ounces) crumbled blue cheese

DRESSING:
1/3 cup sugar
1/3 cup canola oil
1/4 cup cider vinegar
1 tablespoon poppy seeds
1-1/4 teaspoons dried minced onion
1 teaspoon Worcestershire sauce
1/2 teaspoon salt
1/4 teaspoon paprika
1/8 teaspoon pepper

1. In a large salad bowl, combine the first five ingredients. In a small bowl, whisk the dressing ingredients. Drizzle over salad; toss to coat.

YIELD: 16 SERVINGS (1 CUP EACH).

NUTRITION FACTS: 1 cup equals 207 calories, 14 g fat (3 g saturated fat), 6 mg cholesterol, 277 mg sodium, 17 g carbohydrate, 2 g fiber, 6 g protein.

Nichole Fischer has been teaching elementary school in Las Vegas for 20 years. "One of the best parts about teaching is knowing that you're sculpting our youth and giving them a firm foundation for learning," she says. "My goal is to make learning fun and meaningful to my students, and to instill in them how important and special each of them are to me and to society."

REUBEN PASTA SALAD

I have German heritage, so I brought this German-influenced salad to my neighbor's Octoberfest party. It was a house full of teachers who gave it an A+.

Nichole Fischer, Las Vegas, Nevada

4 cups uncooked egg noodles

1/3 cup packed brown sugar

1/4 cup olive oil

1/4 cup Dijon mustard

2 tablespoons cider vinegar

1-1/2 teaspoons caraway seeds

6 cups coleslaw mix

8 ounces sliced deli corned beef, cut into strips

1/4 cup shredded Swiss cheese

1. In a large saucepan, cook the noodles according to package directions.
2. Meanwhile, in a small saucepan over low heat, combine the brown sugar, oil, mustard, vinegar and caraway seeds. Cook and stir for 3-5 minutes or until heated through.
3. Drain noodles. In a large bowl, combine the coleslaw mix, noodles, corned beef and warm dressing; toss to coat. Sprinkle with cheese. Serve warm or at room temperature. Refrigerate leftovers.

YIELD: 16 SERVINGS (3/4 CUP EACH).

NUTRITION FACTS: 3/4 cup equals 131 calories, 5 g fat (1 g saturated fat), 21 mg cholesterol, 267 mg sodium, 16 g carbohydrate, 1 g fiber, 5 g protein.

Teacher, Socastee High School

**Myrtle Beach,
South Carolina**

Over the past decade, educator Christine Green has taught everything from physical science and biology to anatomy and physiology. Seeing her students succeed is what she calls the highlight of her career. "That is what the job is about," she says. "I know that they finally understand what I have been trying so hard to convey." She's also proud to teach at a school that Newsweek Magazine included in the top 5 percent of high schools in the nation.

MEDITERRANEAN PASTA SALAD

My mom always encouraged us to try different foods. She made it her mission in life to expose us to new recipes with unique flavor combinations. This salad reminds me of my mom in how it makes eating new flavors exciting.

Christine Green, Conway, South Carolina

1 package (12 ounces) tricolor spiral pasta

2-1/2 cups quartered and thinly sliced cucumbers

1-1/4 cups grape tomatoes, halved

1 jar (5-3/4 ounces) pimiento-stuffed olives, drained and halved

1/2 cup chopped green pepper

1/2 cup chopped sweet yellow pepper

2 tablespoons capers, drained

1 cup (4 ounces) crumbled feta cheese

6 slices provolone cheese, chopped

1 cup shredded Parmesan cheese, divided

1/4 pound hard salami, cubed

1 cup Italian salad dressing

1. Cook pasta according to package directions. Drain pasta and rinse in cold water.

2. In a large bowl, combine the cucumbers, tomatoes, olives, peppers, capers and pasta. Stir in the feta and provolone cheeses, 1/2 cup Parmesan cheese and salami. Add dressing; toss to coat. Sprinkle with remaining Parmesan cheese.

YIELD: 18 SERVINGS (3/4 CUP EACH).

NUTRITION FACTS: 3/4 cup equals 222 calories, 13 g fat (4 g saturated fat), 18 mg cholesterol, 715 mg sodium, 18 g carbohydrate, 1 g fiber, 9 g protein.

HUNGARIAN MUSHROOM SOUP

You'll think you are eating at a fine restaurant when you taste this rich, golden soup. It's so delicious!

Staff, Griffin Creek Elementary, Medford, Oregon

Sandy Vaughn, Central Point, Oregon

1 large sweet onion, chopped

1/4 cup butter, cubed

3/4 pound sliced fresh mushrooms

3 tablespoons all-purpose flour

1 tablespoon paprika

1 teaspoon dill weed

3/4 teaspoon salt

1/4 teaspoon coarsely ground pepper

1 can (14-1/2 ounces) chicken broth

1 cup 2% milk

1 tablespoon soy sauce

1/2 cup sour cream

2 teaspoons lemon juice

1. In a large saucepan, saute onion in butter for 2 minutes. Add mushrooms; cook 4-5 minutes longer or until mushrooms are tender.

2. Stir in the flour, paprika, dill, salt and pepper until blended. Gradually stir in the broth, milk and soy sauce. Bring to a boil; cook and stir for 2 minutes or until thickened. Reduce heat; cover and simmer for 15 minutes.

3. Just before serving, stir in the sour cream and lemon juice (do not boil).

YIELD: 4 SERVINGS.

NUTRITION FACTS: 1 cup equals 275 calories, 18 g fat (12 g saturated fat), 57 mg cholesterol, 1,249 mg sodium, 20 g carbohydrate, 3 g fiber, 8 g protein.

ORZO WITH SPINACH AND PINE NUTS

I have shared this salad many times with the teachers at my school. They enjoy it so much that they request it. It's best to put the tomatoes on the salad just before serving so they won't wilt from the heat and moisture. In my opinion, the dish would not be as delectable if you substituted another vinegar for the balsamic vinegar.

Teacher, Highland School, Skokie, Illinois

Kate Whitehead, Lindenhurst, Illinois

---

1 package (16 ounces) orzo pasta
1 cup pine nuts
1 garlic clove, minced
1/2 teaspoon dried basil
1/2 teaspoon crushed red pepper flakes
1/4 cup olive oil
1 tablespoon butter
2 packages (6 ounces each) fresh baby spinach
1 teaspoon salt
1/4 teaspoon pepper
1/4 cup balsamic vinegar
2 cups (8 ounces) crumbled feta cheese
1 large tomato, finely chopped

1. In a large saucepan, cook the pasta according to package directions.
2. Meanwhile, in a Dutch oven over medium heat, cook the pine nuts, garlic, basil and pepper flakes in oil and butter just until nuts are lightly browned.
3. Add the spinach, salt and pepper; cook and stir 4-5 minutes longer or just until spinach is wilted. Transfer to a large bowl.
4. Drain pasta. Stir into spinach mixture. Drizzle with vinegar; sprinkle with cheese and tomato.

YIELD: 12 SERVINGS (3/4 CUP EACH).

NUTRITION FACTS: 3/4 cup equals 313 calories, 15 g fat (4 g saturated fat), 13 mg cholesterol, 411 mg sodium, 33 g carbohydrate, 3 g fiber, 12 g protein.

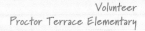

As a parent volunteer, Elizabeth Charpiot wears many hats. She helps in the classroom, grades papers, chaperones field trips and more. Elizabeth describes Proctor Terrace Elementary as a small school that gets "major results in students going on to being in the top of their graduating class."

SOUTHWESTERN CORN BREAD

I put a wonderful twist on my Grandma's classic corn bread. The teachers at my kids' school thought it was sensational. Any extra flavored butter can be kept in the refrigerator for about a week and used in other recipes or on toast.

Elizabeth Charpiot, Santa Rosa, California

2 cups all-purpose flour

2 cups yellow cornmeal

1/2 cup sugar

4 teaspoons baking powder

1 teaspoon baking soda

1 teaspoon salt

1 teaspoon dried minced garlic

1 teaspoon dried minced onion

1 teaspoon paprika

1 teaspoon chili powder

2 cups buttermilk

1/2 cup canola oil

2 eggs

1 jar (7 ounces) roasted sweet red peppers, drained, patted dry and chopped

1 cup frozen corn, thawed

1/4 cup minced chives

CHILI HONEY-LIME BUTTER:

1/2 cup butter, softened

1 tablespoon lime juice

1 tablespoon honey

1 teaspoon chili powder

1 teaspoon grated lime peel

1. In a large bowl, combine the first 10 ingredients. In a small bowl, whisk the buttermilk, oil and eggs. Stir into the dry ingredients just until moistened. Fold in the red peppers, corn and chives.

2. Transfer to a greased 13-in. x 9-in. baking dish. Bake at 400° for 23-28 minutes or until a toothpick inserted near the center comes out clean. Remove to a wire rack.

3. In a small bowl, combine the butter, lime juice, honey, chili powder and lime peel. Serve with warm corn bread.

YIELD: 15 SERVINGS (1/2 CUP BUTTER).

NUTRITION FACTS: 1 piece with 1-1/2 teaspoons butter equals 317 calories, 15 g fat (5 g saturated fat), 46 mg cholesterol, 488 mg sodium, 40 g carbohydrate, 2 g fiber, 6 g protein.

Teacher
Chiddix Junior High School

Normal, Illinois

LeAnn Fujimoto has taught math and science on the Einstein team at Chiddix Junior High School for nearly her entire teaching career. She has been honored with the Illinois Math and Science Academy's 1999 Caring to Challenge Award and was recognized as a 2007 Turner N. Whiley Teacher of the Year. In addition to teaching, LeAnn coaches volleyball for the Illini Elite Volleyball Club. Whether teaching or coaching, LeAnn lives by the philosophy, "Children don't care what you know until they know that you care!"

SESAME SPAGHETTI SALAD WITH PEANUTS

I love the sweet and spicy combination of the Asian-styled sauce in this recipe. This salad can be made a day ahead.

LeAnn Fujimoto, Normal, Illinois

1 package (1 pound) spaghetti

1/3 cup sesame oil

1/4 cup canola oil

1 teaspoon crushed red pepper flakes

1/4 cup reduced-sodium soy sauce

3 tablespoons honey

1-1/2 teaspoons kosher salt

1/2 cup dry roasted peanuts, chopped

1/4 cup minced fresh cilantro

2 tablespoons sesame seeds, toasted

1. Cook spaghetti according to package directions.
2. Meanwhile, in a small saucepan over medium heat, heat the sesame oil, canola oil and pepper flakes until oil is fragrant. Remove from the heat. Stir in the soy sauce, honey and salt; set aside.
3. Drain spaghetti and rinse in cold water; transfer to a large bowl. Add the peanuts, cilantro, sesame seeds and oil mixture; toss to coat. Chill until serving.

YIELD: 10 SERVINGS.

NUTRITION FACTS: 3/4 cup salad equals 358 calories, 18 g fat (2 g saturated fat), 0 cholesterol, 595 mg sodium, 42 g carbohydrate, 2 g fiber, 8 g protein.

SAUSAGE STUFFING MUFFINS

This recipe puts stuffing into a muffin form for a special presentation. I made these when I cooked my first Thanksgiving dinner. You can also bake the stuffing in a greased baking dish with equally delicious results.

Teacher, Hartselle Junior High School, Hartselle, Alabama

Tricia Bibb, Hartselle, Alabama

1 pound bulk pork sausage

4 celery ribs, chopped

2 medium onions, chopped

1/4 cup butter, cubed

1 package (14 ounces) crushed corn bread stuffing

2 medium apples, peeled and chopped

1 package (6 ounces) dried cranberries

1 cup chopped pecans

1 teaspoon salt

1 teaspoon pepper

2 to 3 cups reduced-sodium chicken broth

2 eggs

2 teaspoons baking powder

1. In a large skillet, cook sausage over medium heat until no longer pink; drain. Transfer to a large bowl; set aside.

2. In the same skillet, saute the celery and onions in butter until tender. Transfer to the bowl; add the stuffing, apples, cranberries, pecans, salt and pepper. Stir in enough broth to reach desired moistness. Whisk eggs and baking powder; add to stuffing mixture.

3. Spoon into 18 greased muffin cups. Bake at 375° for 20-25 minutes or until lightly browned. Cool for 10 minutes. Run a knife around the edges of the muffin cups to loosen. Serve immediately.

YIELD: 1-1/2 DOZEN.

NUTRITION FACTS: 1 muffin equals 258 calories, 14 g fat (4 g saturated fat), 39 mg cholesterol, 625 mg sodium, 30 g carbohydrate, 3 g fiber, 6 g protein.

DEEP-FRIED RICE BALLS

My mother moved in with us about eight years ago and started making this side dish. Now I've taken over the duty of making these unique rice balls. Everyone in our family is thrilled to see them on the table.

Staff, Fairfield Elementary School, Virginia Beach, Virginia

Elizabeth Blake, Chesapeake, Virginia

4-1/2 cups water

2 cups uncooked long grain rice

2 tablespoons butter

1 teaspoon salt

1/2 teaspoon pepper

4 eggs, beaten

1/3 cup grated Parmesan cheese

2 tablespoons dried parsley flakes

1-3/4 cups seasoned bread crumbs

Oil for deep-fat frying

1. In a large saucepan, bring the water, rice, butter, salt and pepper to a boil. Reduce heat; cover and simmer for 15-18 minutes or until liquid is absorbed and rice is tender. Cool slightly.

2. In a large bowl, combine the eggs, cheese, parsley and rice. Cover and refrigerate for 20 minutes. Place bread crumbs in a shallow bowl. Shape 1/2 cupfuls of rice mixture into balls; roll in bread crumbs.

3. In a deep-fat fryer or electric skillet, heat oil to 375°. Fry rice balls, a few at a time, for 2-3 minutes or until golden brown. Drain on paper towels.

YIELD: 12 SERVINGS.

NUTRITION FACTS: 1 rice ball equals 343 calories, 20 g fat (3 g saturated fat), 77 mg cholesterol, 461 mg sodium, 34 g carbohydrate, 1 g fiber, 7 g protein.

STRAWBERRY & PECAN SALAD

Fresh strawberries and crunchy pecans star in this salad that always proves to be a crowd-pleaser. I never have any leftovers to bring home.

Teacher, McIntire Elementary, Fulton, Missouri

Sharon Meyer, Fulton, Missouri

1/3 cup canola oil

1/4 cup plus 3 tablespoons sugar, divided

2 tablespoons white vinegar

2 tablespoons grated onion

1/2 teaspoon ground mustard

1/4 teaspoon salt

1/2 cup pecan halves

2 heads leaf lettuce, torn

1 cup sliced fresh strawberries

1/2 cup shredded Monterey Jack cheese

1/3 cup sunflower kernels

1. In a small bowl, whisk the oil, 1/4 cup sugar, vinegar, onion, mustard and salt until sugar is completely dissolved; set the dressing aside.

2. Place pecans in a small heavy skillet. Cook over medium heat for 1-2 minutes until nuts are toasted. Sprinkle with remaining sugar. Cook and stir for 2-4 minutes or until sugar is melted. Spread on foil to cool. Break apart.

3. In a large serving bowl, combine the lettuce, strawberries, cheese, sunflower kernels and sugared pecans. Drizzle with vinaigrette; toss to coat.

YIELD: 8 SERVINGS.

NUTRITION FACTS: 3/4 cup equals 247 calories, 19 g fat (3 g saturated fat), 6 mg cholesterol, 149 mg sodium, 16 g carbohydrate, 2 g fiber, 4 g protein.

TOSSED SALAD WITH CILANTRO VINAIGRETTE

This is not a salad you'll see everywhere. It features a unique mix of veggies tossed with romaine lettuce. Everybody asks for seconds once they've tried it.

Teacher, Riverview Elementary, Elkhart, Indiana

Lari Montesino, Elkhart, Indiana

1/3 cup olive oil
1/4 cup minced fresh cilantro
1/4 cup lime juice
1/8 teaspoon salt

8 cups torn romaine
1 medium zucchini, chopped
1 medium cucumber, chopped
1 medium sweet yellow pepper, chopped
5 to 10 radishes, sliced

1. In a small bowl, whisk the oil, cilantro, lime juice and salt.
2. In a large bowl, combine the romaine, zucchini, cucumber, yellow pepper and radishes. Drizzle with dressing; toss to coat. Serve immediately.

YIELD: 16 SERVINGS (3/4 CUP EACH).

NUTRITION FACTS: 3/4 cup equals 53 calories, 5 g fat (1 g saturated fat), 0 cholesterol, 23 mg sodium, 3 g carbohydrate, 1 g fiber, 1 g protein. DIABETIC EXCHANGE: 1 fat.

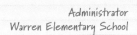

Administrator
Warren Elementary School

Warren, Illinois

Dee Dee Calow is in her 21st year in education. "I spent the first 12 years teaching first and second grade in Wisconsin before returning to Warren where I attended school," says Dee Dee, who is currently a principal for preschool through eighth grade at the Warren Community Unit District #205. "It is great to watch children grow up into young adults and see what they go on to do with their lives."

GARDEN-FRESH POTATO SALAD

A parent from a school where I previously taught gave me this recipe—I think of that parent and child every time I make this potato salad.

Dee Dee Calow, Warren, Illinois

3 pounds small red potatoes, quartered

1 pound fresh green beans, trimmed and cut in half

1/3 cup olive oil

1/4 cup red wine vinegar

1/4 cup minced fresh basil

2 tablespoons minced fresh parsley

1-1/2 teaspoons salt

1/2 teaspoon pepper

6 hard-cooked eggs, sliced

1 cup grape tomatoes

1. Place potatoes in a large saucepan and cover with water. Bring to a boil. Reduce heat; cover and cook for 4 minutes. Stir in the beans; cover and cook 10-12 minutes longer or vegetables are tender. Drain.

2. In a small bowl, whisk the oil, vinegar, basil, parsley, salt and pepper. Pour over potato mixture; toss to coat. Cover and refrigerate for at least 1 hour.

3. Stir before serving; top with eggs and tomatoes.

YIELD: 20 SERVINGS (3/4 CUP EACH).

NUTRITION FACTS: 3/4 cup equals 113 calories, 5 g fat (1 g saturated fat), 64 mg cholesterol, 202 mg sodium, 13 g carbohydrate, 2 g fiber, 4 g protein. DIABETIC EXCHANGES: 1 starch, 1 fat.

BAKED CRANBERRY PEACH SAUCE

This ruby red peach sauce is just fantastic and so versatile. It would be great on ham, pork or turkey and as a topping for waffles, pound cake or ice cream.

Teacher, Mountain Pointe High School, Phoenix, Arizona

Kimberly Swimmer, Phoenix, Arizona

---

5 cups fresh or frozen cranberries, thawed

1 cup flaked coconut

1 cup chopped peeled fresh or frozen peaches, thawed

1 cup orange marmalade

3/4 cup sugar

1/2 cup water

1. In a large bowl, combine all ingredients. Pour into a greased 13-in. x 9-in. baking dish. Bake, uncovered, at 350° for 35-40 minutes or until cranberries are tender. Serve warm or cold. Refrigerate leftovers.

YIELD: 16 SERVINGS (1/4 CUP EACH).

NUTRITION FACTS: 1/4 cup equals 132 calories, 2 g fat (2 g saturated fat), 0 cholesterol, 27 mg sodium, 30 g carbohydrate, 2 g fiber, trace protein.

Teacher
Wasatch Junior High School
Salt Lake City, Utah

Malee Jergensen has taught in Salt Lake City, Utah, for 29 years. She currently teaches seventh grade pre-algebra and seventh and eighth grade algebra. When she isn't teaching formulas to her students, she loves to bake and try new recipes. "It is one of my favorite hobbies," she says. "I like to try new recipes and bring them to school and share them with my colleagues."

PARMESAN ARTICHOKE SOUP

This unique cream-based soup has a splendid flavor combination with artichokes, sun-dried tomatoes and Parmesan cheese.

Malee Jergensen, Murray, Utah

4 celery ribs, finely chopped

1 medium onion, finely chopped

1/2 cup finely chopped carrot

1/2 cup butter, cubed

3 garlic cloves, minced

1 cup all-purpose flour

4-1/2 teaspoons minced fresh thyme or 1-1/2 teaspoons dried thyme

3/4 teaspoon salt

1/2 teaspoon pepper

2 cartons (32 ounces each) reduced-sodium chicken broth

3 bay leaves

1 quart heavy whipping cream

1-1/2 cups shredded Parmesan cheese

1 jar (7-1/2 ounces) marinated quartered artichoke hearts, drained and coarsely chopped

1/4 cup sun-dried tomatoes (not packed in oil), chopped

1. In a large saucepan, saute the celery, onion and carrot in butter until tender. Add the garlic; cook 1 minute longer. Stir in the flour, thyme, salt and pepper until blended; gradually add broth. Add bay leaves. Bring to a boil. Cook and stir for 2 minutes or until thickened.

2. Reduce heat; whisk in the cream, cheese, artichokes and tomatoes. Bring to a gentle boil. Simmer, uncovered, for 5-10 minutes or until flavors are blended. Discard bay leaves.

YIELD: 12 SERVINGS (3 QUARTS).

NUTRITION FACTS: 1 cup equals 473 calories, 43 g fat (25 g saturated fat), 136 mg cholesterol, 936 mg sodium, 15 g carbohydrate, 1 g fiber, 9 g protein.

CONFETTI JICAMA SALAD

I love jicama dipped in citrus and sprinkled with salt and jalapenos. So when I needed to bring a salad to a 4th of July picnic, I decided to use this crunchy vegetable as the star.

Staff, Ridgeview Elementary, Yucaipa, California

Jan Ruiz, Yucaipa, California

1/2 medium jicama, peeled and julienned

1-1/3 cups julienned seedless cucumber

1 each small sweet red, orange and yellow pepper, julienned

1/2 cup thinly sliced red onion

3 green onions, chopped

DRESSING:

1/3 cup minced fresh cilantro

1 jalapeno pepper, seeded and finely chopped

2 tablespoons lime juice

2 tablespoons orange juice concentrate

2 tablespoons olive oil

1 garlic clove, minced

1 teaspoon sugar

1/2 teaspoon salt

1/4 teaspoon pepper

1/8 teaspoon cayenne pepper

1. In a large bowl, combine the jicama, cucumber, peppers and onions.

2. In a small bowl, whisk the cilantro, jalapeno, lime juice, juice concentrate, oil, garlic and seasonings. Pour over the salad; toss to coat. Cover and refrigerate for at least 1 hour. Stir before serving.

YIELD: 6 SERVINGS.

EDITOR'S NOTE: We recommend wearing disposable gloves when cutting hot peppers. Avoid touching your face.

NUTRITION FACTS: 1 cup equals 96 calories, 5 g fat (1 g saturated fat), 0 cholesterol, 203 mg sodium, 13 g carbohydrate, 4 g fiber, 1 g protein. DIABETIC EXCHANGES: 2 vegetable, 1 fat.

HAM AND CHEDDAR SCONES

A good friend of mine frequently makes these scones and shares them with me. They are so good and pretty, too! You can see the flecks of cheese, ham and green onions.

Teacher, Lake Los Anageles Elementary, Palmdale, California

Felicity La Rue, Palmdale, California

3 cups all-purpose flour
1/2 cup sugar
2 tablespoons baking powder
1/2 teaspoon salt
2 cups heavy whipping cream

1 cup diced fully cooked ham
1/2 cup diced cheddar cheese
4 green onions, thinly sliced

1. In a large bowl, combine the flour, sugar, baking powder and salt. Stir in cream just until moistened. Stir in the ham, cheese and onions. Turn onto a floured surface; knead 10 times.

2. Transfer dough to a greased baking sheet. Pat into a 9-in. circle. Cut into 12 wedges, but do not separate. Bake at 400° for 20-25 minutes or until golden brown. Serve warm.

YIELD: 1 DOZEN.

NUTRITION FACTS: 1 scone equals 326 calories, 18 g fat (11 g saturated fat), 66 mg cholesterol, 498 mg sodium, 34 g carbohydrate, 1 g fiber, 8 g protein.

Staff, Carl Sandburg School

Kirkland, Washington

Hilda Fallas values her job as a server in the cafeteria at Carl Sandburg School. Not only does she have the opportunity to interact with the children on a daily basis, she also acts as a translator for some of the parents who do not speak English.

SWEET POTATO SOUP

Subtle ginger and peanut butter flavor make this dazzling orange soup unique. It has a mild, not spicy, taste with an Asian flair.

Hilda Fallas, Bothell, Washington

1 large onion, chopped

1 medium sweet red pepper, chopped

2 medium carrots, chopped

2 teaspoons canola oil

1 teaspoon minced fresh gingerroot

1 garlic clove, minced

1/2 teaspoon cayenne pepper

1/2 teaspoon coarsely ground pepper

1 carton (32 ounces) plus 1 can (14-1/2 ounces) reduced-sodium chicken broth

1 can (14-1/2 ounces) diced tomatoes, undrained

1 large sweet potato, peeled and cubed

2/3 cup creamy peanut butter

2 teaspoons honey

4 green onions, chopped

1. In a large saucepan, saute the onion, red pepper and carrots in oil for 3 minutes. Stir in the ginger, garlic, cayenne and pepper; cook 2 minutes longer. Add the broth, tomatoes and sweet potato. Bring to a boil. Reduce heat; cover and simmer for 15-20 minutes or until potatoes are tender.

2. Cool slightly. In a blender, cover and process soup in batches until smooth. Return all to pan and heat through. Stir in peanut butter and honey. Cook and stir until peanut butter is melted. Garnish servings with green onions.

YIELD: 8 SERVINGS (2 QUARTS).

NUTRITION FACTS: 1 cup equals 213 calories, 12 g fat (2 g saturated fat), 0 cholesterol, 655 mg sodium, 20 g carbohydrate, 4 g fiber, 9 g protein.

Teacher
Grace Evangelical Lutheran School

Menomonee Falls, Wisconsin

Kimberly Knuppenburg teaches kindergarten in the very room where she attended kindergarten. "One of my favorite things about teaching is watching a child read for the first time," she says. "Their excitement and eagerness to read at this level is such an amazing journey, and I am so blessed that I get to lead the children through this walk."

THAI CHICKEN PIZZA

This is the recipe I make for my friends on "girl's night." It is simple to prepare, but full of flavor.

Kimberly Knuppenburg, Menomonee Falls, Wisconsin

1 prebaked 12-inch pizza crust

2/3 cup Thai peanut sauce

2 tablespoons reduced-sodium soy sauce

2 tablespoons creamy peanut butter

1 cup shredded cooked chicken breast

1 cup (4 ounces) shredded part-skim mozzarella cheese

3 green onions, chopped

1/2 cup bean sprouts

1/2 cup shredded carrot

1. Place crust on an ungreased 12-in. pizza pan or baking sheet. In a small bowl, combine the peanut sauce, soy sauce and peanut butter. Add chicken; toss to coat. Spread over crust; sprinkle with cheese and onions.

2. Bake at 400° for 10-12 minutes or until cheese is melted. Top with bean sprouts and carrot.

YIELD: 6 SERVINGS.

NUTRITION FACTS: 1 slice equals 361 calories, 15 g fat (4 g saturated fat), 29 mg cholesterol, 1,183 mg sodium, 35 g carbohydrate, 3 g fiber, 23 g protein.

Goodyear, Arizona

Kathy Fox teaches earth and space science and coaches the girls varsity soccer team at Estrella Foothills High School. "I truly enjoy educating our youth and helping them succeed, either in the classroom or on the soccer field," she says. "The best part of my position is interacting with the students and seeing them light up with excitement when they understand something that I am teaching."

PORK TENDERLOIN WITH DRIED CHERRIES

I love cherries, especially since I grew up in Michigan. Plus, they pair so nicely with pork. Here is a wonderful skillet dish that takes just minutes to cook. It is fabulous for both weeknights and company dinners.

Kathy Fox, Goodyear, Arizona

3/4 cup chicken broth

1/3 cup dried tart cherries

1/4 cup brandy

1 teaspoon minced fresh thyme or 1/4 teaspoon dried thyme

1/8 teaspoon ground allspice

1 pork tenderloin (1 pound), cut into 1-inch slices

1/2 teaspoon salt, divided

1/2 teaspoon pepper, divided

1 tablespoon butter

1 shallot, minced

1/4 cup heavy whipping cream

1. In a small saucepan, combine the first five ingredients. Bring to a boil; cook until liquid is reduced to 1/2 cup. Set aside and keep warm.

2. Flatten pork to 1/2-in. thickness; sprinkle with 1/4 teaspoon salt and 1/4 teaspoon pepper. In a large skillet, brown pork in butter; remove and keep warm.

3. In the same skillet, saute shallot in drippings until tender. Add cream, reserved cherry mixture and remaining salt and pepper, stirring to dissolve browned bits from pan. Bring to a boil; cook until liquid is reduced to sauce consistency. Return pork to the pan; cook until no longer pink.

YIELD: 4 SERVINGS.

NUTRITION FACTS: 3 ounces cooked pork with 1 tablespoon sauce equals 269 calories, 12 g fat (7 g saturated fat), 92 mg cholesterol, 551 mg sodium, 11 g carbohydrate, 1 g fiber, 24 g protein.

BACON & TOMATO-TOPPED MEAT LOAF

I started with a traditional recipe I had that called for horseradish and then added a few other complementary flavors. The results were a moist meat loaf with visible bits of veggies and plenty of savory flavor.

Teacher, Eastside Elementary, Warren, Arkansas

Cheryl Moring, New Edinburg, Arkansas

1 small onion, finely chopped
1 celery rib, finely chopped
1 small green pepper, finely chopped
1 tablespoon canola oil
1 garlic clove, minced
1 egg, lightly beaten
1 tablespoon prepared horseradish
1 tablespoon dry red wine or beef broth
1 teaspoon prepared mustard
1 teaspoon Worcestershire sauce
1 cup soft bread crumbs
1 tablespoon all-purpose flour
1 tablespoon brown sugar
1 teaspoon salt

1 teaspoon Cajun seasoning
1 teaspoon pepper
1/2 teaspoon chili powder
1 pound lean ground beef (90% lean)
1/2 pound bulk pork sausage
1/2 pound bacon strips

TOPPING:
1 can (14-1/2 ounces) diced tomatoes, drained
1 can (8 ounces) tomato sauce

1. In a large skillet, saute the onion, celery and green pepper in oil until tender. Add garlic; cook 1 minute longer. Transfer to a large bowl; cool slightly.

2. Add the egg, horseradish, wine, mustard, Worcestershire sauce, bread crumbs, flour, brown sugar and seasonings. Crumble beef and sausage over mixture and mix well. Pat into an ungreased 9-in. x 5-in. loaf pan. Place bacon strips over meat loaf; tuck in ends.

3. Bake meat loaf, uncovered, at 350° for 55 minutes. Combine the diced tomatoes and tomato sauce; spoon over loaf. Bake 5-10 minutes longer or until no pink remains and a meat thermometer reads 160°.

YIELD: 6 SERVINGS.

NUTRITION FACTS: 1 slice equals 472 calories, 34 g fat (11 g saturated fat), 122 mg cholesterol, 1,353 mg sodium, 16 g carbohydrate, 2 g fiber, 25 g protein.

CHICKEN TORTELLINI IN CREAM SAUCE

Kids and adults alike will devour this quick pasta dinner. It's prepared at home, but tastes like restaurant fare. I like to serve it with a Caesar salad.

Teacher, Burns High School, Lawndale, North Carolina

Julie Kamlade, Shelby, North Carolina

1 package (19 ounces) frozen cheese tortellini
1 cup fresh broccoli florets
1 garlic clove, minced
2 tablespoons butter
1 cup shredded Parmesan cheese
1 cup heavy whipping cream
1/2 teaspoon Italian seasoning
1/4 teaspoon salt
1/8 teaspoon pepper
1-1/3 cups cubed cooked chicken breast
Minced fresh basil, optional

1. In a large saucepan, cook the tortellini according to package directions; add broccoli during the last 5 minutes of cooking.

2. Meanwhile, in a large skillet, saute garlic in butter until tender. Stir in the cheese, cream and seasonings. Bring to a boil; reduce heat. Simmer, uncovered, for 7-9 minutes or until slightly thickened. Add chicken; heat through.

3. Drain tortellini and broccoli; toss with chicken mixture. Sprinkle with basil if desired.

YIELD: 4 SERVINGS.

NUTRITION FACTS: 1-1/2 cups (calculated without basil) equals 685 calories, 43 g fat (25 g saturated fat), 168 mg cholesterol, 929 mg sodium, 40 g carbohydrate, 2 g fiber, 36 g protein.

Teacher
Andrew Cooke Magnet School

Waukegan, Illinois

Julie Ahern has been teaching second grade for 18 years. Last year, her school, Andrew Cooke Magnet School, was the recipient of a Pepsi Refresh grant and, as a result, has been featured in commercials.

PARMESAN PORK CUTLETS

The aroma of these cutlets cooking makes my kids eager to come to the dinner table. It's a no-fuss solution to busy weeknights and hungry kiddos.

Julie Ahern, Waukegan, Illinois

1 pork tenderloin (1 pound)

1/3 cup all-purpose flour

2 eggs, lightly beaten

1 cup dry bread crumbs

1/4 cup grated Parmesan cheese

1 teaspoon salt

1/4 cup olive oil

Lemon wedges

1. Cut the pork diagonally into eight slices; pound each to 1/4-in. thickness.

2. Place flour and eggs in separate shallow bowls. In another shallow bowl, combine the bread crumbs, cheese and salt. Dip pork in the flour, eggs, then bread crumb mixture.

3. In a large skillet, cook pork in oil in batches over medium heat for 2-3 minutes on each side or until crisp and meat juices run clear. Remove and keep warm. Serve pork cutlets with lemon wedges.

YIELD: 4 SERVINGS.

NUTRITION FACTS: 2 cutlets equals 376 calories, 21 g fat (5 g saturated fat), 162 mg cholesterol, 626 mg sodium, 15 g carbohydrate, 1 g fiber, 29 g protein.

Teacher
Lake Park Elementary School

Lake Park, Georgia

Bridget Corbett has been teaching kindergarten reading, language arts and math for 10 years. "The best part of my position is working with and teaching 5- and 6-year-olds, many of who have never been to school before," she says. Her greatest satisfaction comes from watching students be able to read and write when the school year is over.

BROCCOLI QUICHE

My mother passed down this quiche recipe to me. She has been making it for over 30 years. You can serve it for brunch, lunch and even dinner. Any leftovers can be frozen and reheated in the microwave later.

Bridget Corbett, Valdosta, Georgia

- 1 refrigerated pie pastry
- 1 package (9 ounces) frozen broccoli cuts, thawed and chopped
- 1 small onion, finely chopped
- 2 tablespoons butter
- 1 cup heavy whipping cream
- 3 eggs
- 1/2 cup mayonnaise
- 1 tablespoon all-purpose flour
- 1 tablespoon chicken broth
- 1/2 teaspoon salt
- 1/8 teaspoon ground nutmeg
- 1/8 teaspoon pepper
- 1-1/2 cups (6 ounces) shredded cheddar cheese

1. Unroll pastry into a 9-in. deep-dish pie plate; flute edges. Line unpricked pastry with a double thickness of heavy-duty foil. Bake at 450° for 8 minutes. Remove foil; bake 5 minutes longer. Cool on a wire rack.

2. In a large skillet, saute broccoli and onion in butter until onion is tender. Remove from the heat. In a large bowl, whisk the cream, eggs, mayonnaise, flour, broth, salt, nutmeg and pepper; stir in the cheese and broccoli mixture. Pour egg mixture into crust.

3. Bake at 350° for 35-40 minutes or until a knife inserted near the center comes out clean. Let quiche stand for 10 minutes before cutting.

YIELD: 6 SERVINGS.

NUTRITION FACTS: 1 piece equals 622 calories, 53 g fat (24 g saturated fat), 214 mg cholesterol, 698 mg sodium, 24 g carbohydrate, 1 g fiber, 13 g protein.

SLOW-COOKED PULLED PORK

Every time I bring this dish to a potluck, I get asked, "Where did you get the pork?" People are surprised to hear me say that I made it. When I tell them how simple the recipe is, they are doubly surprised. The two-step process fits the demanding schedule of any teacher.

Teacher, Lafayette High School, Wilwood, Missouri

Betsy Rivas, Chesterfield, Missouri

2 tablespoons brown sugar

4-1/2 teaspoons paprika

2 tablespoons coarsely ground pepper, divided

1 tablespoon kosher salt

1 teaspoon chili powder

1/2 teaspoon cayenne pepper

1 boneless pork shoulder butt roast (3 to 4 pounds), cut in half

1 cup cider vinegar

1/4 cup beef broth

1/4 cup barbecue sauce

2 tablespoons Worcestershire sauce

1-1/2 teaspoons hickory Liquid Smoke, optional

10 kaiser rolls, split

1. In a small bowl, combine brown sugar, paprika, 1 tablespoon pepper, salt, chili powder and cayenne. Rub over roast; cover and refrigerate for 8 hours or overnight.

2. Place roast in a 4- or 5-qt. slow cooker. Combine vinegar, broth, barbecue sauce, Worcestershire sauce, Liquid Smoke, if desired, and remaining pepper; pour over roast. Cover and cook on low for 8-10 hours or until meat is tender.

3. Remove meat from slow cooker; cool slightly. Shred meat with two forks and return to the slow cooker; heat through. Using a slotted spoon, place 1/2 cup on each roll.

YIELD: 10 SERVINGS.

NUTRITION FACTS: 1 sandwich equals 419 calories, 16 g fat (5 g saturated fat), 81 mg cholesterol, 1,076 mg sodium, 36 g carbohydrate, 2 g fiber, 29 g protein.

CARAMEL-PECAN FRENCH TOAST BAKE

For a sensational dish for a Sunday brunch, try this ooey-gooey French toast. Prepare it the night before so all you need to do is bake it and make the syrup the following day.

Teacher, Harper Elementary, Harper, Kansas

Brad Shue, Harper, Kansas

1 cup packed brown sugar
1/2 cup butter, cubed
2 tablespoons light corn syrup
1 cup chopped pecans, divided
8 slices French bread (3/4 inch thick)
6 eggs
1-1/2 cups 2% milk
1-1/2 teaspoons ground cinnamon
1 teaspoon ground nutmeg
1 teaspoon vanilla extract
1/4 teaspoon salt

SAUCE:
1/2 cup packed brown sugar
1/4 cup butter, cubed
1 tablespoon light corn syrup

1. In a small saucepan, combine the brown sugar, butter and corn syrup. Bring to a boil. Reduce heat; cook and stir for 3-4 minutes or until thickened. Pour into a greased 13-in. x 9-in. baking dish. Sprinkle with 1/2 cup chopped pecans; top with bread slices.

2. In a large bowl, whisk eggs, milk, cinnamon, nutmeg, vanilla and salt; pour evenly over bread. Sprinkle with remaining pecans. Cover and refrigerate for 8 hours or overnight.

3. Remove from the refrigerator 30 minutes before baking. Bake, uncovered, at 350° for 30-35 minutes or until a knife inserted near the center comes out clean.

4. Meanwhile, in a small saucepan, combine sauce ingredients. Bring to a boil. Reduce heat; cook and stir for 2 minutes or until thickened. Serve with French toast.

YIELD: 8 SERVINGS.

NUTRITION FACTS: 1 piece equals 559 calories, 33 g fat (14 g saturated fat), 207 mg cholesterol, 398 mg sodium, 60 g carbohydrate, 2 g fiber, 9 g protein.

Robert Taylor has been the head custodian at Bonjour Elementary School since 1982. In the 58-year history of Bonjour, there have only been three head custodians caring for the building. It's a tight-knit community—even some former students have returned to teach. "In 1982, the first year I took over as head custodian, our current gym teacher Jenea Ledou was also beginning her history with Bonjour as a kindergartener," Robert says.

TRIPLE PEPPER STEAK SANDWICHES

Separate parts of this recipe can be made ahead of time, and the sandwich can be assembled quickly for a weeknight meal. This fork-and-knife sandwich works very well with leftover grilled steak or chicken.

Robert Taylor, Shawnee, Kansas

2 boneless beef top loin steaks (1 inch thick and 8 ounces each)

1/4 teaspoon salt

1/8 teaspoon pepper

1 large sweet onion, thinly sliced

1 cup sliced fresh mushrooms

1 poblano pepper, thinly sliced

2 tablespoons plus 2 teaspoons butter, divided

2 tablespoons chopped onion

1 garlic clove, minced

1/2 cup heavy whipping cream

1 chipotle pepper in adobo sauce, minced

1/2 teaspoon ground cumin

1/4 teaspoon chicken bouillon granules

1 loaf (14 ounces) ciabatta bread

4 slices pepper Jack cheese

1. Sprinkle steaks with salt and pepper. Grill, covered, over medium heat or broil 3-4 in. from the heat for 7-9 minutes on each side or until the meat reaches desired doneness (for medium-rare, a meat thermometer should read 145°; medium, 160°; well-done, 170°). Let stand for 5 minutes before slicing.

2. Meanwhile, in a large skillet, saute sliced onion, mushrooms and poblano pepper in 2 tablespoons butter until tender. Remove from the heat; stir in sliced steak.

3. In a small saucepan, saute the chopped onion in remaining butter until tender. Add the garlic; cook 1 minute longer. Stir in the cream, chipotle, cumin and bouillon; cook and stir until thickened.

4. Cut ciabatta in half horizontally, then cut into four equal portions. Place cheese on bottom bread slices; top with steak mixture, chipotle cream sauce and remaining bread. Cook on a panini maker or indoor grill for 3-4 minutes or until bread is browned and cheese is melted.

YIELD: 4 SERVINGS.

EDITOR'S NOTE: We recommend wearing disposable gloves when cutting hot peppers. Avoid touching your face.

NUTRITION FACTS: 1 sandwich equals 768 calories, 37 g fat (20 g saturated fat), 145 mg cholesterol, 1,013 mg sodium, 71 g carbohydrate, 4 g fiber, 43 g protein.

Honeoye Falls, New York

Even though Manor Intermediate School houses more than 700 students, school secretary Linda Bacci says the school has a warm, family feel about it. "We are more like a family at Manor than just a group of teachers and staff. The best part of my job is being able to help parents, students and our great staff on a daily basis," she says.

BEEF STEW WITH SESAME SEED BISCUITS

Warm and hearty comfort food is what this dinner is all about. This has it all...homemade biscuits, tender meat and an assortment of veggies.

Linda Bacci, Livonia, New York

1 pound beef stew meat, cut into 1-inch cubes

2 tablespoons olive oil

1-1/2 cups chopped onions

1 cup chopped celery

1 garlic clove, minced

1 tablespoon all-purpose flour

1-1/2 cups water

1 cup diced tomatoes

1/2 cup Burgundy wine or beef broth

1/3 cup tomato paste

1 tablespoon sugar

3/4 teaspoon salt

1/2 teaspoon Worcestershire sauce

1/4 teaspoon pepper

2 cups cubed peeled potatoes

2 cups sliced fresh carrots

1 can (4 ounces) mushroom stems and pieces, drained

1/4 cup sour cream

SESAME SEED BISCUITS:

1-1/4 cups all-purpose flour

2 teaspoons baking powder

1/2 teaspoon salt

1/4 cup shortening

3/4 cup sour cream

2 tablespoons 2% milk

1 tablespoon sesame seeds

1. In a Dutch oven, brown beef in oil in batches. Remove and keep warm. In the same pan, saute onions and celery until tender. Add garlic; cook 1 minute longer.

2. Stir in flour until blended. Gradually add water; stir in the tomatoes, wine, tomato paste, sugar, salt, Worcestershire sauce, pepper and beef. Bring to a boil. Reduce heat; cover and simmer for 1-1/4 hours.

3. Add potatoes and carrots; cook for 30-45 minutes longer or until beef and vegetables are tender. Stir in mushrooms and sour cream. Transfer to a greased 13-in. x 9-in. baking dish.

4. For biscuits, in a large bowl, combine the flour, baking powder and salt. Cut in shortening until mixture resembles coarse crumbs. Stir in sour cream just until moistened.

5. Turn onto a lightly floured surface; knead 8-10 times. Roll out to 1/2-in. thickness; cut with a floured 2-in. biscuit cutter. Brush with milk; sprinkle with sesame seeds. Arrange over stew.

6. Bake at 400° for 30-35 minutes or until the biscuits are golden brown.

YIELD: 5 SERVINGS.

NUTRITION FACTS: 1.333 cups equals 636 calories, 31 g fat (11 g saturated fat), 89 mg cholesterol, 1,029 mg sodium, 59 g carbohydrate, 6 g fiber, 27 g protein.

CREAMY CLAM LINGUINE

This is a fast but special entree that I made up when my sons were home. They loved it so much they continue to request it whenever they visit. You can use the juice from the canned clams, but bottled clam juice gives a better flavor.

Teacher, T.C. Cherry Elementary, Bowling Green, Kentucky

Margie Clevenger, Bowling Green, Kentucky

1 pound linguine

1 medium onion, chopped

1/4 cup butter, cubed

2 tablespoons olive oil

4 garlic cloves, minced

3 tablespoons all-purpose flour

2 cups chicken broth

1 cup clam juice

1/2 cup heavy whipping cream

3 cans (6-1/2 ounces each) minced clams, drained

1/2 cup minced fresh parsley

1/4 teaspoon dried oregano

1/4 teaspoon chipotle hot pepper sauce

1/8 teaspoon salt

1/8 teaspoon pepper

1/8 teaspoon crushed red pepper flakes

2/3 cup grated Parmesan cheese

1. Cook linguine according to package directions.

2. Meanwhile, in a large saucepan, saute onion in butter and oil. Add garlic; saute for 1-2 minutes longer. Stir in flour until blended; gradually add the broth, clam juice and cream. Bring to a boil; cook and stir for 2 minutes or until thickened.

3. Add the clams and seasonings; cook and stir for 2-3 minutes or until heated through. Drain linguine. Add pasta and cheese to sauce; toss to coat.

YIELD: 8 SERVINGS.

NUTRITION FACTS: 1 cup equals 419 calories, 18 g fat (9 g saturated fat), 55 mg cholesterol, 788 mg sodium, 49 g carbohydrate, 3 g fiber, 16 g protein.

Teacher
Sylvan Elementary School

Sylvania, Ohio

Pamela Hesselbart has been in the education field for 33 years and the third grade teacher at Sylvan Elementary School for 27 years. Sylvan Elementary was built in the 1970s, and Pamela's father was a member of the school board. Her favorite aspect of being a teacher is seeing the diversity in her students. "The best part of the job is getting to know young people of all backgrounds and cultures, ever diverse, and yet ever the same," she says.

CURRIED CHICKEN RICE SALAD

Since I usually make and serve this salad while my teacher friends and I are on summer break, I always associate this recipe with relaxed good times! This recipe is best made ahead so that the flavors can mingle.

Pamela Hesselbart, Sylvania, Ohio

1 package (6.6 ounces) toasted almond rice pilaf

2 cups cubed cooked chicken

3/4 cup diced celery

1/2 cup dried cranberries

1/2 cup golden raisins

1/2 cup mayonnaise

1/3 cup chutney

3 tablespoons sour cream

2 tablespoons lemon juice

1 teaspoon curry powder

2 medium apples, cubed

8 lettuce leaves

1/4 cup sliced almonds, toasted

1. Cook rice pilaf according to package directions; cool. In a large bowl, combine the chicken, celery, cranberries, raisins and rice.

2. In a small bowl, combine the mayonnaise, chutney, sour cream, lemon juice and curry powder; stir in apples. Add to rice mixture; toss to coat. Cover and refrigerate for at least 2 hours.

3. Serve on lettuce; garnish with almonds.

YIELD: 6 SERVINGS.

NUTRITION FACTS: 1-1/2 cups equals 506 calories, 24 g fat (4 g saturated fat), 53 mg cholesterol, 573 mg sodium, 55 g carbohydrate, 4 g fiber, 19 g protein.

EGGS BENEDICT BRUNCH BRAID

Here's a great make-ahead brunch entree to serve during the holidays and at potlucks. It has all the ingredients of a classic eggs Benedict encased in puff pastry. You can refrigerate the assembled braid overnight, or freeze it for up to two weeks—just be sure to cover it tightly with plastic wrap so the pastry doesn't dry out. Before baking, brush strudel with egg wash. Add 20 minutes to baking time if the strudel is frozen.

Volunteer, Loon Lake Elementary, Wixom, Michigan

Sarah Strohl, Commerce Township, Michigan

3 egg yolks
1 tablespoon lemon juice
1/4 teaspoon salt
1/4 teaspoon Dijon mustard
Dash cayenne pepper
1/2 cup unsalted butter, melted
BRAID:
1 tablespoon unsalted butter
6 eggs
1/2 teaspoon salt
1/4 teaspoon pepper
1 sheet frozen puff pastry, thawed
6 slices Canadian bacon
2 tablespoons minced chives, divided
1 teaspoon water

1. In a blender, combine the first five ingredients. Cover and process on high. While processing, gradually add butter in a steady stream until combined. Set aside.

2. In a large skillet, melt butter over medium-high heat. Whisk five eggs, salt and pepper; add to skillet. Cook and stir until barely set; stir in sauce.

3. On a lightly greased baking sheet, roll out pastry into a 12-in. x 10-in. rectangle. Layer Canadian bacon and egg mixture down center of rectangle; sprinkle with 1 tablespoon minced chives.

4. On each long side, cut 1/2-in.-wide strips. Starting at one end, fold alternating strips at an angle across filling; pinch ends to seal. Whisk remaining egg and water; brush over braid.

5. Bake at 375° for 20-25 minutes or until golden brown and eggs are completely set. Let stand for 5 minutes before cutting. Sprinkle with remaining chives.

YIELD: 8 SERVINGS.

NUTRITION FACTS: 1 slice equals 354 calories, 27 g fat (12 g saturated fat), 275 mg cholesterol, 523 mg sodium, 18 g carbohydrate, 2 g fiber, 10 g protein.

Teacher, Rossville Elementary

Rossville, Georgia

Debbie Shannon learned about Rossville Elementary's librarian position when her husband went in for an interview and mentioned his wife had just received her library science degree. "We were pleasantly surprised when they hired us both," she says. That was 10 years ago, and she still couldn't wish to work for a better school. "We've got a bunch of great kids and families who really grab your heart. And I couldn't find a better faculty."

CHICKEN MARSALA LASAGNA

I love Chicken Marsala, but most recipes do not serve a crowd. This version is one I invented. It makes enough for 12 people.

2nd place

Debbie Shannon, Ringgold, Georgia

4 teaspoons Italian seasoning, divided

1 teaspoon salt

12 ounces boneless skinless chicken breasts, cubed

1 tablespoon olive oil

1/4 cup finely chopped onion

1/2 cup butter, cubed

12 garlic cloves, minced

1/2 pound sliced baby portobello mushrooms

1-1/2 cups beef broth

3/4 cup marsala wine, divided

1/4 teaspoon coarsely ground pepper

3 tablespoons cornstarch

1/2 cup finely chopped fully cooked ham

1 carton (15 ounces) ricotta cheese

1 package (10 ounces) frozen chopped spinach, thawed and squeezed dry

2 cups (8 ounces) shredded Italian cheese blend

1 cup grated Parmesan cheese, divided

2 eggs, lightly beaten

12 lasagna noodles, cooked, rinsed and drained

1. Combine 2 teaspoons Italian seasoning and salt; sprinkle over chicken. In a large skillet, saute chicken in oil until no longer pink. Remove and keep warm.

2. In the same skillet, cook onion in butter over medium heat for 2 minutes. Add garlic; cook 2 minutes longer. Stir in mushrooms; cook 4-5 minutes longer or until tender.

3. Stir in the broth, 1/2 cup wine and pepper; bring to a boil. Combine the cornstarch and remaining wine until smooth; stir into the pan. Bring to a boil; cook and stir for 2 minutes or until thickened. Stir in ham and chicken.

4. In a large bowl, combine the ricotta cheese, spinach, Italian cheese blend, 3/4 cup Parmesan cheese, eggs and the remaining Italian seasoning. Spread 1 cup chicken mixture into a greased 13-in. x 9-in. baking dish. Layer with three noodles, about 3/4 cup chicken mixture and about 1 cup ricotta mixture. Repeat layers three times.

5. Cover and bake at 350° for 40 minutes. Sprinkle with the remaining Parmesan cheese. Bake, uncovered, for 10-15 minutes or until bubbly and cheese is melted. Let stand for 10 minutes before cutting.

YIELD: 12 SERVINGS.

NUTRITION FACTS: 1 piece equals 388 calories, 20 g fat (12 g saturated fat), 107 mg cholesterol, 749 mg sodium, 27 g carbohydrate, 2 g fiber, 24 g protein.

"Having a job where you are guaranteed smiles, stories and hugs on a daily basis is pretty awesome," says Martha Muellenberg of her job as a first grade teacher at Dakota Valley Elementary. Martha has also shared her artistic talents with the school. She painted murals near the library entrance that depicted scenes from the books "Where the Wild Things Are" and "No David!"

SPINACH ARTICHOKE PIZZA

I came up with this tempting pizza pie while experimenting with spinach and artichokes in different recipes. Needless to say, it's a frequent request from friends and colleagues.

Martha Muellenberg, Vermillion, South Dakota

1 package (1/4 ounce) active dry yeast
3/4 cup warm water (110° to 115°)
1/2 teaspoon sugar
4 teaspoons olive oil
3/4 teaspoon salt
1-3/4 to 2 cups all-purpose flour
TOPPINGS:
1 cup Alfredo sauce
3 cups fresh baby spinach
1 cup (4 ounces) shredded part-skim mozzarella cheese
3/4 cup crumbled feta cheese
1/2 cup shredded Parmesan cheese
3/4 cup water-packed artichoke hearts, rinsed, drained
    and chopped
1/2 teaspoon dried oregano

1. In a large bowl, dissolve yeast in warm water; stir in sugar. Let stand for 5-10 minutes. Add oil, salt and 1 cup flour. Beat until smooth. Stir in enough of the remaining flour to form a soft dough.
2. Turn onto a floured surface; knead until smooth and elastic, about 6-8 minutes. Place in a greased bowl, turning once to grease the top. Cover and let rise in a warm place until doubled, about 1 hour.
3. Grease a 15-in. x 10-in. x 1-in. baking pan. Punch down dough. Roll out to fit prepared pan.
4. Spread with Alfredo sauce. Layer with the spinach and cheeses. Sprinkle with artichokes and dried oregano. Bake at 400° for 18-22 minutes or until crust is lightly browned.

YIELD: 6 SERVINGS.

NUTRITION FACTS: 1 piece equals 351 calories, 15 g fat (8 g saturated fat), 35 mg cholesterol, 873 mg sodium, 35 g carbohydrate, 2 g fiber, 17 g protein.

BBQ CHICKEN PIZZAS

Grilled pizzas are so much fun to do with company on a warm summer night. The dough is easy to work with, and grilling it gives the crust deliciously different flavor. Plus, each person can adjust the ingredients as they see fit.

Teacher, Chinn Elementary, Kansas City, Missouri

Cara Langer, Overland Park, Missouri

2 packages (1/4 ounce each) active dry yeast

1 cup warm water (110° to 115°)

1/4 cup whole wheat flour

3 tablespoons olive oil

1 tablespoon honey

1 teaspoon salt

2-1/4 to 2-3/4 cups all-purpose flour

TOPPINGS:

3/4 pound boneless skinless chicken breasts, cut into 1/2-inch pieces

1/2 medium red onion, thinly sliced and separated into rings

2 tablespoons olive oil, divided

3 garlic cloves, minced

1 cup barbecue sauce

2 cups (8 ounces) shredded smoked Gouda cheese

1 cup (4 ounces) shredded Asiago cheese

1/2 cup pickled pepper rings

Minced fresh basil leaves, optional

1. In a large bowl, dissolve yeast in warm water. Add the whole wheat flour, oil, honey, salt and 1-1/2 cups flour. Beat until smooth. Stir in enough remaining flour to form a soft dough.

2. Turn onto a floured surface; knead until smooth and elastic, about 6-8 minutes. Place in a greased bowl, turning once to grease the top. Cover and let rise in a warm place until doubled, about 1 hour.

3. Punch dough down. On a lightly floured surface, divide dough into four portions. Roll each into a 10-in. circle; build up edges slightly. Cover and let rest for 10 minutes.

4. Meanwhile, in a large skillet, saute chicken and onion in 1 tablespoon oil until chicken is no longer pink. Add garlic; cook 1 minute longer. Stir in barbecue sauce; heat through. Remove from the heat and set aside.

5. Moisten a paper towel with cooking oil; using long-handled tongs, lightly coat the grill rack. Brush both sides of dough with remaining oil. Grill dough, covered, over medium heat for 1-2 minutes or until the crust is lightly browned. Remove from the grill.

6. Layer the grilled side of each pizza with the chicken mixture, cheeses and pepper rings. Return the pizzas to the grill.

7. Cover and cook for 4-5 minutes or until the crust is lightly browned and cheese is melted, rotating the pizzas halfway through cooking to ensure an evenly browned crust. Sprinkle with basil if desired.

YIELD: 4 INDIVIDUAL PIZZAS.

NUTRITION FACTS: 1 pizza (calculated without basil) equals 920 calories, 44 g fat (18 g saturated fat), 136 mg cholesterol, 1,741 mg sodium, 80 g carbohydrate, 5 g fiber, 50 g protein.

FRENCH BEEF STEW

"Special" and "sensational" are two words that come to mind when I think of this stew. One bite and you'll know why. It makes a lot, but the recipe can easily be halved.

Staff, Illini Central CUSD 189, Mason City, Illinois

John Maxson, Mason City, Illinois

---

5 pounds beef sirloin tip roast, cut into 1-inch cubes

1-1/2 teaspoons salt

1/2 teaspoon pepper

3 tablespoons olive oil

2 large sweet onions, chopped

3 medium carrots, sliced

5 tablespoons butter, divided

6 garlic cloves, minced

2 pounds assorted fresh mushrooms, such as portobello, shiitake and/or oyster), sliced

4 large Yukon Gold potatoes, cubed

1 carton (32 ounces) beef broth

1 cup dry red wine or additional beef broth

1 tablespoon minced fresh basil or 1 teaspoon dried basil

3 tablespoons all-purpose flour

1 cup heavy whipping cream

2/3 cup crumbled blue cheese

1. Sprinkle beef with salt and pepper. In a stockpot, brown the beef in oil in batches. Remove and keep warm.

2. In the same pan, saute onions and carrots in 2 tablespoons butter for 4 minutes. Add garlic; cook 2 minutes longer. Stir in mushrooms, potatoes, broth, wine, basil and beef. Bring to a boil. Reduce heat; cover and simmer for 1-1/4 hours. Uncover; simmer 20-30 minutes longer or until beef is tender.

3. In a small saucepan, melt remaining butter. Stir in flour until smooth; gradually add cream. Bring to a boil; cook and stir for 2 minutes or until thickened. Stir into stew; heat through. Sprinkle with cheese.

YIELD: 20 SERVINGS (1 CUP EACH).

NUTRITION FACTS: 1 cup equals 336 calories, 16 g fat (8 g saturated fat), 100 mg cholesterol, 517 mg sodium, 18 g carbohydrate, 2 g fiber, 27 g protein.

Staff, Heritage Elementary

Nibley, Utah

Nothing can turn a bad day around for Jessica Kempton like her students. "I may come to work one day, weighed down with my own cares and burdens, feeling like I'm pretty insignificant in the world. Then a child asks me to sharpen his pencil and laughs in delight when I pretend to prick my finger on the tip, and I no longer feel insignificant," says Jessica, who is a reading aide.

CREAMY PESTO SHRIMP LINGUINE

I rely on this fantastic dish whenever I want to impress friends. They never suspect how easy it is to make. The flavorful pesto cream sauce is even more delectable than a typical Alfredo sauce.

Jessica Kempton, Logan, Utah

8 ounces linguine

1 pound uncooked large shrimp, peeled and deveined

1/4 cup butter, cubed

2 cups heavy whipping cream

1 cup grated Parmesan cheese

1/3 cup prepared pesto

1/4 teaspoon pepper

1. Cook linguine according to package directions.
2. Meanwhile, in a large skillet, saute shrimp in butter until shrimp turn pink. Remove and set aside. Add cream to the pan; bring to a gentle boil. Reduce heat; cook, uncovered, for 4-6 minutes or until slightly thickened, stirring occasionally.
3. Stir in the Parmesan cheese, pesto and pepper until smooth. Return shrimp to the pan; heat through. Drain linguine; serve with sauce.

YIELD: 4 SERVINGS.

NUTRITION FACTS: 1 cup linguine with 1 cup sauce equals 1,000 calories, 73 g fat (41 g saturated fat), 355 mg cholesterol, 727 mg sodium, 48 g carbohydrate, 3 g fiber, 40 g protein.

GRILLED SALMON KYOTO

The men in my family went on a fishing trip to Alaska and brought home an abundance of fish. The cooks in the family swapped fish recipes so we could experiment with different ways to prepare the bounty. My mom shared this recipe with us, and it has become a favorite.

Staff, Jefferson Elementary School, Pierre, South Dakota

Sandy Zimmerman, Pierre, South Dakota

1/3 cup reduced-sodium soy sauce

1/4 cup thawed orange juice concentrate

2 tablespoons canola oil

2 tablespoons tomato sauce

1 tablespoon finely chopped green onion

1 garlic clove, minced

1 teaspoon lemon juice

1/2 teaspoon minced fresh gingerroot

1/2 teaspoon prepared mustard

4 salmon steaks or fillets (1 inch thick)

1. In a small bowl, whisk the first nine ingredients until well blended. Pour 1/2 cup marinade into a large resealable plastic bag. Add the salmon; seal bag and turn to coat. Refrigerate for up to 1 hour. Set aside remaining marinade for basting.

2. Drain salmon and discard marinade. Moisten a paper towel with cooking oil; using long-handled tongs, lightly coat the grill rack. Grill salmon, covered, over high heat or broil 3-4 in. from the heat for 3 minutes. Turn; grill or broil 2-7 minutes longer or until fish flakes easily with a fork, basting occasionally with reserved marinade.

YIELD: 4 SERVINGS.

NUTRITION FACTS: 1 salmon steak equals 425 calories, 26 g fat (5 g saturated fat), 114 mg cholesterol, 675 mg sodium, 6 g carbohydrate, trace fiber, 40 g protein.

GRILLED WHISKEY CHOPS

This is a family favorite for summertime gatherings. The molasses butter nicely contrasts with the whiskey and peppercorn taste of the chops.

Teacher, North Side Intermediate School, Anderson, Indiana

Kelly Melling, Frankton, Indiana

1/4 cup butter, softened

1 tablespoon molasses

1/2 teaspoon ground cinnamon

1/2 teaspoon lemon juice

3 tablespoons coarsely ground pepper

1/3 cup whiskey

1/2 teaspoon salt

4 bone-in pork loin chops (3/4 inch thick)

1. In a small bowl, combine the butter, molasses, cinnamon and lemon juice; chill until serving.

2. Place pepper in a shallow bowl. In another shallow bowl, combine the whiskey and salt. Dip chops in whiskey mixture, then pepper.

3. Moisten a paper towel with cooking oil; using long-handled tongs, lightly coat the grill rack. Grill chops, covered, over medium heat or broil 4 in. from the heat for 4-5 minutes on each side or until a meat thermometer reads 160°. Serve with molasses butter.

YIELD: 4 SERVINGS.

NUTRITION FACTS: 1 pork chop with 1 tablespoon butter mixture equals 459 calories, 30 g fat (14 g saturated fat), 141 mg cholesterol, 286 mg sodium, 7 g carbohydrate, 1 g fiber, 37 g protein.

A+ Recipes from SCHOOLS Across America

WHITE CHICKEN CHILI

Lime, cumin and cilantro really create a burst of flavor in this zesty chicken chili. It's a healthier alternative to the traditional variety, and never disappoints.

Teacher, Walter Johnson Middle School, Morganton, North Carolina

Donna Lindecamp, Morganton, North Carolina

2 cans (14-1/2 ounces each) chicken broth

3 bone-in chicken breast halves (8 ounces each), skin removed

1 large onion, chopped

2 garlic cloves, minced

1 teaspoon ground cumin

1 teaspoon dried oregano

1/2 teaspoon salt

1/4 teaspoon cayenne pepper

2 cans (15-1/2 ounces each) great northern beans, rinsed and drained

1-1/2 cups frozen white corn

1/3 cup lime juice

Sour cream, shredded white cheddar cheese and/or minced fresh cilantro, optional

1. In a large saucepan, combine the first eight ingredients. Bring to a boil. Reduce heat; cover and simmer for 35-40 minutes or until a meat thermometer reads 170°. Remove chicken from broth; allow to cool.

2. Remove meat from bones; discard bones. Cube chicken and return to pan. Mash half of the beans. Add all of the beans, corn and lime juice to chicken mixture. Return to a boil. Reduce heat; cover and simmer for 15-20 minutes or until flavors are blended.

3. Serve with sour cream, cheese and cilantro if desired.

YIELD: 7 SERVINGS.

NUTRITION FACTS: 1 cup equals 229 calories, 3 g fat (1 g saturated fat), 41 mg cholesterol, 887 mg sodium, 30 g carbohydrate, 8 g fiber, 22 g protein.

Maylene, Alabama

Holly Jackson became one of the assistant principals at Creek View Elementary after spending five years teaching second and third grades. In her new role she handles attendance, discipline, school safety, technology integration and provides student support. "Something special about Creek View Elementary is that during the 2010-2011 school year, we enrolled 20 sets of twins!"

GRILLED ROSEMARY CHICKEN

This moist, tender chicken has a hint of rosemary flavor. It's so easy to throw together, which makes it a great weeknight dish. I always prepare extra pieces of chicken so that we can use it later in the week. It's splendid the first day grilled and leftovers make fantastic chicken salad.

Holly Jackson, Calera, Alabama

2/3 cup ranch salad dressing

3 tablespoons olive oil

3 tablespoons Worcestershire sauce

2 tablespoons dried rosemary, crushed

2 teaspoons dried basil

2 teaspoons white wine vinegar

2 teaspoons lemon juice

1-1/4 teaspoons dried oregano

1-1/4 teaspoons honey

1/2 teaspoon salt

1/4 teaspoon pepper

6 boneless skinless chicken breast halves
   (5 ounces each)

1. In a large resealable plastic bag, combine first 11 ingredients. Flatten chicken to 1/2-in. thickness; add to bag. Seal and turn to coat. Refrigerate for 8 hours or overnight.

2. Drain chicken and discard marinade. Moisten a paper towel with cooking oil; using long-handled tongs, lightly coat the grill rack. Grill chicken, covered, over medium heat or broil 4 in. from the heat for 4-7 minutes on each side or until a meat thermometer reads 170°.

YIELD: 6 SERVINGS.

NUTRITION FACTS: 1 chicken breast half equals 211 calories, 9 g fat (2 g saturated fat), 80 mg cholesterol, 207 mg sodium, 2 g carbohydrate, trace fiber, 29 g protein.

SWEET & SASSY BABY BACK RIBS

My family loves this recipe so much that I always have to triple it when the entire gang is home. I usually make three to four slabs. Any extras taste great reheated the next day.

Teacher, Brooklyn Elementary, Brooklyn, Michigan

Terri Kandell, Addison, Michigan

2 cups ketchup

2 cups cider vinegar

1 cup dark corn syrup

1/4 cup packed brown sugar

1/4 cup root beer

1/2 teaspoon salt

1/2 teaspoon garlic powder

1/2 teaspoon onion powder

1/2 teaspoon hot pepper sauce

4 pounds pork baby back ribs

1. In a large saucepan, combine the first nine ingredients. Bring to a boil. Reduce heat; simmer, uncovered, for 20-25 minutes or until slightly thickened, stirring occasionally. Set aside 3 cups for basting and serving.

2. Brush remaining sauce over ribs. Place bone side down on a rack in a large shallow roasting pan. Cover tightly with foil; bake at 325° for 1-1/2 to 2 hours or until tender.

3. Moisten a paper towel with cooking oil; using long-handled tongs, lightly coat the grill rack. Grill the ribs, covered, over medium heat for 15-25 minutes or until browned, turning and brushing occasionally with some of the reserved sauce. Cut into serving-size pieces; serve with sauce.

YIELD: 8 SERVINGS.

NUTRITION FACTS: 1 serving equals 605 calories, 31 g fat (11 g saturated fat), 122 mg cholesterol, 1,084 mg sodium, 56 g carbohydrate, trace fiber, 25 g protein.

WHITE BEAN TUNA SALAD

I love tuna, and this recipe is a great way to use the canned variety. The Mediterranean flavors really pack a punch.

Volunteer, Hawarden Hills Academy, Riverside, California

Laureen Pittman, Riverside, California

VINAIGRETTE:

1/2 cup olive oil

1/4 cup white wine vinegar

2 to 3 tablespoons lemon juice

2 tablespoons snipped fresh dill

1 tablespoon Dijon mustard

1 tablespoon honey

1/2 teaspoon kosher salt

1/4 teaspoon pepper

SALAD:

1 can (15 ounces) white kidney or cannellini beans, rinsed and drained

2 cans (5 ounces each) white water-packed tuna, drained

1 cup chopped roasted sweet red peppers

1/2 cup chopped red onion

1/2 cup chopped pitted Greek olives

1/2 cup chopped oil-packed sun-dried tomatoes

1/2 cup minced fresh parsley

2 teaspoons minced fresh oregano

6 leaves red leaf lettuce

1. In a small bowl, whisk all the vinaigrette ingredients until well blended.

2. In a large bowl, combine the beans, tuna, red peppers, onion, olives, tomatoes, parsley and oregano. Drizzle with the vinaigrette; gently toss to coat. Serve on lettuce.

YIELD: 6 SERVINGS.

NUTRITION FACTS: 3/4 cup equals 367 calories, 24 g fat (3 g saturated fat), 20 mg cholesterol, 849 mg sodium, 21 g carbohydrate, 4 g fiber, 15 g protein.

TUSCAN SAUSAGE AND POTATO SOUP

Here's a soup that's bound to be popular with the whole family. Though it feels special, it's actually fairly simple to make. I like serving it with warm fresh rolls.

Teacher, Burton Elementary, Erie, Pennsylvania

Lisa Sinicki, Erie, Pennsylvania

1-1/2 pounds bulk Italian sausage

3 pounds potatoes, peeled and sliced

3 cans (14-1/2 ounces each) chicken broth

2 cups water

1 cup chopped sweet onion

2 garlic cloves, minced

1/4 teaspoon salt

1/8 teaspoon pepper

3 cups chopped Swiss chard

2 cups heavy whipping cream

8 bacon strips, cooked and crumbled

1. In a large skillet, cook sausage over medium heat until no longer pink. Drain; set aside.

2. In a Dutch oven, combine the potatoes, broth, water, onion, garlic, salt and pepper. Bring to a boil. Reduce heat; cover and simmer for 18-22 minutes or until potatoes are tender.

3. Stir in the Swiss chard, cream, bacon and sausage. Bring to a boil. Reduce heat; simmer, uncovered, for 5 to 10 minutes or until chard is tender.

YIELD: 10 SERVINGS (3-3/4 QUARTS).

NUTRITION FACTS: 1-1/2 cups equals 400 calories, 29 g fat (15 g saturated fat), 101 mg cholesterol, 1,073 mg sodium, 23 g carbohydrate, 2 g fiber, 12 g protein.

Teacher
Sabetha Elementary School

Sabetha, Kansas

Karen Aeschliman has been teaching fourth grade language arts at Sabetha Elementary School for the past 23 years. "I love to see kids get really excited about a good book," says Karen, who makes an effort to share some of her favorite books with the students, as well. Karen also likes to cook and always gets a chuckle out of seeing a student at the grocery store. "They are amazed to see their teacher comes there, too!"

HERBED LEMON CHICKEN

This is a sensational recipe for busy cooks. You can put the chicken in the marinade the day before, and it will be ready to grill when you come home from work the next night. In the winter, I grill the chicken on my indoor electric grill. It's so easy and always turns out terrific.

Karen Aeschliman, Sabetha, Kansas

1 cup mayonnaise

1/4 cup lemon juice

2 tablespoons white wine or chicken broth

1 tablespoon garlic powder

1 tablespoon dried oregano

1/4 teaspoon pepper

6 boneless skinless chicken breast halves
   (5 ounces each)

1. In a small bowl, combine the first six ingredients. Pour 3/4 cup marinade into a large resealable plastic bag. Add chicken seal bag and turn to coat. Refrigerate for at least 8 hours or overnight. Cover and refrigerate remaining marinade.

2. Drain chicken and discard marinade. Moisten a paper towel with cooking oil; using long-handled tongs, lightly coat the grill rack. Grill chicken, covered, over medium heat or broil 4 in. from the heat for 5 minutes. Turn chicken; grill or broil 4-9 minutes longer or until a meat thermometer reads 170°, basting occasionally with reserved marinade.

YIELD: 6 SERVINGS.

NUTRITION FACTS: 1 chicken breast equals 374 calories, 27 g fat (4 g saturated fat), 89 mg cholesterol, 229 mg sodium, 2 g carbohydrate, trace fiber, 29 g protein.

SOUTHWESTERN SHRIMP WITH SALSA

I prefer to grill in the summer, especially when it means I can prepare this tasty shrimp dish. If you want to get fancy with the presentation, serve it in a chilled martini glass. Cook the rice and shrimp ahead and refrigerate until serving.

Teacher, Sarah Winnemucca Elementary, Reno, Nevada

Lindsay Matuszak, Reno, Nevada

2 tablespoons olive oil

1 tablespoon chili powder

1 teaspoon garlic salt

1 teaspoon ground coriander

1 teaspoon dried oregano

1/2 teaspoon ground cumin

1/2 teaspoon pepper

20 uncooked jumbo shrimp, peeled and deveined

1 cup uncooked saffron rice

AVOCADO-CORN SALSA:

1 medium ripe avocado, peeled and cubed

2 to 3 tablespoons lime juice

1-1/2 cups frozen corn, thawed

1 medium tomato, peeled, seeded and chopped

2 jalapeno peppers, seeded and minced

1/4 cup minced fresh cilantro

1 green onion, chopped

1/8 teaspoon salt

1/8 teaspoon pepper

1. In a large resealable plastic bag, combine the first seven ingredients. Add shrimp; seal and turn to coat. Refrigerate for 30 minutes.

2. Meanwhile, cook rice according to package directions.

3. In a small bowl, combine avocado and lime juice; toss to coat. Add the remaining ingredients; gently stir to combine.

4. Drain shrimp and discard marinade. Thread shrimp onto metal or soaked wooden skewers. Moisten a paper towel with cooking oil; using long-handled tongs, lightly coat the grill rack.

5. Grill shrimp, covered, over medium heat or broil 4 in. from the heat for 6-9 minutes or until shrimp turn pink, turning once. Serve with rice and salsa.

YIELD: 4 SERVINGS.

EDITOR'S NOTE: We recommend wearing disposable gloves when cutting hot peppers. Avoid touching your face.

NUTRITION FACTS: 5 shrimp with 1/2 cup rice and 3/4 cup salsa equals 461 calories, 16 g fat (2 g saturated fat), 154 mg cholesterol, 1,254 mg sodium, 55 g carbohydrate, 7 g fiber, 28 g protein.

SPICY APRICOT CHICKEN THIGHS

Chicken thighs are inexpensive and make a great dinner for a large group. The apricot glaze gives the meat a tempting gloss, while a few minutes in the broiler crisps the skin to perfection. Leftovers are great the next day, too! Just turn oven on 375° and heat chicken for 10–15 minutes.

Teacher, Farwell Elementary, Spokane, Washington

Marcy Gallinger, Deer Park, Washington

3 tablespoons minced fresh rosemary or 1 tablespoon dried rosemary, crushed

2 tablespoons brown sugar

2 teaspoons salt

2 teaspoons pepper

1 teaspoon crushed red pepper flakes

12 bone-in chicken thighs (about 5 pounds)

SAUCE:

1 jar (12 ounces) apricot preserves

1/4 cup rice vinegar

1 tablespoon honey

2 teaspoons minced fresh rosemary or 1/2 teaspoon dried rosemary, crushed

1. In a small bowl, combine the first five ingredients; rub over chicken. Place chicken, skin side up, on a rack in a shallow roasting pan. Bake at 375° for 35-40 minutes or until a meat thermometer reads 180°.

2. Meanwhile, in a small saucepan, combine sauce ingredients; bring to a boil over medium-high heat, stirring frequently. Reduce heat; simmer, uncovered, for 5 minutes, stirring the sauce occasionally.

3. Turn chicken. Spoon some sauce over chicken. Broil 4-6 in. from the heat for 3-5 minutes or until browned. Turn chicken again; baste with sauce. Broil for 2-3 minutes longer or until browned. Serve with remaining sauce.

YIELD: 6 SERVINGS.

NUTRITION FACTS: 2 chicken thighs with 4-1/2 teaspoons sauce equals 626 calories, 29 g fat (8 g saturated fat), 163 mg cholesterol, 950 mg sodium, 46 g carbohydrate, trace fiber, 46 g protein.

Administrator, Taft School

Watertown, Connecticut

Lisa Keys has been a certified physician assistant since 1981. Prior to joining Taft School, she worked at Westover School for 18 years and, prior to that, in a private practice. Lisa is the head of the Taft Community Health and Wellness Committee and a member of the American Academy of Physician Assistants. She has two children, both Taft graduates, and currently resides in Middlebury with her husband, Bill, and dog, Deacon. Lisa enjoys making jewelry and is an award-winning competitive cook.

MAHOGANY-GLAZED MUSHROOM BURGERS

This burger is covered with a few of my favorite things... portobello mushrooms, goat cheese, basil and Mascarpone. They get quite juicy, so serve them with extra napkins.

Lisa Keys, Middlebury, Connecticut

1/4 cup maple syrup

1/4 cup Kahlua (coffee liqueur)

1/4 cup reduced-sodium soy sauce

10 ounces sliced baby portobello mushrooms

1/2 cup thinly sliced red onion

2 tablespoons olive oil

1/4 teaspoon kosher salt

1/8 teaspoon pepper

CHEESE SPREAD:

1/2 cup Mascarpone cheese

1/2 cup crumbled goat cheese

1/4 cup minced fresh parsley

2 tablespoons minced fresh basil or 2 teaspoons dried basil

1/8 teaspoon pepper

BURGERS:

1-1/2 pounds ground beef

1 teaspoon kosher salt

1/2 teaspoon pepper

6 hard rolls, split

1. In a small saucepan, combine the maple syrup, Kahlua and soy sauce. Bring to a boil; cook for 8 minutes or until liquid is reduced by half.

2. In a large skillet, saute mushrooms and onion in oil until tender. Add the salt, pepper and 1/4 cup of Kahlua mixture. Cook and stir until liquid is almost evaporated.

3. In a small bowl, combine the cheese spread ingredients; cover and refrigerate until serving.

4. Crumble beef into a large bowl. Sprinkle with salt and pepper; mix well. Shape into six patties.

5. Grill burgers, covered, over medium heat for 6 minutes. Turn; grill 5-8 minutes longer or until a meat thermometer reads 160° and juices run clear, basting occasionally with remaining Kahlua mixture. Grill rolls, uncovered, for 1-2 minutes or until toasted.

6. Spread the rolls with cheese spread; top with burgers and mushroom mixture. Replace tops.

YIELD: 6 SERVINGS.

NUTRITION FACTS: 1 burger equals 674 calories, 40 g fat (17 g saturated fat), 128 mg cholesterol, 1,238 mg sodium, 45 g carbohydrate, 3 g fiber, 32 g protein.

SPICY COCONUT CHICKEN STRIPS

My family has always enjoyed Thai food, but we really love chicken curry. Since we have a two-year-old son, I wanted to make something that he would eat. His favorite food is chicken strips, so I started making them with some curry flavor. Now my family prefers these even more than my original chicken curry.

Teacher, Eduprize Charter School, Queen Creek, Arizona

Daniel Fox, Queen Creek, Arizona

2 eggs
1/2 cup coconut milk
2 tablespoons red curry paste
1 tablespoon cornstarch
1 cup flaked coconut
1 cup all-purpose flour
4 teaspoons chili powder
12 chicken tenderloins
Oil for deep-fat frying

PEANUT DIPPING SAUCE:
1/4 cup chunky peanut butter
1/4 cup coconut milk
3 tablespoons 2% milk
4-1/2 teaspoons reduced-sodium soy sauce
3 garlic cloves, minced
1 tablespoon minced fresh cilantro
1 tablespoon brown sugar
1 tablespoon lime juice

1. In a shallow bowl, whisk eggs, coconut milk, curry paste and cornstarch until smooth. In another shallow bowl, combine coconut, flour and chili powder. Dip chicken in egg mixture, then coat with coconut mixture.

2. In an electric skillet or deep fryer, heat oil to 375°. Fry the chicken, a few at a time, for 2-3 minutes on each side or until golden brown. Drain on paper towels.

3. In a microwave-safe bowl, combine the sauce ingredients. Cover and microwave on high for 45 seconds or until heated through, stirring once. Serve with chicken.

YIELD: 4 SERVINGS (2/3 CUP SAUCE).

NUTRITION FACTS: 3 tenderloins with 2 tablespoons plus 2 teaspoons sauce equals 638 calories, 42 g fat (15 g saturated fat), 124 mg cholesterol, 580 mg sodium, 40 g carbohydrate, 4 g fiber, 31 g protein.

CHEESY MAC & CHEESE

Everyone comes home for dinner when I make this crowd-pleasing homemade macaroni and cheese. It also receives great compliments at potlucks.

Teacher, Wood Elementary School, Tempe, Arizona

Debra Sult, Chandler, Arizona

2 cups uncooked elbow macaroni
1 tablespoon all-purpose flour
1 cup heavy whipping cream
1 cup half-and-half cream
1/4 cup sour cream
1 egg
1/2 teaspoon ground mustard
1/2 teaspoon cayenne pepper
1/4 teaspoon salt
1/4 teaspoon pepper
1/8 teaspoon ground nutmeg
8 ounces Monterey Jack cheese, cubed
8 ounces cheddar cheese, cubed
2 cups (8 ounces) shredded cheddar cheese

1. Cook macaroni according to package directions. Meanwhile, in a large bowl, whisk the flour, cream, half-and-half, sour cream, egg, ground mustard, cayenne, salt, pepper and nutmeg until smooth.

2. Drain pasta. Transfer to a greased 2-1/2-qt. baking dish. Stir in cubed cheeses. Top with cream mixture. Sprinkle with the shredded cheese.

3. Bake, uncovered, at 350° for 30-40 minutes or until bubbly and golden brown.

YIELD: 8 SERVINGS.

NUTRITION FACTS: 1 cup equals 563 calories, 43 g fat (28 g saturated fat), 172 mg cholesterol, 648 mg sodium, 18 g carbohydrate, 1 g fiber, 25 g protein.

Teacher
Willow Valley Middle School

Wellsville, Utah

Stacie Gomm has dual roles at Willow Valley Middle School where she acts as both assistant principal and classroom teacher. In addition to working with a great group of students, Stacie says she couldn't ask for a better school location. "The school is set at the foot of a huge mountain in Wellsville, Utah...it's just a beautiful area."

PASTA ARRABBIATA (ANGRY PASTA)

I learned how to make this while I was visiting Italy one summer. Add more or less crushed red pepper to decide how "angry" you would like your pasta.

Stacie Gomm, Providence, Utah

1/2 pound bacon strips, chopped

2 garlic cloves, minced

1/3 cup olive oil

3 cans (15 ounces each) tomato puree

6 fresh basil leaves, thinly sliced

1/2 to 1 teaspoon crushed red pepper flakes

3 cups uncooked penne pasta

Grated Parmesan cheese

1. In a large skillet, cook bacon over medium heat until crisp. Remove bacon to paper towels with a slotted spoon; discard the drippings.

2. In the same skillet, saute garlic in olive oil for 1 minute. Add the tomato puree, basil, pepper flakes and bacon. Bring to a boil; reduce heat and simmer 15 minutes to allow flavors to blend, stirring occasionally.

3. Meanwhile, cook pasta according to package directions; drain. Serve with sauce; sprinkle with Parmesan cheese.

YIELD: 6 SERVINGS.

NUTRITION FACTS: 1 cup pasta with 3/4 cup sauce (calculated without cheese) equals 460 calories, 28 g fat (7 g saturated fat), 42 mg cholesterol, 925 mg sodium, 31 g carbohydrate, 3 g fiber, 20 g protein.

SHRIMP-STUFFED POBLANO PEPPERS

I created this dish for my mother when she moved back to our hometown. Since my mom really enjoys shrimp and slightly spicy food, I decided to create shrimp-stuffed poblanos to surprise her. She was delighted with it.

Staff, Lanier Elementary School, Tampa, Florida

Tina Garcia-Ortiz, Tampa, Florida

4 large poblano peppers
2 tablespoons butter, melted, divided
1 teaspoon coarsely ground pepper
1/2 teaspoon kosher salt
1 small onion, finely chopped
2 celery ribs, chopped
4 ounces cream cheese, softened
1 pound chopped cooked peeled shrimp
1-3/4 cups shredded Mexican cheese blend
1-1/2 cups cold cooked rice
2 tablespoons lemon juice
2 teaspoons dried cilantro flakes
1/2 teaspoon onion powder
1/2 teaspoon garlic powder

TOPPING:

1 cup panko (Japanese) bread crumbs
1/4 cup grated Parmesan cheese
2 tablespoons butter, melted

1. Cut peppers in half lengthwise and discard seeds. Place the peppers, cut sides down, in an ungreased 15-in. x 10-in. x 1-in. baking pan. Brush with 1 tablespoon butter; sprinkle with pepper and salt. Bake, uncovered, at 350° for 10-15 minutes or until tender.

2. Meanwhile, in a large skillet, saute onion and celery in the remaining butter until tender. Stir in the cream cheese until melted. Add the shrimp, cheese blend, rice, lemon juice and seasonings; heat through. Spoon into pepper halves.

3. Place on an ungreased 15-in. x 10-in. x 1-in. baking pan. Combine topping ingredients; sprinkle over peppers. Bake, uncovered, at 350° for 10-15 minutes or until topping is golden brown.

YIELD: 8 SERVINGS.

EDITOR'S NOTE: We recommend wearing disposable gloves when cutting hot peppers. Avoid touching your face.

NUTRITION FACTS: 1 stuffed pepper half equals 361 calories, 21 g fat (13 g saturated fat), 153 mg cholesterol, 541 mg sodium, 20 g carbohydrate, 2 g fiber, 23 g protein.

Marysville, Washington

Suzanne Francis has been a paraprofessional at Liberty Elementary School since 1990. She describes the staff and students as very caring. "The students have donated money to the American Red Cross for Haiti, for leukemia and to Japan after the tsunami disaster."

MUSHROOM-ARTICHOKE BRUNCH BAKE

While the potatoes are baking, take care of the rest of the prep work for this recipe. The original recipe makes a pretty vegetarian egg bake. However, you can also add a layer of little smoked sausages cut lengthwise in half over the artichokes to create a more substantial meal.

Suzanne Francis, Marysville, Washington

3 cups frozen shredded hash brown potatoes, thawed

2 tablespoons butter, melted, divided

1/2 teaspoon salt

2-1/2 cups sliced fresh mushrooms

1 can (14 ounces) water-packed artichoke hearts, rinsed, drained and quartered

3 cups (12 ounces) shredded cheddar cheese

12 eggs

1-3/4 cups 2% milk

1 can (4 ounces) chopped green chilies, drained

1. Place potatoes in a greased 13-in. x 9-in. baking dish; drizzle with 1 tablespoon butter and sprinkle with salt. Bake at 350° for 20-25 minutes or until lightly browned.

2. Meanwhile, in a small skillet, saute mushrooms in remaining butter until tender. Place artichokes on paper towels; pat dry. Sprinkle mushrooms, artichokes and cheese over potatoes. In a large bowl, whisk the eggs, milk and green chilies; pour over cheese.

3. Bake, uncovered, for 40-45 minutes or until a knife inserted near the center comes out clean. Let stand for 5 minutes before serving.

YIELD: 12 SERVINGS.

NUTRITION FACTS: 1 slice equals 239 calories, 16 g fat (9 g saturated fat), 249 mg cholesterol, 493 mg sodium, 9 g carbohydrate, 1 g fiber, 15 g protein.

Volunteer
Watkins Glen Middle School

Watkins Glen, New York

With kids at two different schools, Brud Holland finds himself doing double volunteer duty at Watkins Glen Middle School and at Watkins Glen High School. But he doesn't mind. "There's nothing like sharing your talents and life experiences with students and inspiring them to try new things. It's especially satisfying to hear them say, 'I can do that!'" he says.

RICOTTA GNOCCHI WITH SPINACH & GORGONZOLA

Gnocchi are thick, soft dumpling-like pasta made from potatoes. In this special dish, the tender pillows of pasta are treated to a creamy white sauce that features butternut squash, spinach and Gorgonzola cheese.

Brud Holland, Watkins Glen, New York

3 large potatoes

3 cups reduced-fat ricotta cheese

1/4 cup grated Romano cheese

2 tablespoons olive oil

1 tablespoon kosher salt

6 eggs

4-1/2 cups cake flour

4 quarts water

SAUCE:

2-2/3 cups cubed peeled butternut squash

1/3 cup thinly sliced fresh basil leaves

1/3 cup water

2 tablespoons plus 2 teaspoons olive oil

2 garlic cloves, peeled and thinly sliced

1-1/4 teaspoons kosher salt

3/4 teaspoon pepper

1-1/3 cups heavy whipping cream

2/3 cup crumbled Gorgonzola cheese

1-1/2 pounds fresh spinach, coarsely chopped

1. Scrub and pierce potatoes. Bake at 400° for 50-55 minutes or until tender. Peel potatoes; press through a potato ricer or strainer into a large bowl. Cool slightly.

2. Add ricotta and Romano cheeses, oil and salt to potato pulp; beat on low speed until smooth. Beat in eggs, one at a time. Add flour; mix well. On a lightly floured surface, knead 10-12 times, forming a soft dough.

3. Divide dough into 16 portions. On a floured surface, roll each portion into a 1/2-in.-thick rope; cut into 3/4-in. pieces. Press and roll each piece with a lightly floured fork.

4. In a Dutch oven, bring water to a boil. Cook gnocchi in batches for 30-60 seconds or until they float. Remove with a slotted spoon and keep warm.

5. In a large saucepan, combine squash, basil, water, oil, garlic, salt and pepper. Bring to a boil. Cover and cook for 4-6 minutes or until squash is tender.

6. Stir in cream and Gorgonzola. Bring to a boil. Reduce heat; simmer, uncovered, for 2 minutes. Add spinach in batches; cook until spinach is wilted. Serve with gnocchi.

YIELD: 8 SERVINGS.

NUTRITION FACTS: 1-1/2 cups gnocchi with 3/4 cup spinach mixture equals 833 calories, 35 g fat (17 g saturated fat), 248 mg cholesterol, 1,420 mg sodium, 101 g carbohydrate, 7 g fiber, 29 g protein.

PESTO CHICKEN SALAD SANDWICHES

Sandwiches are a teacher's lunchtime staple. The prepared pesto and roasted peppers add a welcome twist to traditional chicken salad.

Teacher, Pequea Elementary School, Willow Street, Pennsylvania

Ellen Finger, Lancaster, Pennsylvania

2/3 cup reduced-fat mayonnaise

1/3 cup prepared pesto

2 tablespoons lemon juice

1/4 teaspoon garlic powder

1/4 teaspoon pepper

3 cups cubed cooked chicken

1 jar (7 ounces) roasted sweet red peppers, drained and chopped

1 celery rib, finely chopped

6 romaine leaves

6 ciabatta rolls, split

1. In a large bowl, combine the first five ingredients. Add the chicken, red peppers and celery; toss to coat. Serve on lettuce-lined rolls.

YIELD: 6 SERVINGS.

NUTRITION FACTS: 1 sandwich equals 636 calories, 24 g fat (5 g saturated fat), 76 mg cholesterol, 1,047 mg sodium, 75 g carbohydrate, 4 g fiber, 33 g protein.

Volunteer
Heritage Christian Academy

Maple Grove, Minnesota

As a parent volunteer, Jamie Miller contributes in various ways in both her daughter's kindergarten class and the school library. "As part of the WAY (We Appreciate You) committee, I contribute food to a monthly teachers' lunch called First Fridays. The teachers love it," she says.

PEPPERONI LASAGNA ROLL-UPS

It tastes like pizza, looks like manicotti and everyone loves it! The dish works great for teacher meetings and potlucks because it can be made well in advance, travels well and is way easier than stuffing filling into manicotti noodles.

Jamie Miller, Maple Grove, Minnesota

16 uncooked lasagna noodles

1/2 pound bulk Italian sausage

1/2 pound sliced baby portobello mushrooms

1/4 cup chopped sweet onion

1 jar (24 ounces) tomato basil pasta sauce

1-1/2 teaspoons brown sugar

1-1/2 teaspoons fennel seed, crushed

1/2 teaspoon dried tarragon

1-1/8 teaspoons salt, divided

1/8 teaspoon crushed red pepper flakes, optional

1 package (3-1/2 ounces) sliced pepperoni

2-1/2 cups (10 ounces) shredded part-skim mozzarella cheese

2-1/2 cups part-skim ricotta cheese

2 cups grated Parmesan cheese, divided

2 eggs, lightly beaten

6 tablespoons minced fresh parsley, divided

3 tablespoons minced fresh basil or 1 tablespoon dried basil

1/2 teaspoon pepper

1. Cook noodles according to package directions.
2. Meanwhile, in a Dutch oven, cook the sausage, mushrooms and onion over medium heat until meat is no longer pink; drain. Transfer to a large bowl. Stir in the pasta sauce, brown sugar, fennel seed, tarragon, 1/8 teaspoon salt and pepper flakes if desired.
3. In the same pan, cook pepperoni for 4-5 minutes or until lightly browned; remove to paper towels to drain.
4. In another large bowl, combine the mozzarella, ricotta, 1 cup Parmesan, eggs, 4 tablespoons parsley, basil, pepper and remaining salt.
5. Drain noodles. Spread 1 cup meat sauce in a greased 13-in. x 9-in. baking dish. Spread 1/4 cup cheese mixture over each noodle; top with 3 or 4 pepperoni slices. Carefully roll up; place seam side down in prepared dish. Top with remaining meat sauce; sprinkle with remaining Parmesan.
6. Cover and bake at 350° for 55-60 minutes or until bubbly. Sprinkle with remaining parsley before serving.

YIELD: 16 SERVINGS.

NUTRITION FACTS: 1 roll-up equals 329 calories, 15 g fat (7 g saturated fat), 68 mg cholesterol, 819 mg sodium, 28 g carbohydrate, 2 g fiber, 21 g protein.

Staff, Hillcrest School

Lebanon, Missouri

In addition to being the administrative assistant to the principal, Linda Rhoads is a mother and a grandmother who loves to cook Sunday lunch for her family. "My husband Jim bakes amazing cookies for everyone, and I love to cook the main meal. We make a great team," she says.

SUNDAY PAELLA

My adult children adore this recipe and look forward to eating it when they come over for lunch on Sundays after church. I do some preparation before leaving for church and finish it when we return home. That is why we call it Sunday Paella.

Linda Rhoads, Lebanon, Missouri

1-1/2 pounds boneless skinless chicken breasts, cubed

3 tablespoons canola oil

1 pound smoked sausage, cut into 1/4-inch slices

1 small onion, chopped

1-1/2 cups uncooked long grain rice

2 teaspoons Italian seasoning

1/4 teaspoon ground turmeric

1/4 teaspoon pepper

3 cups chicken broth

1-1/2 pounds uncooked medium shrimp, peeled and deveined

1 can (28 ounces) diced tomatoes, undrained

1-1/2 cups frozen peas, thawed

1 tablespoon sugar

1. In a Dutch oven, cook and stir chicken in oil over medium heat until no longer pink. Add sausage and onion; cook 3-4 minutes longer. Add the rice, Italian seasoning, turmeric and pepper; cook and stir for 3-4 minutes or until the rice is lightly browned.

2. Add broth. Bring to a boil. Reduce heat; cover and simmer for 14-18 minutes or until rice is almost tender. Stir in the shrimp, tomatoes, peas and sugar; cover and cook for 10-15 minutes or until shrimp turn pink, stirring occasionally.

YIELD: 8 SERVINGS.

NUTRITION FACTS: 1-1/2 cups equals 570 calories, 24 g fat (8 g saturated fat), 190 mg cholesterol, 1,309 mg sodium, 41 g carbohydrate, 4 g fiber, 44 g protein.

PORK TENDERLOIN WITH CILANTRO-LIME PESTO

Scrumptious, elegant, easy...what more could you want in a recipe? The homemade cilantro-jalapeno pesto has a wonderful blend of flavors and goes deliciously well with the pork.

Teacher, Kahoa Elementary, Lincoln, Nebraska

Jerri Gradert, Lincoln, Nebraska

- 1/4 cup chopped green onions
- 2 tablespoons minced fresh gingerroot
- 2 tablespoons lime juice
- 2 tablespoons orange juice
- 1 tablespoon minced garlic
- 1 tablespoon minced fresh cilantro
- 1 teaspoon chopped seeded jalapeno pepper
- 1/2 teaspoon pepper
- 2 tablespoons olive oil
- 2 pork tenderloins (1 pound each)
- 1/2 cup shredded pepper Jack cheese
- 1/4 cup sunflower kernels, toasted and chopped
- 1/2 cup crumbled cooked bacon

1. In a small food processor, combine the first eight ingredients; cover and process until blended. While processing, gradually add oil in a steady stream.

2. Make a lengthwise slit down the center of each tenderloin to within 1/2 in. of bottom. Open tenderloin so it lies flat; cover with plastic wrap. Flatten to 3/4-in. thickness.

3. Remove the plastic wrap; spread a fourth of the pesto mixture over each tenderloin. Sprinkle each with the cheese, sunflower kernels and bacon. Close the tenderloins; tie at 1-1/2-in. to 2-in. intervals with kitchen string and secure ends with toothpicks. Spread the remaining pesto over the tenderloins. Cover; refrigerate for several hours or overnight.

4. Place tenderloins on a rack in a shallow baking pan. Bake at 425° for 25-30 minutes or until a meat thermometer reads 160°. Cover and let stand for 10 minutes before slicing.

YIELD: 6 SERVINGS.

EDITOR'S NOTE: We recommend wearing disposable gloves when cutting hot peppers. Avoid touching your face.

NUTRITION FACTS: 5 ounces cooked pork equals 308 calories, 16 g fat (4 g saturated fat), 96 mg cholesterol, 411 mg sodium, 4 g carbohydrate, 1 g fiber, 36 g protein.

SHRIMP MAC & CHEESE SALAD

My mother had a recipe similar to this one, but no one could find it. After an exhaustive search on the Internet, I decided to re-create the salad from memory. Mom thinks I did a pretty good job!

Teacher, Bladenboro Middle School, Bladenboro, North Carolina

Daphne DeLaney, Lake Waccamaw, North Carolina

4 cups uncooked elbow macaroni

1/4 cup butter, cut up

1/4 cup all-purpose flour

1-1/2 cups half-and-half cream

4 ounces Gouda cheese, shredded

1/2 cup shredded cheddar cheese

1/2 cup shredded part-skim mozzarella cheese

2 pounds peeled and deveined cooked medium shrimp, cut into pieces

1 cup chopped onion

1 cup chopped sweet red pepper

1 cup mayonnaise

1/2 cup chopped celery

1/2 cup chopped dill pickle

1/8 teaspoon salt

1/8 teaspoon pepper

8 lettuce leaves

1. Cook macaroni according to package directions; drain and set aside.

2. Meanwhile, in a large saucepan, melt butter. Stir in flour until smooth; gradually add cream. Bring to a boil; cook and stir for 2 minutes or until thickened. Remove pan from the heat; add cheeses, stirring until melted. Add macaroni; stir to coat. Transfer to a large bowl; cool to room temperature.

3. In another large bowl, combine the shrimp, onion, red pepper, mayonnaise, celery, pickle, salt and pepper. Fold in cooled macaroni mixture; cover and chill. Serve on lettuce.

YIELD: 16 SERVINGS.

NUTRITION FACTS: 1 cup equals 345 calories, 21 g fat (7 g saturated fat), 124 mg cholesterol, 368 mg sodium, 19 g carbohydrate, 1 g fiber, 19 g protein.

BACON CHEESEBURGER MEATBALL SUBS

I love combining some of my favorite dishes into a brand-new creation. Here's a culinary experiment that is a meatball and a bacon cheeseburger rolled into one. This hearty dish will please the meat lovers in your gang.

Teacher, Estates Elementary School, Naples, Florida

Cyndy Gerken, Naples, Florida

2 eggs, lightly beaten

1 tablespoon Worcestershire sauce

2 medium onions, finely chopped

2/3 cup seasoned bread crumbs

1/3 cup grated Parmesan cheese

3 tablespoons minced fresh parsley or 1 tablespoon dried parsley flakes

8 garlic cloves, minced

2 tablespoons minced fresh basil or 2 teaspoons dried basil

1 tablespoon minced fresh oregano or 1 teaspoon dried oregano

1/8 teaspoon kosher salt

1/8 teaspoon pepper

1/8 teaspoon crushed red pepper flakes

3/4 pound ground beef

2/3 pound ground veal

2/3 pound ground pork

24 cubes cheddar cheese (1/2-inch each)

8 cooked bacon strips, cut into thirds

8 lettuce leaves

8 submarine buns, split and toasted

1 cup barbecue sauce, warmed

1. In a large bowl, combine the first 12 ingredients. Crumble the meats over the mixture and mix well; divide into 24 portions.

2. Wrap each cheese cube with a cut bacon strip. Shape one portion of the meat mixture around each bacon-wrapped cheese cube. Place the meatballs on a greased rack in a shallow baking pan.

3. Bake, uncovered, at 400° for 20-25 minutes or until meat is no longer pink. Drain on paper towels. Serve on lettuce-lined buns with barbecue sauce.

YIELD: 8 SANDWICHES.

NUTRITION FACTS: 1 sandwich with 3 meatballs and 2 tablespoons sauce equals 784 calories, 29 g fat (11 g saturated fat), 150 mg cholesterol, 1,594 mg sodium, 85 g carbohydrate, 5 g fiber, 43 g protein.

Staff
Northeast Community College

Norfolk, Nebraska

Joan Kollars' career at Northeast Community College Library began in 1999. "Because we have a small staff, we have all been cross-trained to fill in all areas of our library,"  *she says. "I also work in circulation and reference as needed." Joan says working in an academic environment is both stimulating and rewarding. "I enjoy meeting and working with students of all ages. There is never a dull moment!"*

ARTICHOKE & SPINACH ENCHILADAS

Surprise your gang with delightful vegetarian enchiladas. The cheesy mushroom, artichoke and spinach filling is a fantastic alternative from the usual ingredients.

Joan Kollars, Norfolk, Nebraska

3 tablespoons butter

3 tablespoons all-purpose flour

1 can (14-1/2 ounces) vegetable broth

1 can (8 ounces) tomato sauce

1-1/2 teaspoons chili powder

3/4 teaspoon ground cumin

ENCHILADAS:

1 large onion, chopped

3 garlic cloves, minced

2 tablespoons olive oil

1/2 pound medium fresh mushrooms, quartered

1 can (14 ounces) water-packed artichoke hearts, rinsed, drained and chopped

1 package (10 ounces) frozen chopped spinach, thawed and squeezed dry

1 carton (15 ounces) ricotta cheese

1 cup (8 ounces) sour cream

2 cups (8 ounces) shredded Monterey Jack cheese, divided

8 whole wheat tortillas (8 inches), warmed

1. In a small saucepan, melt the butter. Stir in the flour until smooth; gradually add broth. Bring to a boil; cook and stir for 2 minutes or until thickened. Stir in the tomato sauce, chili powder and cumin. Simmer, uncovered, for 6-8 minutes or until slightly thickened. Spread 3/4 cup sauce into a greased 13-in. x 9-in. baking dish. Set aside remaining sauce.

2. In a large skillet, saute onion and garlic in oil until tender. Stir in mushrooms; cook 3 minutes longer. Add artichokes and spinach; cook for 4-5 minutes. Remove from the heat; stir in the ricotta cheese, sour cream and 1 cup Monterey Jack cheese.

3. Place 2/3 cup mushroom mixture down the center of each tortilla. Roll up and place seam side down in prepared dish. Pour reserved sauce over the top; sprinkle with remaining Monterey Jack cheese.

4. Bake enchiladas, uncovered, at 375° for 20-25 minutes or until heated through.

YIELD: 8 SERVINGS.

NUTRITION FACTS: 1 enchilada equals 506 calories, 29 g fat (15 g saturated fat), 77 mg cholesterol, 933 mg sodium, 37 g carbohydrate, 3 g fiber, 21 g protein.

ITALIAN WEDDING SOUP

You don't have to be Italian to love this easy-to-make soup! It's a hit with everyone who tries it and makes a great meal with hot crusty Italian bread or garlic bread.

Staff, Prairie Trace Elementary, Carmel, Indiana

Mary Sheetz, Carmel, Indiana

2 eggs, lightly beaten

1/2 cup dry bread crumbs

1/4 cup minced fresh parsley

2 tablespoons grated Parmesan cheese

1 tablespoon raisins, finely chopped

3 garlic cloves, minced

1/4 teaspoon crushed red pepper flakes

1/2 pound lean ground beef (90% lean)

1/2 pound bulk spicy pork sausage

2 cartons (32 ounces each) reduced-sodium chicken broth

1/2 teaspoon pepper

1-1/2 cups cubed rotisserie chicken

2/3 cup uncooked acini di pepe pasta

1/2 cup fresh baby spinach, cut into thin strips

Shredded Parmesan cheese, optional

1. In a large bowl, combine the first seven ingredients. Crumble beef and sausage over mixture and mix well. Shape meat into 1/2-in. balls.

2. In a Dutch oven, brown meatballs in small batches; drain. Add broth and pepper; bring to a boil. Reduce heat; simmer, uncovered, for 10 minutes. Stir in chicken and pasta; cook 5-7 minutes longer or until pasta is tender. Stir in spinach; cook until wilted. Sprinkle individual servings with shredded Parmesan cheese if desired.

YIELD: 9 SERVINGS (2-1/4 QUARTS).

NUTRITION FACTS: 1 cup equals 253 calories, 10 g fat (4 g saturated fat), 94 mg cholesterol, 797 mg sodium, 18 g carbohydrate, 1 g fiber, 21 g protein.

Rossford, Ohio

Sandy Komisarek brought her background in advertising-marketing and medical transcription to the education field in 2005. In addition to any clerical support Sandy provides to the school's principal, she is responsible for making school purchases, maintaining the purchasing budget, coordinating graduation and acting as co-advisor of the sophomore class. "Being involved with young people keeps me energized, inspires me to be the best I can possibly be and teaches me to embrace change," she says.

TURKEY CORDON BLEU WITH ALFREDO SAUCE

For our annual Kentucky Derby party, I wanted to create a twist on a traditional Kentucky Hot Brown sandwich. This casserole version stars tender turkey, smoky ham and melted cheese, but the crispy bacon really sets the dish apart.

Sandy Komisarek, Swanton, Ohio

8 slices part-skim mozzarella cheese

8 thin slices deli honey ham

8 turkey breast cutlets

2 cups panko (Japanese) bread crumbs

2 eggs, lightly beaten

1/2 cup all-purpose flour

1/2 teaspoon salt

1/4 teaspoon pepper

1/4 cup canola oil

1 jar (15 ounces) Alfredo sauce, warmed

8 bacon strips, cooked and crumbled

1/4 cup grated Parmesan cheese

1. Place one slice mozzarella cheese and ham on each cutlet. Roll up each from a short side and secure with toothpicks.

2. Place bread crumbs and eggs in separate shallow bowls. In another shallow bowl, combine the flour, salt and pepper. Dip turkey in the flour mixture, eggs, then bread crumbs.

3. In a large skillet, brown turkey in oil in batches. Place in a greased 13-in. x 9-in. baking dish. Bake, uncovered, at 350° for 20-25 minutes or until turkey juices run clear. Discard toothpicks.

4. Spoon Alfredo sauce over turkey. Sprinkle with bacon and Parmesan cheese.

YIELD: 8 SERVINGS.

NUTRITION FACTS: 1 turkey roll-up with about 3 tablespoons sauce equals 455 calories, 24 g fat (10 g saturated fat), 147 mg cholesterol, 910 mg sodium, 18 g carbohydrate, 1 g fiber, 39 g protein.

MAPLE-GLAZED CORNED BEEF

Corned beef gets a touch of sweetness with a maple syrup glaze. Even people who say they don't care for corned beef will ask for seconds when served this tasty version passed down to me from my great-grandmother.

Teacher, Corona Foothills Middle School, Vail, Arizona

Gayle Macklin, Vail, Arizona

2 corned beef briskets with spice packets
  (3 pounds each)

1 large sweet onion, sliced

12 garlic cloves, peeled and halved

1/4 cup kosher salt

1/4 cup whole peppercorns

8 bay leaves

2 tablespoons dried basil

2 tablespoons dried oregano

4 quarts water

3 cups beef broth

1/4 cup maple syrup

1/3 cup packed brown sugar

1. Place the briskets and contents of the spice packets in a stockpot. Add onion, garlic, salt, peppercorns, bay leaves, basil and oregano. Pour in water and beef broth. Bring to a boil. Reduce heat; cover and simmer for 2-1/2 to 3 hours or until meat is tender.

2. Transfer meat to a broiler pan. Brush with maple syrup; sprinkle with brown sugar. Broil 4-6 in. from the heat for 2-3 minutes or until beef is glazed. Thinly slice across the grain.

YIELD: 12 SERVINGS.

NUTRITION FACTS: 3 ounces cooked beef equals 439 calories, 30 g fat (10 g saturated fat), 156 mg cholesterol, 2,014 mg sodium, 11 g carbohydrate, 0 fiber, 29 g protein.

I'M STUFFED FRENCH TOAST

I enjoyed a similar dish at a restaurant and was able to re-create it at home. The fruit adds a special touch.

Teacher, Waterloo High School, Waterloo, New York

Melissa Kerrick, Auburn, New York

2 medium ripe bananas, sliced

2 tablespoons brown sugar

1 teaspoon banana or vanilla extract

1 package (8 ounces) reduced-fat cream cheese

8 slices oat bread (1/2 inch thick)

2 eggs

2/3 cup evaporated milk

1-1/4 teaspoons ground cinnamon

1-1/4 teaspoons vanilla extract

1 tablespoon butter

1 cup sliced fresh strawberries or frozen unsweetened sliced strawberries, thawed

1/2 cup fresh blueberries or frozen unsweetened blueberries

1 tablespoon sugar

Confectioners' sugar

1. In a large skillet coated with cooking spray, saute bananas with brown sugar. Stir in banana extract. In a small bowl, beat cream cheese until smooth. Add the banana mixture; beat well. Spread on four slices of bread; top with the remaining bread.

2. In a shallow bowl, whisk eggs, milk, cinnamon and vanilla. Dip both sides of sandwiches in egg mixture.

3. In a large skillet, toast sandwiches in butter for 2-3 minutes on each side or until golden brown.

4. Meanwhile, in a small saucepan, combine the strawberries, blueberries and sugar; heat through. Serve with French toast; sprinkle with confectioners' sugar.

YIELD: 4 SERVINGS.

NUTRITION FACTS: 1 stuffed French toast with 1/4 cup berries (calculated without confectioners' sugar) equals 496 calories, 22 g fat (13 g saturated fat), 167 mg cholesterol, 659 mg sodium, 58 g carbohydrate, 5 g fiber, 17 g protein.

Administrator, St. Thomas More
Catholic School

Baton Rouge, Louisiana

*Two weeks after Judy
Armstrong accepted the
principal position at
St. Thomas More
Catholic School,
Hurricane Katrina hit
Louisiana. "That is when
I realized just how caring and
dedicated our faculty is," Judy
says. "Within a week, and while
schools were officially closed, the
faculty came to school to help
with a nursing home staying in
our gym and 436 displaced
students." She added that
dedicated and caring spirit
is part of what makes her
job so enjoyable.*

ANDOUILLE-STUFFED PORK LOIN

A faculty potluck favorite, this andouille-stuffed and bacon-wrapped pork loin is full of bold flavors, and yet is fairly simple to prepare. This recipe may be prepared ahead, covered, refrigerated and baked just before needed to provide a wonderful warm entree.

Judy Armstrong, Prairieville, Louisiana

1/4 cup Dijon mustard

2 tablespoons apricot preserves

1 tablespoon minced fresh rosemary or 1 teaspoon dried rosemary, crushed

1 tablespoon minced fresh thyme or 1 teaspoon dried thyme

3 garlic cloves, minced

2 boneless pork loin roasts (2 pounds each)

1 teaspoon salt

1 teaspoon pepper

4 fully cooked andouille sausage links (about 1 pound)

12 bacon strips

1/2 cup chicken broth

1/2 cup white wine or additional chicken broth

1. In a small bowl, combine the first five ingredients. Set aside.
2. Make a lengthwise slit down the center of each roast to within 1/2 in. of bottom. Open roast so it lies flat; cover with plastic wrap. Flatten slightly. Remove plastic wrap. Season with salt and pepper.
3. Arrange two sausage links in center of each roast. Close roasts; brush with mustard mixture. Wrap each roast with bacon. Tie several times with kitchen string; secure ends with toothpicks. Place on a rack in a shallow roasting pan. Pour broth and wine into roasting pan.
4. Bake, uncovered, at 400° for 55-60 minutes or until a meat thermometer inserted into the pork loin reads 160°. Discard string and toothpicks. Let pork roast stand for 10 minutes before slicing.

YIELD: 12 SERVINGS.

NUTRITION FACTS: 5 ounces cooked pork equals 332 calories, 17 g fat (6 g saturated fat), 131 mg cholesterol, 842 mg sodium, 5 g carbohydrate, trace fiber, 39 g protein.

CAJUN SHRIMP

There is plenty of sauce with these savory shrimp. You can serve them over linguine, beans or rice for an inviting dinner. I usually have some fresh bread on the side to soak up the flavorful sauce.

Teacher, Hutchison High School, Fairbanks, Alaska

Mark Oppe, North Pole, Alaska

2 garlic cloves, minced

3 tablespoons butter

1/2 cup amber beer or beef broth

1 teaspoon pepper

1 teaspoon Worcestershire sauce

1/2 teaspoon salt

1/2 teaspoon dried thyme

1/2 teaspoon dried rosemary, crushed

1/2 teaspoon crushed red pepper flakes

1/4 teaspoon cayenne pepper

1/8 teaspoon dried oregano

1 pound uncooked large shrimp, peeled and deveined

1. In a large skillet, saute garlic in butter for 1 minute. Add the beer and seasonings. Bring to a boil. Reduce heat to medium-high. Add shrimp; cook and stir for 3-4 minutes or until shrimp turn pink.

YIELD: 4 SERVINGS.

NUTRITION FACTS: 1/2 cup equals 191 calories, 10 g fat (6 g saturated fat), 160 mg cholesterol, 505 mg sodium, 3 g carbohydrate, trace fiber, 19 g protein.

Parent Teacher
Organization Officer
Sallas Mahone Elementary School

Valdosta, Georgia

Although Rita Combs has her hands full with two children, Lucy and Lucas, she still finds time to volunteer at Sallas Mahone Elementary School, where Lucy is in fourth grade. Rita came to the United States from Italy in 1999. Her love of traditional Italian food comes through in her culinary creations. "I love to cook, and all our family and friends love my food," she says.

TUSCAN BURGERS WITH PESTO MAYO

Everyone will need to bring their appetite when you serve these hearty burgers. They have a bit of Italian flair with the use of pancetta, pesto and mozzarella cheese. Try them...you'll love them!

Rita Combs, Valdosta, Georgia

1/4 cup mayonnaise

1/4 cup prepared pesto, divided

3 ounces sliced pancetta, finely chopped

1/4 teaspoon pepper

1/8 teaspoon kosher salt

1 pound ground beef

1 small red onion, cut into 4 slices

1 large tomato, cut into 4 slices

1 tablespoon olive oil

8 ounces fresh mozzarella cheese, cut into 4 slices

4 Italian rolls, split

1 cup fresh arugula or fresh baby spinach

1. In a small bowl, combine mayonnaise and 2 tablespoons pesto; cover and chill until serving. In a large bowl, combine the pancetta, pepper, salt and remaining pesto. Crumble beef over mixture and mix well. Shape into four patties.

2. Brush the onion and tomato slices with oil. Grill onion over medium heat for 4-6 minutes on each side or until crisp-tender. Grill tomato for 1-2 minutes on each side or until lightly browned.

3. Grill burgers, covered, over medium heat for 5-7 minutes on each side or until a meat thermometer reads 160° and juices run clear. Top burgers with mozzarella cheese. Grill 1 minute longer or until the cheese is melted. Spread cut sides of rolls with pesto mayonnaise; top with burgers, onion, tomato slices and arugula.

YIELD: 4 SERVINGS.

NUTRITION FACTS: 1 burger equals 833 calories, 58 g fat (20 g saturated fat), 142 mg cholesterol, 1,015 mg sodium, 32 g carbohydrate, 2 g fiber, 42 g protein.

Hutchinson, Kansas

Cooking with middle school students can provide some interesting culinary results, says Denise Pounds, an education aide for family and consumer sciences. "We've had some students misread a recipe and use a 1/4 cup of garlic powder instead of 1/4 teaspoon!" When she isn't teaching, cooking or creating new recipes, Denise enjoys knitting.

BBQ HOEDOWN TACOS

Here's a family-friendly twist on traditional tacos. It's easy to make after a long day at work. I serve it on toasted flour tortillas, which is a healthy alternative to a fried shell. To toast the flour tortillas, fold them in half, without creasing. Pop them into a long slotted toaster and toast to golden brown. They'll be in a taco shape and ready to eat.

Denise Pounds, Hutchinson, Kansas

1 pound ground beef

1 small onion, chopped

3/4 cup barbecue sauce

1 can (4 ounces) chopped green chilies

1 teaspoon ground coriander

1 teaspoon ground cumin

1/2 teaspoon salt

2 cups angel hair coleslaw mix

1/4 cup green goddess salad dressing

8 flour tortillas (6 inches), warmed

8 slices pepper Jack cheese

1. In a large nonstick skillet, cook beef and onion over medium heat until meat is no longer pink; drain. Stir in the barbecue sauce, chilies, coriander, cumin and salt. Bring to a boil. Reduce heat; simmer, uncovered, for 5-7 minutes or until heated through.

2. In a small bowl, combine coleslaw mix and salad dressing; toss to coat. On each tortilla, layer cheese, beef mixture and coleslaw; fold to close.

YIELD: 4 SERVINGS.

NUTRITION FACTS: 2 tacos equals 722 calories, 44 g fat (16 g saturated fat), 126 mg cholesterol, 1,803 mg sodium, 40 g carbohydrate, 3 g fiber, 41 g protein.

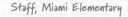

Staff, Miami Elementary

Lafayette, Indiana

As the school secretary at Miami Elementary, Laura Ehlers gets a lot of enjoyment from her day-to-day interactions with students. The students also provide a good dose of laughter. "At the beginning of the school year, I asked a student which bus he rode?," she recalls. "He answered, 'The yellow one.'"

SPECIAL SAUERBRATEN

After simmering in the slow cooker for hours, the rump roast is fork-tender and takes on the flavors of the sauce. My family looks forward to having this home-style meal. I serve it with mashed potatoes and corn.

Laura Ehlers, Lafayette, Indiana

1 beef rump roast or bottom round roast
  (3 to 4 pounds), cut in half
1 tablespoon olive oil
1-1/2 cups cider vinegar
1 medium onion, chopped
2/3 cup packed brown sugar
1 envelope onion soup mix
1/3 cup shredded carrot
2 tablespoons beef bouillon granules
1 tablespoon Worcestershire sauce
1 bay leaf
1 garlic clove, minced
1 teaspoon salt
1 teaspoon celery seed
1 teaspoon ground ginger
1/2 teaspoon mixed pickling spices
1/4 teaspoon ground allspice
1/4 teaspoon pepper
1/4 cup cornstarch
1/2 cup water

1. In a large skillet, brown meat in oil on all sides. Transfer meat and drippings to a 5-qt. slow cooker. In a large bowl, combine the vinegar, onion, sugar, soup mix, carrot, bouillon, Worcestershire sauce and seasonings; pour over roast. Cover and cook on low for 6-8 hours or until tender.

2. Remove meat to a serving platter; keep warm. Strain cooking juices, discarding vegetables and seasonings.

3. Skim fat from the cooking juices; transfer juices to a large saucepan. Bring to a boil. Combine cornstarch and water until smooth; gradually stir into the pan. Bring to a boil; cook and stir for 2 minutes or until thickened. Serve with beef.

YIELD: 6 SERVINGS.

NUTRITION FACTS: 6 ounces cooked beef with 2/3 cup gravy equals 470 calories, 13 g fat (4 g saturated fat), 136 mg cholesterol, 1,706 mg sodium, 37 g carbohydrate, 1 g fiber, 46 g protein.

N'ORLEANS SHRIMP WITH BEANS & RICE

Thirty minutes is all it takes to place this tasty shrimp dish on the table. It's quick for weeknight meals but special enough to serve dinner guests.

Teacher, Buckhorn Elementary School, Valrico, Florida

Elaine Holmes, Brandon, Florida

1/4 cup butter, softened

1 garlic clove, minced

3/4 cup chopped red onion, divided

1-1/2 pounds uncooked large shrimp, peeled and deveined

1/4 cup chopped tomatoes

1/4 cup minced fresh parsley

1 tablespoon lemon juice

2-1/2 teaspoons Creole seasoning, divided

1/2 cup white wine or chicken broth

3 cups cooked long grain rice

1 can (16 ounces) kidney beans, rinsed and drained

1. In a small bowl, combine butter and garlic. In a large skillet, saute 1/4 cup onion in 3 tablespoons butter mixture until tender. Add the shrimp, tomatoes, parsley, lemon juice and 1-1/2 teaspoons Creole seasoning; cook 1 minute longer. Stir in wine. Bring to a boil; cook until liquid is almost evaporated and shrimp turn pink.

2. Meanwhile, in a large saucepan, saute remaining onion and Creole seasoning in remaining butter mixture. Add rice and beans; heat through. Serve with shrimp.

YIELD: 4 SERVINGS.

EDITOR'S NOTE: The following spices may be substituted for 1 teaspoon Creole seasoning: 1/4 teaspoon each salt, garlic powder and paprika; and a pinch each of dried thyme, ground cumin and cayenne pepper.

NUTRITION FACTS: 3/4 cup shrimp mixture with 1 cup rice mixture equals 533 calories, 14 g fat (8 g saturated fat), 237 mg cholesterol, 885 mg sodium, 57 g carbohydrate, 7 g fiber, 39 g protein.

Okatie, South Carolina

As the data specialist at Okatie Elementary School, Lisa Nelson meets and greets the school's new enrollments, maintains the student records and information database and handles the state reporting. She said she truly enjoys her job and puts just as much dedication into it as she does her second love, cooking. "At work and at home, I have my tasters, my critics and my supporters who guide me with my love of cooking," she says.

BAYOU OKRA SAUSAGE STEW

My husband and I worked on this recipe together. We make a big pot and freeze it to enjoy all winter long. We also have added sauteed shrimp for a delicious addition to this stew.

Lisa Nelson, Bluffton, South Carolina

1 pound smoked sausage, halved lengthwise and cut into 1/4-inch slices

2 large onions, chopped

1 large green pepper, chopped

8 green onions, sliced

1 cup minced fresh parsley

1/4 cup olive oil

6 garlic cloves, minced

1 cup white wine

1 can (28 ounces) diced tomatoes, undrained

1 package (16 ounces) frozen sliced okra

1 can (8 ounces) tomato sauce

2 tablespoons soy sauce

1 tablespoon Louisiana-style hot sauce

Hot cooked rice

1. In a Dutch oven, saute the first five ingredients in oil until the vegetables are tender. Add garlic; cook 1 minute longer. Add wine, stirring to loosen browned bits from pan.

2. Stir in the tomatoes, okra, tomato sauce, soy sauce and hot sauce; bring to a boil. Reduce heat; simmer, uncovered, for 4-5 minutes or until okra is tender. Serve with rice.

YIELD: 9 SERVINGS.

NUTRITION FACTS: 1 cup (calculated without rice) equals 274 calories, 20 g fat (7 g saturated fat), 34 mg cholesterol, 1,011 mg sodium, 13 g carbohydrate, 4 g fiber, 10 g protein.

ARGENTINE LASAGNA

My family is from Argentina, which has a strong Italian heritage and large cattle ranches. This all-in-one lasagna is packed with meat, cheese and veggies.

Teacher, St. Vincent de Paul Elementary School, Omaha, Nebraska

Sylvia Maenenr, Omaha, Nebraska

1 pound ground beef

1 large sweet onion, chopped

1/2 pound sliced fresh mushrooms

1 garlic clove, minced

1 can (15 ounces) tomato sauce

1 can (6 ounces) tomato paste

1/4 teaspoon pepper

4 cups (16 ounces) shredded part-skim mozzarella cheese, divided

1 jar (15 ounces) Alfredo sauce

1 carton (15 ounces) ricotta cheese

3 cups frozen peas, thawed

1 package (10 ounces) frozen chopped spinach, thawed and squeezed dry

1 package (9 ounces) no-cook lasagna noodles

Fresh basil leaves and grated Parmesan cheese, optional

1. In a Dutch oven, cook the beef, onion, mushrooms and garlic over medium heat until meat is no longer pink; drain. Stir in tomato sauce, tomato paste, pepper and 2 cups mozzarella cheese; set aside.

2. In a large bowl, combine the Alfredo sauce, ricotta cheese, peas and spinach.

3. Spread 1 cup meat sauce into a greased 13-in. x 9-in. baking dish. Layer with four noodles, 1-1/4 cups meat sauce and 1-1/4 cups spinach mixture. Repeat layers three times. Sprinkle with remaining cheese. (Pan will be full.)

4. Cover and bake at 350° for 45 minutes. Uncover; bake 10 minutes longer or until cheese is melted. Let stand for 10 minutes before cutting. Garnish with basil and serve with Parmesan cheese if desired.

YIELD: 12 SERVINGS.

NUTRITION FACTS: 1 piece (calculated without Parmesan cheese and basil) equals 406 calories, 18 g fat (10 g saturated fat), 69 mg cholesterol, 598 mg sodium, 33 g carbohydrate, 4 g fiber, 28 g protein.

BLACKENED CATFISH WITH MANGO AVOCADO SALSA

A delightful and tasty rub takes this recipe from good to fantastic. While the fish is sitting, you can easily assemble the salsa. My family thinks this is marvelous and you will, too.

Teacher
Southampton Road Elementary School, Westfield, Massachusetts

Laura Fisher, Westfield, Massachusetts

2 teaspoons dried oregano

2 teaspoons ground cumin

2 teaspoons paprika

2-1/4 teaspoons pepper, divided

3/4 teaspoon salt, divided

4 catfish fillets (6 ounces each)

1 medium mango, peeled and cubed

1 medium ripe avocado, peeled and cubed

1/3 cup finely chopped red onion

2 tablespoons minced fresh cilantro

2 tablespoons lime juice

2 teaspoons olive oil

1. Combine the oregano, cumin, paprika, 2 teaspoons pepper and 1/2 teaspoon salt; rub over fillets. Refrigerate for at least 30 minutes.

2. Meanwhile, in a small bowl, combine the mango, avocado, red onion, cilantro, lime juice and remaining salt and pepper. Chill until serving.

3. In a 10-in. cast iron skillet, cook fillets in oil over medium heat for 5-7 minutes on each side or until fish flakes easily with a fork. Serve with salsa.

YIELD: 4 SERVINGS (2 CUPS SALSA).

NUTRITION FACTS: 1 fillet with 1/2 cup salsa equals 376 calories, 22 g fat (4 g saturated fat), 80 mg cholesterol, 541 mg sodium, 17 g carbohydrate, 6 g fiber, 28 g protein. DIABETIC EXCHANGES: 5 lean meat, 1 starch, 1/2 fat.

Teacher
Centreville Middle School

Centreville, Maryland

Marlena Liimatainen never thought she would end up teaching sixth grade mathematics in Maryland. "Yet, suddenly, I find myself in my seventh year at Centreville Middle School," she says. "Being relatively new to Maryland's Eastern Shore, I have enjoyed becoming part of Centreville's community and seeing young students continue down the road of lifelong learning."

CHEESE TORTELLINI AND KALE SOUP

A steaming bowl of this hearty soup is always a welcome dish with both my family and neighbors. I often serve it when we get together during the cold months to watch football games. I add crusty bread, sliced cheese and grapes to round out the meal.

Marlena Liimatainen, Denton, Maryland

3 Italian sausage links (4 ounces each), sliced

1 medium onion, finely chopped

1 cup chopped fennel bulb

4 garlic cloves, minced

1-1/2 teaspoons minced fresh thyme

1/2 teaspoon crushed red pepper flakes

2 tablespoons olive oil

2 cartons (32 ounces each) reduced-sodium chicken broth

1 cup water

4 cups chopped fresh kale

1 can (15 ounces) white kidney or cannellini beans, rinsed and drained

1 package (9 ounces) refrigerated cheese tortellini

1. In a large saucepan, cook the sausage, onion, fennel, garlic, thyme and pepper flakes in oil until sausage is no longer pink; drain. Add broth and water; bring to a boil.

2. Stir in kale and beans; return to a boil. Reduce heat; simmer, uncovered, until kale is tender. Add tortellini; simmer, uncovered, for 7-9 minutes or until tender.

YIELD: 12 SERVINGS (3 QUARTS).

NUTRITION FACTS: 1 cup equals 180 calories, 8 g fat (3 g saturated fat), 20 mg cholesterol, 641 mg sodium, 18 g carbohydrate, 2 g fiber, 10 g protein. DIABETIC EXCHANGES: 1 starch, 1 medium-fat meat, 1/2 fat.

BUTTERNUT SQUASH ENCHILADAS

When you want to go meatless for a meal, try this deliciously different spin on a Southwestern favorite. It's fabulous.

Teacher, Burns Park Elementary, Ann Arbor, Michigan

Rachel Erdstein, Ann Arbor, Michigan

1 medium butternut squash (3-1/2 to 4 pounds)

1 medium sweet red pepper, chopped

1/2 cup chopped onion

1 garlic clove, minced

1 teaspoon canola oil

1 teaspoon ground cumin

1/2 teaspoon chili powder

1/2 teaspoon pepper

1/4 teaspoon salt

1 package (12 ounces) frozen vegetarian meat crumbles, thawed

1 can (10 ounces) enchilada sauce, divided

8 flour tortillas (8 inches), warmed

1 cup (4 ounces) shredded reduced-fat Mexican cheese blend, divided

1. Cut squash in half; discard seeds. Place squash cut side down in a 15-in. x 10-in. x 1-in. baking pan coated with cooking spray. Bake at 350° for 55-65 minutes or until tender. Cool slightly; scoop out pulp and set aside.

2. In a large nonstick skillet coated with cooking spray, cook the red pepper, onion and garlic in oil until tender. Stir in the cumin, chili powder, pepper and salt; cook 1 minute longer. Stir in crumbles and reserved squash; heat through.

3. Spread 1/4 cup enchilada sauce into a 13-in. x 9-in. baking dish coated with cooking spray. Place about 3/4 cup squash mixture down the center of each tortilla; top squash mixture with 1 tablespoon cheese. Roll up and place seam side down in prepared dish. Pour remaining enchilada sauce over the top; sprinkle with remaining cheese.

4. Bake, uncovered, at 350° for 25-35 minutes or until heated through.

YIELD: 8 SERVINGS.

EDITOR'S NOTE: Vegetarian meat crumbles are a nutritious protein source made from soy. Look for them in the natural foods freezer section.

NUTRITION FACTS: 1 enchilada equals 346 calories, 9 g fat (2 g saturated fat), 10 mg cholesterol, 801 mg sodium, 53 g carbohydrate, 9 g fiber, 19 g protein.

CALIFORNIA CHICKEN SALAD

Since I purchase cooked chicken breast at the store, I only have to cook the pasta for a healthy, delectable dinner. With minimal cooking, this is great for the summer.

Staff, Canfield Village Middle School, Canfield, Ohio

Regina Reynolds, Struthers, Ohio

2 cups uncooked whole wheat spiral pasta

1/4 cup mayonnaise

1/4 cup sour cream

4-1/2 teaspoons 2% milk

1 tablespoon sugar

1 tablespoon balsamic vinegar

1 teaspoon salt

1/4 teaspoon pepper

2 cups cubed cooked chicken breast

1 large tart apple, chopped

1 cup green grapes, halved

1/2 cup unsweetened pineapple tidbits

1/3 cup mandarin oranges

1 celery rib, finely chopped

14 Boston or Bibb lettuce leaves

1. Cook pasta according to package instructions. Drain pasta and rinse in cold water.

2. In a large bowl, combine the mayonnaise, sour cream, milk, sugar, vinegar, salt and pepper. Stir in the chicken, apple, grapes, pineapple, oranges, celery and cooked pasta. Chill until serving.

3. Spoon 1/2 cup onto each lettuce leaf.

YIELD: 14 SERVINGS.

NUTRITION FACTS: 1/2 cup chicken salad equals 127 calories, 5 g fat (1 g saturated fat), 20 mg cholesterol, 209 mg sodium, 13 g carbohydrate, 2 g fiber, 8 g protein. DIABETIC EXCHANGES: 1 lean meat, 1/2 starch, 1/2 fruit, 1/2 fat.

Coach
Glasgow Elementary

St. Louis, Missouri

Karla Sheeley is an instructional coach at Glasgow Elementary. Although this is Karla's first year coaching, she has been in education for 18 years. "I work with both teachers and students grades K-5. My role is to develop a partnership with teachers to improve instruction for their students," she explains. "I love my position as a coach because I get the best of both worlds— working with my peers, the teachers and students."

CHIPOTLE-BLACK BEAN CHILI

I love soup weather, especially when I can warm up with this chili. The whole can of chipotles in adobo make this a pretty spicy chili, but you can cut back and adjust to your taste.

Karla Sheeley, Worden, Illinois

1 tablespoon Creole seasoning

1 beef top sirloin steak (2 pounds),
    cut into 1/2-inch cubes

3 tablespoons olive oil

1 large sweet onion, chopped

3 chipotle peppers in adobo sauce,
    seeded and finely chopped

2 tablespoons minced garlic

1/3 cup masa harina

2 tablespoons chili powder

2 tablespoons Worcestershire sauce

1 tablespoon ground cumin

1 teaspoon ground cinnamon

1/4 teaspoon salt

1/4 teaspoon cayenne pepper

4 cups reduced-sodium beef broth

1 can (28 ounces) diced tomatoes, undrained

3 cans (15 ounces each) black beans, rinsed and drained

Shredded cheddar cheese and/or finely chopped red onion, optional

1. Place Creole seasoning in a large resealable plastic bag. Add beef, a few pieces at a time, and shake to coat.

2. In a Dutch oven, saute beef in oil in batches. Stir in the onion, chipotle peppers and garlic. Cook 3 minutes longer or until onion is tender. Drain.

3. Stir in the masa harina, chili powder, Worcestershire sauce, cumin, cinnamon, salt and cayenne. Cook and stir for 3-5 minutes. Stir in beef broth and diced tomatoes. Bring to a boil. Reduce heat; simmer, uncovered, for 45 minutes or until the beef is tender.

4. Stir in beans; heat through. Garnish with cheddar cheese and/or red onion if desired.

YIELD: 10 SERVINGS (3 QUARTS).

EDITOR'S NOTE: We recommend wearing disposable gloves when cutting hot peppers. Avoid touching your face.

NUTRITION FACTS: 1-1/4 cups (calculated without garnishes) equals 314 calories, 8 g fat (2 g saturated fat), 39 mg cholesterol, 900 mg sodium, 31 g carbohydrate, 8 g fiber, 28 g protein. DIABETIC EXCHANGES: 4 lean meat, 2 starch.

Teacher
Mountainside Elementary School

Mendon, Utah

*Karen Ensign is a
third-grade teacher at
Mountainside Elementary
in Mendon, Utah. "This
is my first year at
Mountainside, as well as
my first year as a teacher,"
she says. "The best part of being
a teacher is the students—I love
my students!"*

HERBED SALMON FILLETS

*On a busy day I turn to this sensational salmon recipe for
dinner. It's fast, healthy and tastes great.*

Karen Ensign, Providence, Utah

2-1/2 pounds salmon fillet

1 tablespoon minced fresh parsley

1 tablespoon minced fresh thyme

1 tablespoon olive oil

3 garlic cloves, minced

2 teaspoons grated lemon peel

2 teaspoons grated lime peel

1/2 teaspoon salt

1/2 teaspoon pepper

1. Place salmon on a large baking sheet coated with cooking
   spray. In a small bowl, combine the remaining ingredients;
   spread over fillet. Bake at 400° for 12-14 minutes or until fish
   flakes easily with a fork. Cut salmon into eight pieces.

YIELD: 8 SERVINGS.

NUTRITION FACTS: 3 ounces cooked salmon equals 238 calories, 15 g fat (3 g saturated fat),
71 mg cholesterol, 219 mg sodium, 1 g carbohydrate, trace fiber, 24 g protein. DIABETIC
EXCHANGES: 4 lean meat, 1 fat.

CURRIED CHICKEN SLOPPY JOES

These delicious sloppy Joes pack a burst of unexpected flavors in every bite. They'll surely jazz up your dinner repertoire. For potlucks, keep the chicken mixture warm in a slow cooker and let everyone fill their own buns.

Volunteer, Heritage Christian Academy, Maple Grove, Minnesota

Jamie Miller, Maple Grove, Minnesota

1-1/4 pounds ground chicken

1 cup chopped sweet onion

1/2 cup chopped sweet orange pepper

2 garlic cloves, minced

1 tablespoon olive oil

2 teaspoons curry powder

1 teaspoon minced fresh gingerroot

1/2 teaspoon coarsely ground pepper

1/4 teaspoon salt

1 can (14-1/2 ounces) petite diced tomatoes, undrained

1 medium tart apple, peeled and diced

1/2 cup golden raisins

3 tablespoons mango chutney

1/4 cup reduced-fat mayonnaise

1 tablespoon Dijon mustard

10 whole wheat hamburger buns, split

1. In a large nonstick skillet, cook chicken over medium heat until no longer pink; drain and set aside.

2. In the same skillet, cook the onion, pepper and garlic in oil until tender. Stir in the curry, ginger, pepper and salt; cook 1 minute longer.

3. Stir in the tomatoes, apple and raisins; bring to a boil. Reduce heat; simmer, uncovered, for 6-8 minutes. Stir in the chutney, mayonnaise, mustard and chicken; heat through. Serve on buns.

YIELD: 10 SERVINGS.

NUTRITION FACTS: 1 sandwich equals 288 calories, 10 g fat (2 g saturated fat), 40 mg cholesterol, 486 mg sodium, 39 g carbohydrate, 5 g fiber, 14 g protein. DIABETIC EXCHANGES: 2 starch, 2 lean meat, 1 vegetable, 1/2 fat.

PASTA WITH EGGPLANT SAUCE

This was my mother's recipe and is a nice way to incorporate eggplant into a meal. The thick, chunky sauce is splendid. I like to have it with a glass of red wine, crusty Italian bread and a tossed salad.

Staff, Cathedral School at Holy Rosary, Rochester, New York

Jean Lawrence, Rochester, New York

1 large eggplant, cut into 1-inch cubes

1/2 cup finely chopped onion

2 tablespoons minced fresh parsley

1 garlic clove, chopped

1/4 cup olive oil

1 can (14-1/2 ounces) Italian stewed tomatoes, cut up

1/2 cup dry red wine or chicken broth

1 can (6 ounces) Italian tomato paste

1 can (4-1/2 ounces) sliced mushrooms, drained

1 teaspoon sugar

1 teaspoon dried oregano

1/2 teaspoon salt

3/4 pound thin spaghetti

Grated Parmesan cheese

1. In a Dutch oven, saute the eggplant, onion, parsley and garlic in oil until tender.

2. Stir in the tomatoes, wine, tomato paste, mushrooms, sugar, oregano and salt. Bring to a boil. Reduce heat; simmer, uncovered, for 10-15 minutes or until sauce is thickened, stirring occasionally.

3. Meanwhile, cook pasta according to package directions. Drain pasta. Serve with sauce. Sprinkle with cheese.

YIELD: 6 SERVINGS.

NUTRITION FACTS: 3/4 cup pasta with 2/3 cup sauce (calculated without Parmesan cheese) equals 385 calories, 11 g fat (1 g saturated fat), 0 cholesterol, 782 mg sodium, 61 g carbohydrate, 7 g fiber, 11 g protein.

GRILLED TANDOORI CHICKEN KABOBS

When I prepare this recipe, it brings back memories of my childhood and my rich Indian heritage. This has a nice spice level, but if you like your food on the mild side, then reduce each spice a little.

Volunteer, Manzanita Elementary School, Gridley, California

Ravinder Aujla, Gridley, California

1-1/4 cups plain yogurt

1/3 cup chopped onion

2 tablespoons lemon juice

2 garlic cloves, minced

2 teaspoons garam masala

2 teaspoons minced fresh gingerroot

1 teaspoon salt

1 teaspoon cayenne pepper

3 drops yellow food coloring, optional

3 drops red food coloring, optional

2 pounds boneless skinless chicken breasts, cut into 1-inch cubes

2 teaspoons minced fresh cilantro

1 medium lemon, cut into six wedges

1. In a large resealable plastic bag, combine the first 10 ingredients. Add the chicken; seal bag and turn to coat. Refrigerate for at least 8 hours or overnight.

2. Drain and discard marinade. Thread chicken onto six metal or soaked wooden skewers. Moisten a paper towel with cooking oil; using long-handled tongs, lightly coat the grill rack.

3. Grill chicken, covered, over medium heat or broil 4 in. from the heat for 10-15 minutes or until juices run clear, turning occasionally. Sprinkle with cilantro; garnish with lemon wedges.

YIELD: 6 SERVINGS.

EDITOR'S NOTE: Look for garam masala in the spice aisle.

NUTRITION FACTS: 1 kabob equals 192 calories, 5 g fat (2 g saturated fat), 88 mg cholesterol, 366 mg sodium, 4 g carbohydrate, trace fiber, 32 g protein. DIABETIC EXCHANGES: 4 lean meat.

Staff
Coronado Elementary School

St. Johns, Arizona

Michelle Ashton is the librarian and intervention aide for kindergarten through third grade. She is very proud of the school's reading achievements, adding, "We are a Reading First school and have been very successful with the program. For example, at the beginning of the 2007-08 school year, 21% of our kindergarten students were at benchmark. By the end of the school year, 84% achieved benchmark, a gain of 63%!"

CHICKEN & TORTELLINI SPINACH SALAD

Not only is this attractive salad easy to make, but it is delicious, light and satisfying.

Michelle Ashton, St. Johns, Arizona

2 packages (9 ounces each) refrigerated cheese tortellini

2 packages (6 ounces each) fresh baby spinach

1 package (22 ounces) frozen grilled chicken breast strips, cut into 1-inch pieces

12 slices red onion, halved

1 cup dried cranberries

1 cup (4 ounces) crumbled feta cheese

BALSAMIC VINAIGRETTE:

1/3 cup olive oil

1/3 cup balsamic vinegar

1 tablespoon tomato paste

2 garlic cloves, minced

1 teaspoon dried oregano

1/8 teaspoon salt

1/8 teaspoon pepper

1/4 cup grated Parmesan cheese

1. In a large saucepan, cook tortellini according to package directions. Meanwhile, in a large bowl, combine the spinach, chicken, onion, cranberries and feta cheese. Drain pasta. Cool for 5 minutes. Add to spinach mixture.

2. For vinaigrette, in a small bowl, whisk the oil, vinegar, tomato paste, garlic, oregano, salt and pepper. Pour over spinach mixture; gently toss to coat. Sprinkle with Parmesan cheese.

YIELD: 9 SERVINGS.

NUTRITION FACTS: 2 cups equals 432 calories, 17 g fat (6 g saturated fat), 74 mg cholesterol, 820 mg sodium, 43 g carbohydrate, 4 g fiber, 30 g protein. DIABETIC EXCHANGES: 3 lean meat, 2-1/2 starch, 1-1/2 fat, 1 vegetable.

PORK MEDALLIONS WITH SQUASH & GREENS

The colors of this dish remind me of autumn, my favorite season. Butternut squash is nutritious as well as colorful. This recipe allows me to prepare it another way that isn't mashed and sweetened. The pork tenderloin medallions are mildly seasoned with rosemary and are very tender.

Teacher, Horace W. Porter School, Columbia, Connecticut

Louise Nowak, Columbia, Connecticut

2 quarts water

4 cups chopped mustard greens

1 medium butternut squash, peeled and
   cut into 1/2-inch cubes

3 medium leeks (white portion only), halved and sliced

3 tablespoons olive oil

2 garlic cloves, minced

1/8 teaspoon crushed red pepper flakes

1-1/2 cups reduced-sodium chicken broth

1/2 teaspoon salt

PORK MEDALLIONS:

2 pork tenderloins (3/4 pound each), cut into eight slices

1/3 cup all-purpose flour

1/2 teaspoon salt

1/4 teaspoon pepper

1/4 teaspoon dried rosemary, crushed

1 teaspoon cornstarch

1/2 cup apple cider or juice

1/3 cup reduced-sodium chicken broth

1 tablespoon olive oil

1 tablespoon butter

1 medium tart apple, peeled and chopped

1. In a large saucepan, bring water to a boil. Add mustard greens; cook, uncovered, for 3-5 minutes or until tender.

2. Meanwhile, in a Dutch oven, saute squash and leeks in oil until tender. Add garlic and pepper flakes; saute 1 minute longer. Stir in broth and salt. Bring to a boil. Reduce heat; simmer, uncovered, for 8 minutes or until liquid has almost evaporated. Drain greens and add to squash mixture; set aside and keep warm.

3. Cover pork with plastic wrap. Flatten to 1/4-in. thickness. Remove plastic. In a large resealable plastic bag, combine the flour, salt, pepper and rosemary. Add pork, a few pieces at a time, and shake to coat.

4. In a small bowl, whisk the cornstarch, apple cider and broth until smooth; set aside.

5. In a large skillet, cook pork in oil and butter until meat juices run clear. Remove and keep warm. Add apple to the pan; cook and stir for 2-4 minutes or until crisp-tender.

6. Stir cornstarch mixture; add to the pan. Bring to a boil; cook and stir for 2 minutes or until thickened. Add pork; heat through. Top with apple mixture; serve with squash mixture.

YIELD: 8 SERVINGS.

NUTRITION FACTS: 3 ounces cooked pork with 3/4 cup squash mixture equals 272 calories, 11 g fat (3 g saturated fat), 51 mg cholesterol, 669 mg sodium, 24 g carbohydrate, 5 g fiber, 20 g protein. DIABETIC EXCHANGES: 2 lean meat, 1-1/2 starch, 1-1/2 fat.

SAVORY OVEN-FRIED CHICKEN

You won't believe how moist this chicken is. It has a nicely seasoned crumb crust that bakes up to a golden color. It's tasty, healthy and easy.

Teacher, Augusta Christian Schools, Martinez, Georgia

Ranee Bullard, Evans, Georgia

1/2 cup buttermilk

1 tablespoon Dijon mustard

2 garlic cloves, minced

1 teaspoon hot pepper sauce

4 bone-in chicken breast halves
   (12 ounces each), skin removed

1/2 cup whole wheat flour

1-1/2 teaspoons paprika

1 teaspoon baking powder

1 teaspoon dried thyme

1/4 teaspoon salt

1/4 teaspoon pepper

Cooking spray

1. In a large resealable plastic bag, combine the buttermilk, mustard, garlic and pepper sauce. Add the chicken; seal bag and turn to coat. Refrigerate for 8 hours or overnight. Drain and discard marinade.

2. In a large resealable plastic bag, combine the flour, paprika, baking powder, thyme, salt and pepper. Add chicken, one at a time, and shake to coat.

3. Place chicken bone side down on a rack in a shallow baking pan. Spritz chicken with cooking spray. Bake, uncovered, at 425° for 50-60 minutes or until a meat thermometer reads 170°.

YIELD: 4 SERVINGS.

NUTRITION FACTS: 1 chicken breast half equals 355 calories, 8 g fat (2 g saturated fat), 153 mg cholesterol, 394 mg sodium, 10 g carbohydrate, 2 g fiber, 58 g protein.

SPICY CHICKEN SAUSAGE LETTUCE WRAPS

I love dishes that you can put together and eat with your hands. I've found that kids really like this fresh-tasting chicken wrap.

Teacher, Dinwiddie Middle School, Dinwiddie, Virginia

Vanessa Campbell, Ford, Virginia

2 cups coleslaw mix

2 cups shredded yellow summer squash

2 medium Asian or Bosc pears, chopped

1/4 cup canola oil

3 tablespoons rice vinegar

1 teaspoon minced fresh gingerroot

1 teaspoon finely chopped crystallized ginger

1/2 teaspoon salt

1-1/2 cups frozen pepper strips, thawed

1 small red onion, thinly sliced

1 package (12 ounces) fully cooked spicy chicken sausage links, cut into 1/2-inch slices

1/4 cup Asian toasted sesame salad dressing

12 Bibb or Boston lettuce leaves

2 tablespoons minced fresh cilantro

1. In a large bowl, combine the coleslaw mix, squash and pears. Whisk together the oil, vinegar, ginger, crystallized ginger and salt; drizzle over slaw mixture. Toss to coat; set aside.

2. In a large nonstick skillet coated with cooking spray, saute peppers and onion until crisp-tender. Add sausage; cook 4-5 minutes longer. Stir in salad dressing; heat through.

3. Spoon sausage mixture onto lettuce leaves. Top with slaw mixture; sprinkle with cilantro. Fold lettuce over filling.

YIELD: 6 SERVINGS.

NUTRITION FACTS: 2 lettuce wraps equals 273 calories, 16 g fat (2 g saturated fat), 37 mg cholesterol, 656 mg sodium, 19 g carbohydrate, 4 g fiber, 12 g protein. DIABETIC EXCHANGES: 2-1/2 fat, 2 lean meat, 1 starch.

Teacher, Cherokee High School

Canton, Georgia

Kathy Carlan has been teaching family and consumer sciences for 32 years, with the past 15 years at Cherokee High School, the oldest high school in the county. Her specific areas of concentration include nutrition and wellness and food science. "Every day is fun; teenagers are amazing to work with," she says. "Teaching at Cherokee High is wonderful because our school has a lot of traditions, and we have a great principal who embraces our history and traditions."

ROASTED VEGETABLE QUESADILLAS

I am always looking for recipes that will encourage students to eat vegetables, and this one has been a huge success. You can also use other vegetables, such as mushrooms, eggplant, asparagus and broccoli. Just remember to roast your vegetables before making the quesadillas.

Kathy Carlan, Canton, Georgia

2 medium red potatoes, quartered and sliced

1 medium zucchini, quartered and sliced

1 medium sweet red pepper, sliced

1 small onion, chopped

2 tablespoons olive oil

1 garlic clove, minced

1/2 teaspoon salt

1/2 teaspoon dried oregano

1/4 teaspoon pepper

1 cup (4 ounces) shredded part-skim mozzarella cheese

1 cup (4 ounces) shredded reduced-fat cheddar cheese

8 whole wheat tortillas (8 inches)

1. In a large bowl, combine the first nine ingredients. Transfer to a 15-in. x 10-in. x 1-in. baking pan. Bake at 425° for 24-28 minutes or until potatoes are tender.

2. In a small bowl, combine cheeses. Place tortillas on a griddle coated with cooking spray. Spread 1/3 cup vegetable mixture over half of each tortilla. Sprinkle with 1/4 cup cheese. Fold over and cook over low heat for 1-2 minutes on each side or until cheese is melted.

YIELD: 8 SERVINGS.

NUTRITION FACTS: 1 quesadilla equals 279 calories, 12 g fat (4 g saturated fat), 18 mg cholesterol, 479 mg sodium, 30 g carbohydrate, 3 g fiber, 12 g protein. DIABETIC EXCHANGES: 2 starch, 1-1/2 fat, 1 lean meat.

TUSCAN PORTOBELLO STEW

This is a heart-healthy, one-skillet meal that is quick and easy to prepare yet elegant enough for company. Vegetarian teachers and students alike appreciate this stew at school potlucks.

Teacher, Youth Initiative High School, Viroqua, Wisconsin

Jane Siemon, Viroqua, Wisconsin

2 large portobello mushrooms, coarsely chopped

1 medium onion, chopped

3 garlic cloves, minced

2 tablespoons olive oil

1/2 cup white wine or vegetable broth

1 can (28 ounces) diced tomatoes, undrained

2 cups chopped fresh kale

1 bay leaf

1 teaspoon dried thyme

1/2 teaspoon dried basil

1/2 teaspoon dried rosemary, crushed

1/4 teaspoon salt

1/4 teaspoon pepper

2 cans (15 ounces each) white kidney or cannellini beans, rinsed and drained

1. In a large skillet, saute the mushrooms, onion and garlic in oil until tender. Add the wine. Bring to a boil; cook until liquid is reduced by half. Stir in the tomatoes, kale and seasonings. Bring to a boil. Reduce heat; cover and simmer for 8-10 minutes.

2. Add beans; heat through. Discard bay leaf.

YIELD: 4 SERVINGS.

NUTRITION FACTS: 1-1/4 cups equals 309 calories, 8 g fat (1 g saturated fat), 0 cholesterol, 672 mg sodium, 46 g carbohydrate, 13 g fiber, 12 g protein. DIABETIC EXCHANGES: 2 starch, 2 vegetable, 1-1/2 fat, 1 lean meat.

THAI CHICKEN LETTUCE WRAPS

This recipe is so flavorful and fresh tasting. The teachers and staff love it because it's fun to put together.

Volunteer, Hawarden Hills Academy, Riverside, California

Laureen Pittman, Riverside, California

1/4 cup rice vinegar

2 tablespoons lime juice

2 tablespoons reduced-fat mayonnaise

2 tablespoons reduced-fat creamy peanut butter

1 tablespoon brown sugar

1 tablespoon reduced-sodium soy sauce

2 teaspoons minced fresh gingerroot

1 teaspoon sesame oil

1 teaspoon Thai chili sauce

1 garlic clove, chopped

3 tablespoons canola oil

1/2 cup minced fresh cilantro

CHICKEN SALAD:

2 cups cubed cooked chicken breast

1 small sweet red pepper, diced

1/2 cup chopped green onions

1/2 cup shredded carrot

1/2 cup unsalted dry roasted peanuts, chopped, divided

6 Bibb or Boston lettuce leaves

1. In a blender, combine the first 10 ingredients. While processing, gradually add oil in a steady stream; stir in cilantro. Set aside.

2. In a large bowl, combine the chicken, red pepper, onions, carrot and 1/4 cup peanuts. Add dressing and toss to coat. Divide among lettuce leaves; sprinkle with remaining peanuts. Fold lettuce over filling.

YIELD: 6 SERVINGS.

NUTRITION FACTS: 1/2 cup chicken salad equals 284 calories, 19 g fat (2 g saturated fat), 38 mg cholesterol, 222 mg sodium, 12 g carbohydrate, 2 g fiber, 19 g protein. DIABETIC EXCHANGES: 2 lean meat, 2 fat, 1 starch.

VEGETABLE BEEF STEW

My Lebanese grandmother passed down this family favorite. We enjoy it often during the winter. Whenever I make it, I think of my grandmother and the wonderful aromas and flavors I associate with her kitchen.

Teacher, Westside Elementary School, Hartman, Arkansas

Mary Robbins, Clarksville, Arkansas

1-1/2 pounds boneless beef chuck roast

1 tablespoon canola oil

1 large sweet onion, chopped

3 garlic cloves, peeled and sliced

3 cups water, divided

1 can (28 ounces) diced tomatoes, undrained

1 medium eggplant, peeled and cut into 3/4-inch cubes

2 medium potatoes, peeled and cut into 3/4-inch cubes

1 can (15 ounces) garbanzo beans or chickpeas, rinsed and drained

1 can (15 ounces) tomato sauce

1 teaspoon ground cinnamon

1/8 teaspoon salt

1/8 teaspoon pepper

1 package (16 ounces) frozen sliced okra, thawed

1-1/2 cups frozen cut green beans, thawed

4-1/2 cups uncooked egg noodles

1. In a stockpot, brown roast in oil on all sides. Remove and set aside. Add onion and garlic to the pan; cook until tender. Return meat to the pan. Add 2 cups water. Bring to a boil. Reduce heat; cover and simmer for 1-1/2 to 2 hours or until meat is tender.

2. Remove meat to a cutting board. Cut into 3/4-in. pieces; return to pan. Stir in the tomatoes, eggplant, potatoes, beans, tomato sauce, cinnamon, salt, pepper and remaining water.

3. Bring to a boil. Reduce heat; cover and simmer for 20-25 minutes or until vegetables are tender, adding okra and green beans during the last 5 minutes of cooking. Meanwhile, cook noodles according to package directions. Serve with stew.

YIELD: 14 SERVINGS.

NUTRITION FACTS: 1 cup stew with 1/3 cup noodles equals 248 calories, 7 g fat (2 g saturated fat), 45 mg cholesterol, 315 mg sodium, 32 g carbohydrate, 6 g fiber, 16 g protein. DIABETIC EXCHANGES: 2 lean meat, 1-1/2 starch, 1 vegetable.

LIME-CILANTRO MARINADE FOR CHICKEN

This marinade is low-calorie and low-sodium. It is wonderful for chicken, but you can also use it on pork or fish.

Staff, Auburn School Department, Auburn, Maine

Roz Walton, Auburn, Maine

1/2 cup minced fresh cilantro

1/4 cup lime juice

1/4 cup orange juice

1/4 cup olive oil

1 tablespoon chopped shallot

1 teaspoon dried minced garlic

1 teaspoon pepper

1/8 teaspoon salt

6 boneless skinless chicken breast halves
  (5 ounces each)

1. In a blender, combine the first eight ingredients; cover and process until smooth. Place marinade in a large resealable plastic bag. Add the chicken; seal bag and turn to coat. Refrigerate for at least 2 hours.

2. Drain and discard marinade. Moisten a paper towel with cooking oil; using long-handled tongs, lightly coat the grill rack. Grill chicken, covered, over medium heat or broil 4 in. from the heat for 5-7 minutes on each side or until a meat thermometer reads 170°.

YIELD: 6 SERVINGS.

NUTRITION FACTS: 1 chicken breast half equals 175 calories, 6 g fat (1 g saturated fat), 78 mg cholesterol, 80 mg sodium, 1 g carbohydrate, trace fiber, 29 g protein. DIABETIC EXCHANGES: 4 lean meat, 1/2 fat.

Teacher
Sam Case Primary

Newport, Oregon

Cathy Rau is the media assistant, more commonly known as librarian, and technology instructor at Sam Case Primary. "I love my job because I get to work with kids and hopefully make a difference in their education and their lives," she says. "The best part of my day is getting to read stories to the kids." To Cathy, Sam Case Primary is more than a school, it's family. "I lost my husband a year ago to cancer, and it was my Sam Case family that helped get me through. I don't know what I would have done without the love and support of the staff, students and families."

WEEKNIGHT PASTA SUPPER

After a long day at school, I want something that is healthy but also quick to prepare. This pasta dish fits my needs!

Cathy Rau, Newport, Oregon

3 cups uncooked bow tie pasta

10 ounces lean ground turkey

8 ounces sliced baby portobello mushrooms

2 garlic cloves, minced

2 teaspoons olive oil

1 can (14-1/2 ounces) fire-roasted diced tomatoes, undrained

1/4 cup dry red wine or chicken broth

5 pitted Greek olives, chopped

1 teaspoon dried basil

1 teaspoon dried oregano

1 teaspoon dried parsley flakes

1/2 teaspoon salt

1/8 teaspoon coarsely ground pepper

2 cups fresh baby spinach, chopped

1 tablespoon grated Parmesan cheese

1. Cook pasta according to package directions.
2. Meanwhile, in a large nonstick skillet, cook turkey until no longer pink; drain. Remove meat; set aside and keep warm.
3. In the same skillet, cook mushrooms and garlic in oil until tender. Stir in the tomatoes, wine, olives, seasonings and turkey. Bring to a boil. Reduce heat; simmer, uncovered, for 10 minutes.
4. Drain pasta. Stir into turkey mixture. Stir in spinach; cook 1-2 minutes longer or until spinach is wilted. Sprinkle with cheese.

YIELD: 4 SERVINGS.

NUTRITION FACTS: 1-1/2 cups equals 411 calories, 11 g fat (3 g saturated fat), 57 mg cholesterol, 751 mg sodium, 52 g carbohydrate, 4 g fiber, 24 g protein.

MANGO-CHUTNEY CHICKEN SALAD

I often make this recipe and eat it at school for lunch. It makes me feel like I've ordered out from a fancy restaurant. It is wonderful as a salad or as a gourmet lunch wrap.

Staff, Heritage Middle School, Meridian, Idaho

Michelle Sichak, Meridian, Idaho

1 carton (6 ounces) plain yogurt
1/4 cup light coconut milk
1-1/2 teaspoons curry powder
2 cups cubed cooked chicken
2 cups green grapes, halved
6 green onions, chopped
1/2 cup dried cranberries
1/3 cup mango chutney
1/4 cup slivered almonds, toasted

1. In a small bowl, whisk the yogurt, milk and curry until smooth.
2. In a large bowl, combine the chicken, grapes, onions and cranberries. Drizzle with yogurt dressing and toss to coat. Fold in mango chutney. Refrigerate for at least 1 hour.
3. Just before serving, sprinkle with almonds.

YIELD: 6 SERVINGS.

NUTRITION FACTS: 1 cup equals 267 calories, 8 g fat (2 g saturated fat), 45 mg cholesterol, 208 mg sodium, 34 g carbohydrate, 2 g fiber, 16 g protein. DIABETIC EXCHANGES: 2 lean meat, 1-1/2 starch, 1/2 fruit, 1/2 fat.

Administrative Assistant
Piney Orchard Elementary

Odenton, Maryland

Joan Sullivan has worked as the secretary at Piney Orchard Elementary since December 2006. She says she never ceases to be amazed at the staff's dedication and willingness to go above and beyond for the students. She also enjoys the school's sense of community. "We see children come and go, succeed and struggle, laugh and cry. We get to know the families and feel we are an integral part of the community," she says.

ALMOND CAKE WITH RASPBERRY SAUCE

This cake is simple but delectable—and it looks elegant. The cake is very moist with great flavor. The drizzle of raspberry sauce not only adds to the enjoyment of the dessert but looks beautiful on the plate.

Joan Sullivan, Gambrills, Maryland

1 can (8 ounces) almond paste

3/4 cup plus 1 tablespoon sugar, divided

1/2 cup butter, softened

3 eggs, lightly beaten

1 tablespoon orange liqueur

1/4 teaspoon almond extract

1/4 cup all-purpose flour

1/4 teaspoon plus 1/8 teaspoon baking powder

1/4 cup confectioners' sugar

1 package (10 ounces) frozen sweetened raspberries, thawed

1. Line an 8-in. round baking pan with parchment paper; coat paper with cooking spray and set aside.

2. In a large bowl, combine the almond paste, 3/4 cup sugar and butter; beat for 2 minutes until blended. Beat in the eggs, liqueur and extract. Combine flour and baking powder; add to creamed mixture just until combined.

3. Spread into prepared pan. Bake at 350° for 40-45 minutes or until a toothpick inserted near center comes out clean. Cool completely on a wire rack.

4. Invert cake onto cake plate; remove parchment paper. Sprinkle with confectioners' sugar.

5. Place raspberries in a food processor; cover and process until pureed. Strain, reserving juice; discard seeds. In a small saucepan over medium heat, cook raspberry juice and remaining sugar for 15-18 minutes or until mixture is reduced to 1/4 cup. Serve with cake.

YIELD: 12 SERVINGS (1/4 CUP SAUCE).

NUTRITION FACTS: 1 slice with 1 teaspoon sauce equals 272 calories, 14 g fat (6 g saturated fat), 73 mg cholesterol, 84 mg sodium, 34 g carbohydrate, 2 g fiber, 4 g protein.

Administrator
Knob Noster Middle School

Knob Noster, Missouri

Dr. Jamie Burkhart is the principal of Knob Noster Middle School. Prior to her current position, she taught science at the school. She has seen quite a bit during her career at this school, including a fire that destroyed part of the school and major flooding when a few pipes burst. But the greatest source of excitement comes from the students with whom she interacts on a daily basis—they bring both joys and challenges into her life. At home, she is a busy wife and a mother to five children.

CHOCOLATE-AMARETTO MOUSSE PIE

My mother made this silky pie when I was a child. It was my father's favorite. The fluffy chocolate–almond filling rests inside a thin chocolate shell. Be warned: It is so rich you should only take a sliver.

Jamie Burkhart, Windsor, Missouri

- 1 teaspoon plus 1/2 cup butter, divided
- 2 cups (12 ounces) semisweet chocolate chips, divided
- 1 can (14 ounces) sweetened condensed milk
- 1/4 teaspoon salt
- 1/4 cup water
- 1/2 cup Amaretto
- 2 cups heavy whipping cream, whipped
- 1/4 cup slivered almonds, toasted

1. Line a 9-in. pan with foil and grease the foil with 1 teaspoon butter; set aside.

2. In a small saucepan over low heat, melt 1 cup chocolate chips with 1/4 cup butter; quickly spread in an even layer in prepared pan. Freeze for 30 minutes.

3. In a small saucepan over low heat, heat the condensed milk, salt and remaining butter and chips until melted; stir until well blended. Gradually stir in water; cook over medium heat for 5 minutes. Add Amaretto; cook for 5 minutes or until thickened, stirring constantly. Cool to room temperature.

4. Fold half of whipped cream into chocolate mixture. Using foil, lift chocolate shell out of pan; gently peel off foil. Return shell to the pie plate; spoon filling into shell. Garnish with remaining whipped cream; sprinkle with almonds. Chill for 3 hours or until set.

YIELD: 8 SERVINGS.

NUTRITION FACTS: 1 piece equals 742 calories, 52 g fat (31 g saturated fat), 128 mg cholesterol, 246 mg sodium, 62 g carbohydrate, 3 g fiber, 8 g protein.

ORANGE & BLACKBERRY PANTHER TART

I took this wonderful tart into school for a potluck during homecoming. I work with fourth-graders, and we typically eat at staggered times starting with kindergarten and working our way up to fourth grade. By the time I got into the lunchroom, my tart was gone—but someone left a nice note telling me how tasty it was.

Staff, Lincoln Grade School, Washington, Illinois

Dianna Wara, Washington, Illinois

1 sheet refrigerated pie pastry
1 package (8 ounces) cream cheese, softened
3 tablespoons confectioners' sugar
2 tablespoons orange marmalade
3 cups fresh blackberries
1/2 cup macadamia nuts, finely chopped
3 tablespoons sugar
1 tablespoon all-purpose flour

1 tablespoon butter, melted
1/2 cup white baking chips
1/2 teaspoon shortening
1/4 teaspoon apple pie spice

1. On a lightly floured surface, roll dough into a 12-in. circle. Transfer to a parchment paper-lined baking sheet.

2. In a small bowl, combine the cream cheese, confectioners' sugar and marmalade. Spread over the pastry to within 1-1/4 in. of edges. Top with blackberries to within 1 in. of cream cheese edge. Fold up edges of pastry over filling, leaving center uncovered.

3. In a small bowl, combine the nuts, sugar, flour and butter; sprinkle over blackberries. Bake at 400° for 35-40 minutes or until crust is golden and filling is bubbly. Using the parchment paper, slide tart onto a wire rack to cool.

4. In a microwave, melt baking chips and shortening; stir until smooth. Stir in apple pie spice. Drizzle over tart.

YIELD: 10 SERVINGS.

NUTRITION FACTS: 1 slice equals 335 calories, 23 g fat (11 g saturated fat), 33 mg cholesterol, 183 mg sodium, 30 g carbohydrate, 3 g fiber, 4 g protein.

MINIATURE PUMPKIN CAKE TOWERS

The faculty at my school hosts a weekly breakfast club. I make these pumpkin treats every autumn and they are gone in minutes. The spice combination is perfect for fall, and it's all wrapped up in a pretty little cake.

Teacher, DeFranco Elementary School, Bangor, Pennsylvania

Deb Lyon, Bangor, Pennsylvania

1 can (15 ounces) solid-pack pumpkin

2 cups sugar

3/4 cup canola oil

4 eggs

2 cups all-purpose flour

2 teaspoons baking powder

2 teaspoons ground cinnamon

1 teaspoon ground nutmeg

1/2 teaspoon salt

1/2 teaspoon ground ginger

SPICED CREAM CHEESE FILLING:

1 package (8 ounces) cream cheese, softened

1/2 cup shortening

1/2 cup butter, softened

1 tablespoon 2% milk

1 teaspoon ground cinnamon

1 teaspoon vanilla extract

3 cups confectioners' sugar

Hot caramel ice cream topping, warmed

1. In a large bowl, beat the pumpkin, sugar, oil and eggs until well blended. Combine the flour, baking powder, cinnamon, nutmeg, salt and ginger; gradually beat into pumpkin mixture until blended. Transfer to two greased 15-in. x 10-in. x 1-in. baking pans; spread batter evenly in pans.

2. Bake at 350° for 20-25 minutes or until a toothpick inserted near the center comes out clean. Cool on wire racks.

3. For filling, in a bowl, beat the cream cheese, shortening and butter until light and fluffy. Beat in the milk, cinnamon and vanilla. Gradually beat in confectioners' sugar until smooth.

4. Using a 3-in. round cookie cutter, cut out 30 circles from cakes. Spread 1 cup filling over 10 cake circles. Top with 10 more cakes and repeat. Top with 10 remaining cakes; pipe remaining filling over tops. Store in the refrigerator. Garnish with ice cream topping.

YIELD: 10 SERVINGS.

NUTRITION FACTS: 1 cake tower equals 830 calories, 46 g fat (15 g saturated fat), 134 mg cholesterol, 361 mg sodium, 100 g carbohydrate, 3 g fiber, 8 g protein.

Teacher
Grandview High School

Grandview, Missouri

Cheryl Landers keeps a busy schedule at Grandview High School, where she teaches family and consumer sciences, acts as chair of the practical arts department, sponsors the ProStart culinary arts program and acts as an adviser to the Family, Career and Community Leaders of America (FCCLA). Working at Grandview is a family affair for Cheryl—her daughter teaches in the same area and her husband works for the maintenance department.

RASPBERRIES WITH WHITE CHOCOLATE SAUCE AND SUGARED ALMONDS

In this dish, just a handful of ingredients makes a stunning dessert. White chocolate ganache contrasts bright, juicy raspberries. Both my daughter and I enjoy this fabulous treat.

Cheryl Landers, LaTour, Missouri

3/4 cup slivered almonds

2 tablespoons sugar

1/2 cup heavy whipping cream

6 ounces white baking chocolate, chopped

1/4 teaspoon orange extract

3 cups fresh raspberries

1. In a small heavy skillet, cook the almonds over medium heat until toasted, about 3 minutes. Sprinkle with sugar; cook and stir for 2-4 minutes or until sugar is melted. Spread on foil to cool.

2. In a small heavy saucepan, bring cream just to a boil. Pour over chocolate; whisk until smooth. Stir in orange extract. Refrigerate until chilled.

3. To serve, divide the raspberries among six martini glasses or dessert dishes. Top each with sauce; sprinkle with almonds.

YIELD: 6 SERVINGS.

NUTRITION FACTS: 1 serving equals 354 calories, 25 g fat (11 g saturated fat), 33 mg cholesterol, 38 mg sodium, 31 g carbohydrate, 6 g fiber, 6 g protein.

Teacher
Hiawassee Elementary

Orlando, Florida

Stephanie McShan says the best part of being a family intervention specialist at Hiawassee Elementary is the opportunity she has every day to positively influence the lives of the entire school body. She also uses her love of baking to make a difference in the lives of those closest to her. "Cooking is a passion that I have always held close to my heart," she says. "I am so excited to represent my school with something that I love as much as I love working with kids."

PINA COLADA CAKE

As an avid baker, I wanted to create something from my heart. I aimed to make a cake that tasted like the perfect pina colada drink, and I feel like I accomplished just that with this recipe.

Stephanie McShan, Apopka, Florida

1 cup butter, softened
2 cups sugar
6 eggs
1 teaspoon coconut extract
3 cups all-purpose flour
1 teaspoon baking powder
1/2 teaspoon baking soda
1 cup (8 ounces) sour cream
1 can (8 ounces) crushed pineapple, undrained

FROSTING:
1 cup butter, softened
4 cups confectioners' sugar
2 teaspoons coconut extract
3 to 4 tablespoons water

FILLING:
1 jar (18 ounces) pineapple preserves
Dried pineapple slices and toasted coconut, optional

1. In a large bowl, cream butter and sugar until light and fluffy. Add the eggs, one at a time, beating well after each addition. Beat in the extract. Combine the flour, baking powder and baking soda; add to the creamed mixture alternately with sour cream, beating well after each addition.

2. In a food processor, cover and pulse the pineapple until almost smooth. Stir into batter. Transfer to three greased and floured 9-in. round baking pans. Bake at 350° for 20-25 minutes or until a toothpick inserted near the center comes out clean.

3. Cool for 10 minutes before removing from pans to wire racks to cool completely.

4. For frosting, in a large bowl, beat butter until fluffy. Beat in the confectioners' sugar, extract and enough water to achieve a spreading consistency.

5. To assemble, place one cake layer on a serving plate; spread with half of the preserves. Repeat layers. Top with remaining cake layer. Frost top and sides. Garnish with pineapple slices and coconut if desired.

YIELD: 12 SERVINGS.

NUTRITION FACTS: 1 slice equals 868 calories, 36 g fat (22 g saturated fat), 199 mg cholesterol, 344 mg sodium, 129 g carbohydrate, 1 g fiber, 7 g protein.

FRENCH APPLE TART

I used to prepare this eye-catching tart with my grandmother. It has a buttery, tender crust that's topped with glossy glazed apple slices.

Teacher, Crespi Carmelite High School, Encino, California

Esteban Vazquez, Encino, California

2 cups all-purpose flour
3/4 cup cold unsalted butter, cubed
1 tablespoon sugar
1/4 teaspoon salt
6 tablespoons ice water
TOPPING:
4 medium tart apples, peeled and sliced
1/2 cup sugar
1/4 cup cold unsalted butter, cubed
1/4 cup apricot preserves
1 tablespoon apple brandy or water

1. In a food processor, combine the flour, butter, sugar and salt; cover and pulse until mixture resembles coarse crumbs. While processing, gradually add water in a steady stream until dough forms a ball. Wrap in plastic wrap. Refrigerate for 1 hour or until easy to handle.

2. Roll out pastry to a 14-in. x 10-in. rectangle; transfer pastry to a baking sheet lined with parchment paper. Beginning at one corner of the pastry, arrange overlapping apple slices diagonally to opposite corner. Repeat rows. Sprinkle with sugar; dot with butter.

3. Bake at 400° for 40-45 minutes or until golden brown and apples are tender. In a small microwave-safe bowl, combine preserves and brandy; microwave on high for 30 seconds or until blended. Brush over warm tart. Serve warm or at room temperature.

YIELD: 12 SERVINGS.

NUTRITION FACTS: 1 slice equals 286 calories, 15 g fat (10 g saturated fat), 40 mg cholesterol, 54 mg sodium, 35 g carbohydrate, 1 g fiber, 2 g protein.

KEY LIME PIE WITH SHORTBREAD MACADAMIA CRUST

Key Lime is my favorite pie. I make this one at least four times a month during the summer months! It's so refreshing. And the shortbread crust gives a richness to the pie that a graham cracker crust doesn't.

Teacher, LeBleu Settlement Elementary, Lake Charles, Louisiana

Brynn LeMaire, Gueydan, Louisiana

1 cup crushed shortbread cookies
1/2 cup finely chopped macadamia nuts
1/3 cup butter, melted
1/4 cup sugar

FILLING:

1 package (8 ounces) cream cheese, softened
1 can (14 ounces) sweetened condensed milk
1/2 cup key lime juice or lime juice
1 cup heavy whipping cream, whipped
1/4 cup coarsely chopped macadamia nuts
Lime slices, optional

1. Combine the cookie crumbs, macadamia nuts, butter and sugar; press onto the bottom and up the sides of a greased 9-in. pie plate. Refrigerate for 30 minutes.

2. For the filling, in a large bowl, beat cream cheese until smooth. Add milk and lime juice; beat until smooth. Pour into the crust. Refrigerate for at least 4 hours. Garnish with whipped cream, macadamia nuts and lime slices if desired.

YIELD: 8 SERVINGS.

NUTRITION FACTS: 1 slice equals 604 calories, 45 g fat (23 g saturated fat), 111 mg cholesterol, 297 mg sodium, 46 g carbohydrate, 1 g fiber, 9 g protein.

A+ Recipes from SCHOOLS Across America

Staff
Illini Elementary School

Fairview Heights, Illinois

As a secretary at Illini Elementary School, Kathleen Hedger wears many hats. But through her varied duties, she is able to interact with everyone affiliated with the school: staff, students and parents. "It has been a great honor to meet many wonderful students and families over the years and to literally watch those students grow day by day," she says. The school is especially meaningful to Kathleen, because her three children, now college students, all attended Illini Elementary.

GRILLED BANANAS FOSTER

I worked at a bed-and-breakfast a few years back, and bananas Foster was a dessert often served with dinner. This wonderful version can be prepared on your outdoor grill. Once you grill them, just add ice cream to the bananas and you have a heavenly dessert—without heating up your kitchen.

Kathleen Hedger, Fairview Heights, Illinois

1/3 cup packed brown sugar

1/4 cup butter, melted

2 tablespoons rum or unsweetened apple juice

4 medium bananas

2 cups vanilla ice cream

1. In a small bowl, combine the brown sugar, butter and rum. Cut each banana into 1-in. slices; place on a double thickness of heavy-duty foil (about 18 in. x 12 in.). Spoon brown sugar mixture over the bananas. Fold foil around banana mixture and seal tightly.

2. Grill, covered, over medium heat for 7-9 minutes or until bananas are tender. Open foil carefully to allow steam to escape. Spoon into four dessert dishes. Serve with ice cream.

YIELD: 4 SERVINGS.

NUTRITION FACTS: 1 banana with 2-1/2 tablespoons sauce and 1/2 cup ice cream equals 423 calories, 19 g fat (12 g saturated fat), 59 mg cholesterol, 142 mg sodium, 60 g carbohydrate, 3 g fiber, 4 g protein.

Volunteer
Fireside Elementary

Louisville, Colorado

Callie Palen-Lowrie is a parent volunteer at Fireside Elementary, where her children are in fourth and second grade. Although she volunteers in the classroom, she has a special interest in helping in the kitchen, lunchroom and school garden as a way to promote healthy living. "The enthusiasm the kids show when they are with me is the reason I give so freely of my time," Callie says.

LEMON CURD CHIFFON PIE

This pie is a showstopper. It's very fresh and tart. I get frequent requests from my gang to make it. Normally, I'm a chocolate lover—but this pie makes me forget about chocolate.

Callie Palen-Lowrie, Louisville, Colorado

9 whole graham crackers, broken into large pieces
1/2 cup chopped pecans
3 tablespoons sugar
1/4 teaspoon vanilla extract
1/8 teaspoon salt
5 tablespoons butter, melted

FILLING:

1-1/2 cups heavy whipping cream
3 tablespoons sugar
3 teaspoons vanilla extract
1 jar (11 ounces) lemon curd
1 package (8 ounces) cream cheese, softened
1 tablespoon grated lemon peel
1-1/2 teaspoons unflavored gelatin
1/3 cup lemon juice
1 tablespoon limoncello

BERRY SAUCE:

1/2 pint fresh raspberries
1/2 pint fresh blueberries
1/2 pint fresh strawberries
1/4 cup sugar

1 tablespoon seedless raspberry jam
1 tablespoon lemon juice
1 tablespoon raspberry liqueur

1. Place the graham crackers, pecans, sugar, vanilla and salt in a food processor; cover and pulse until mixture resembles fine crumbs. Add the butter; process until blended.

2. Press crumb mixture onto the bottom and up the sides of a greased 9-in. deep-dish pie plate. Bake at 350° for 10-12 minutes or until light golden brown. Cool completely on a wire rack.

3. In a bowl, combine cream, sugar and vanilla. Beat until stiff peaks form; set aside. In a large bowl, beat the lemon curd, cream cheese and lemon peel until blended; set aside.

4. Sprinkle gelatin over lemon juice; let stand for 1 minute. Microwave on high for 20 seconds. Stir and let stand for 1 minute or until gelatin is completely dissolved. Stir in limoncello. Gradually beat into lemon curd mixture until well blended. Fold in whipped cream; pour into the crust. Refrigerate for 3 hours or until set.

5. In a saucepan over medium heat, combine berries, sugar and jam. Cook and stir for 3-5 minutes or until fruit is softened. In a blender, cover and process berry mixture for 1-2 minutes or until blended. Strain, reserving juice. Discard seeds.

6. Return juice to the saucepan; cook for 15-18 minutes or until reduced to desired consistency, stirring occasionally. Stir in lemon juice and raspberry liqueur. Chill for 1 hour. Garnish servings with sauce.

YIELD: 8 SERVINGS.

NUTRITION FACTS: 1 piece with 4-1/2 teaspoons sauce equals 684 calories, 43 g fat (23 g saturated fat), 140 mg cholesterol, 327 mg sodium, 69 g carbohydrate, 2 g fiber, 6 g protein.

Teacher
Blue Ridge Elementary

Seneca, South Carolina

Lora Roth teaches fifth grade at Blue Ridge Elementary. Additionally, she is a coach for the school's FIRST Robotics Lego League team. The team went to the state championship after their research project won first place in their region. "The theme was Body Forward, so our team focused on cerebral palsy," she says. "We designed a football launcher for a classmate. It attaches to his wheelchair!"

STRAWBERRY-LEMON CREPE CAKE

Each year, for my husband's birthday, I make him a different lemon cake—a tradition started by his mother. A few years ago, I made a lemon crepe cake, and it was really tasty. This spring, I added fresh strawberries and the cake was unforgettable! I like to make the crepe batter and lemon curd the night before and assemble it all the next morning.

Lora Roth, Seneca, South Carolina

1 teaspoon unflavored gelatin

2 tablespoons cold water

4 eggs

1 cup sugar

3/4 cup lemon juice

6 egg yolks

2 tablespoons grated lemon peel

6 tablespoons butter, cubed

CREPES:

1-1/4 cups 2% milk

3 eggs

1/3 cup melted butter

1 teaspoon vanilla extract

3/4 cup all-purpose flour

1/2 cup sugar

1/4 teaspoon salt

FILLING/TOPPING:

1-1/2 cups heavy whipping cream

1/4 cup confectioners' sugar

1 package (16 ounces) fresh strawberries, hulled and thinly sliced

1. Sprinkle gelatin over cold water; let stand for 5 minutes.

2. In a small heavy saucepan over medium heat, whisk the eggs, sugar, lemon juice, egg yolks and lemon peel until blended. Add butter; cook, whisking constantly, until the mixture is thickened and coats the back of a spoon. Remove from the heat; stir in the softened gelatin until completely dissolved. Transfer to a large bowl; cool. Press waxed paper onto the surface of lemon curd; refrigerate overnight or until chilled.

3. Meanwhile, for crepes, in a small bowl, whisk the milk, eggs, melted butter and vanilla. Combine the flour, sugar and salt; add to milk mixture and mix well. Cover and refrigerate for 2 hours or overnight.

4. Heat a lightly greased 8-in. nonstick skillet over medium heat; pour 2 tablespoons batter into center of skillet. Lift and tilt pan to coat bottom evenly. Cook until top appears dry; turn and cook 15-20 seconds longer. Remove to a wire rack. Repeat with remaining batter, greasing skillet as needed. When cool, stack crepes with waxed paper or paper towels in between.

5. In a large bowl, beat cream until it begins to thicken. Add confectioners' sugar; beat until stiff peaks form. Set aside 1 cup for topping; cover and refrigerate. In a large bowl, gradually whisk whipped cream into lemon curd.

6. To assemble, place one crepe on a cake plate. Spread with 3 tablespoons of the filling and layer with 2 tablespoons of the strawberries. Repeat layers until 15 crepes are used (save remaining crepes for another use). Cover cake and remaining lemon curd mousse; refrigerate until serving.

7. Just before serving, top cake with whipped cream. Garnish with remaining strawberries. Serve with additional lemon curd mousse.

YIELD: 10 SERVINGS PLUS 5 LEFTOVER CREPES.

NUTRITION FACTS: 1 slice with a scant 1/4 cup lemon curd mousse equals 461 calories, 30 g fat (17 g saturated fat), 328 mg cholesterol, 186 mg sodium, 42 g carbohydrate, 1 g fiber, 8 g protein.

DEVIL'S FOOD CAKE

This is my grandmother's homemade chocolate cake. I remember that she often had it ready when my family came to visit. The creamy chocolate custard filling makes it so sinful, and everything is topped with a fluffy white frosting.

Teacher, Palmer Lake Elementary, Brooklyn Park, Minnesota

Bonnie Capper-Eckstein, Maple Grove, Minnesota

4 egg whites
1/2 cup butter, softened
1-3/4 cups sugar
1 teaspoon vanilla extract
2 cups all-purpose flour
1/2 cup baking cocoa
1/2 teaspoon baking soda
1/4 teaspoon salt
1 cup water

PUDDING:
1 cup sugar
1/4 cup all-purpose flour
1/2 teaspoon salt
2 cups 2% milk
2 egg yolks, beaten
3 ounces unsweetened chocolate, chopped
1 tablespoon butter
1 teaspoon vanilla extract

FROSTING:
1 cup sugar
3 egg whites
3 tablespoons cold water
2 tablespoons light corn syrup
1/2 teaspoon cream of tartar
1/8 teaspoon salt
1 teaspoon vanilla extract

1. Place the egg whites in a large bowl; let stand at room temperature for 30 minutes. Meanwhile, in a large bowl, cream butter and sugar until light and fluffy. Beat in vanilla. Combine the flour, cocoa, baking soda and salt; add to the creamed mixture alternately with water, beating well after each addition.

2. Beat egg whites with clean beaters until stiff peaks form; fold into batter. Transfer to a greased 13-in. x 9-in. baking pan. Bake at 350° for 30-35 minutes or until a toothpick inserted near the center comes out clean. Cool on a wire rack.

3. For pudding, in a heavy saucepan, combine sugar, flour and salt. Stir in milk until smooth. Cook and stir over medium-high heat until thickened and bubbly. Reduce heat to low; cook and stir 2 minutes longer. Remove from the heat.

4. Stir a small amount of hot mixture into egg yolks; return all to the pan, stirring constantly. Bring to a gentle boil; cook and stir 2 minutes longer. Remove from the heat. Stir in chocolate until smooth. Stir in butter and vanilla. Cool to room temperature, stirring occasionally. Spread over cake.

5. In a large heavy saucepan, combine the sugar, egg whites, water, corn syrup, cream of tartar and salt over low heat. With a hand mixer, beat on low speed for 1 minute. Continue beating on low over low heat until frosting reaches 160°, about 8-10 minutes.

6. Pour into a large bowl; add vanilla. Beat on high until stiff peaks form, about 7 minutes. Spread over the cake. Store in the refrigerator.

YIELD: 12 SERVINGS.

NUTRITION FACTS: 1 piece cake equals 495 calories, 14 g fat (8 g saturated fat), 60 mg cholestero 342 mg sodium, 88 g carbohydrate, 2 g fiber, 8 g protein.

Teacher
Leland CUSD #1

Leland, Illinois

As a teacher in a small K-12 grade school, Carrie Price gets to develop close relationships with students and witness their educational journeys from beginning to end. The school's largest graduating class, the class of 1972, consisted of just 36 students. "I enjoy being able to really get to know the students and see how they progress through the years," says Carrie, who teaches sixth grade.

PEPPERMINT CHEESECAKE

People are thrilled when they see me coming with this rich, smooth cheesecake. It's always a crowd-pleaser—not only does it look sensational, but it's also scrumptious!

Carrie Price, Ottawa, Illinois

2-1/2 cups cream-filled chocolate sandwich
    cookie crumbs
1/3 cup butter, melted
5 packages (8 ounces each) cream cheese, softened
1 cup sugar
1 cup (8 ounces) sour cream
3 tablespoons all-purpose flour
3 teaspoons vanilla extract
1 teaspoon peppermint extract
3 eggs, lightly beaten
1 package (10 ounces) Andes creme de menthe baking chips or 2 packages (4.67 ounces each) mint Andes candies, chopped

TOPPING:
1 package (8 ounces) cream cheese, softened
1/3 cup sugar
1 carton (12 ounces) frozen whipped topping, thawed
Miniature candy canes, optional

1. Place a greased 9-in. springform pan on a double thickness of heavy-duty foil (about 18 in. square). Securely wrap foil around pan.

2. In a small bowl, combine cookie crumbs and butter. Press onto the bottom and 1 in. up the sides of the prepared pan. Place pan on a baking sheet. Bake at 325° for 12-14 minutes or until set. Cool on a wire rack.

3. In a large bowl, beat cream cheese and sugar until smooth. Beat in the sour cream, flour and extracts. Add eggs; beat on low speed just until combined. Fold in chips. Pour into crust. (Pan will be full.) Place springform pan in a large baking pan; add 1 in. of hot water to larger pan.

4. Bake at 325° for 1-1/4 to 1-1/2 hours or until center is just set and top appears dull. Remove springform pan from water bath. Cool on a wire rack for 10 minutes. Carefully run a knife around edge of the pan to loosen; cool 1 hour longer. Refrigerate overnight. Remove sides of pan.

5. For topping, in a large bowl, beat cream cheese and sugar until smooth. Stir one-fourth whipped topping into mixture; fold in remaining whipped topping. Spread or pipe onto the cheesecake. Garnish with miniature candy canes if desired.

YIELD: 16 SERVINGS.

NUTRITION FACTS: 1 slice (calculated without candy canes) equals 711 calories, 51 g fat (33 g saturated fat), 153 mg cholesterol, 424 mg sodium, 52 g carbohydrate, 2 g fiber, 10 g protein.

Teacher
A. Hein Elementary

Elk Grove, California

Denise Nakamoto has taught both kindergarten and fourth grade during her 24 years as an educator. "The most rewarding part of my job is being a positive influence in students' lives," she says. "My goal is to help them grow to become caring, thinking, problem-solving adults who maintain a love of learning. I am privileged to see the 'light bulbs' go on when they learn something new and celebrate their effort and personal growth."

ELEGANT FRESH BERRY TART

This elegant tart was my first original creation. If other fresh fruits are used, adjust simple syrup flavor to match.

Denise Nakamoto, Elk Grove, California

1/2 cup butter, softened

1/3 cup sugar

1/2 teaspoon grated orange peel

1/4 teaspoon orange extract

1/8 teaspoon vanilla extract

1 cup all-purpose flour

FILLING:

1 package (8 ounces) cream cheese, softened

1/4 cup sugar

1/2 teaspoon lemon juice

SYRUP:

1/2 cup water

1 tablespoon sugar

1 tablespoon red raspberry or strawberry preserves

1/4 teaspoon lemon juice

TOPPING:

1 pound fresh strawberries, sliced

1 cup fresh raspberries

2 medium kiwifruit, peeled and sliced

1/2 cup fresh blueberries

1. In a small bowl, cream butter and sugar until light and fluffy. Add the orange peel and extracts. Gradually add flour until mixture forms a ball. Press into a greased 11-in. fluted tart pan with a removable bottom. Bake at 375° for 10-12 minutes or until golden brown. Cool on a wire rack.

2. For filling, in a small bowl, beat the cream cheese, sugar and lemon juice until smooth. Spread over crust. Cover and refrigerate for 30 minutes or until set.

3. Meanwhile, in a small saucepan, bring the water, sugar, preserves and lemon juice to a boil. Reduce heat; simmer, uncovered, for 10 minutes. Set aside to cool.

4. Arrange the strawberries, raspberries, kiwi and blueberries over filling. Brush with sugar mixture. Cover and refrigerate for at least 1 hour before serving.

YIELD: 16 SERVINGS.

NUTRITION FACTS: 1 slice equals 186 calories, 11 g fat (7 g saturated fat), 31 mg cholesterol, 83 mg sodium, 21 g carbohydrate, 2 g fiber, 2 g protein.

CARROT CAKE CUPCAKES

This recipe is so special to me, because it was passed down from my grandmother to my mother and now to me. This family classic is now often requested for any type of work function.

Teacher, Camp Ernst Middle School, Burlington, Kentucky

Leann Schmid, Covington, Kentucky

2 cups sugar

1-1/4 cups canola oil

3 eggs

1 teaspoon vanilla extract

2-1/2 cups all-purpose flour, divided

2 teaspoons ground cinnamon

1 teaspoon baking soda

1/2 teaspoon salt

2 cups grated carrots

1 can (8 ounces) unsweetened crushed
  pineapple, undrained

1 cup raisins

FROSTING:

4 ounces cream cheese, softened

1/4 cup butter, softened

2-1/2 cups confectioners' sugar

1 tablespoon 2% milk

1. In a large bowl, beat the sugar, oil, eggs and vanilla until well blended. Combine 2 cups flour, cinnamon, baking soda and salt; gradually beat into sugar mixture until blended. Stir in carrots and pineapple. Toss the raisins with the remaining flour until coated; fold into batter.

2. Fill paper-lined muffin cups two-thirds full. Bake at 350° for 20-25 minutes or until a toothpick inserted near the center comes out clean. Cool for 10 minutes before removing from pans to wire racks to cool completely.

3. For frosting, in a small bowl, beat cream cheese and butter until fluffy. Add confectioners' sugar and milk; beat until smooth. Frost cupcakes. Refrigerate leftovers.

YIELD: 28 CUPCAKES.

NUTRITION FACTS: 1 cupcake equals 287 calories, 14 g fat (3 g saturated fat), 31 mg cholesterol, 125 mg sodium, 40 g carbohydrate, 1 g fiber, 2 g protein.

BLACK FOREST FUDGE SAUCE

I've used this velvety fudge sauce studded with cherries for years, and everyone raves about its addicting taste. This fudge sauce is so luscious I could just eat it with a spoon!

Teacher, Meadowmere Elementary School, Grandview, Missouri

Linda Pace, Lees Summit, Missouri

2 cups (16 ounces) sour cream
1 cup sugar
1 cup baking cocoa

1 jar (6 ounces) maraschino cherries, drained and chopped
3 teaspoons vanilla extract
1/4 teaspoon almond extract
Ice cream

1. In a small heavy saucepan, combine the sour cream, sugar and cocoa. Cook and stir over medium-low heat until sugar is dissolved and mixture is smooth. Stir in cherries and extracts. Serve warm over ice cream. Refrigerate leftovers.

YIELD: 24 SERVINGS (2 TABLESPOONS EACH).

NUTRITION FACTS: 2 tablespoons (calculated without ice cream) equals 126 calories, 7 g fat (4 g saturated fat), 25 mg cholesterol, 15 mg sodium, 13 g carbohydrate, 1 g fiber, 2 g protein.

Staff
Sunset Lake Elementary School

Vicksburg, Michigan

Working as the office aide at Sunset Lake Elementary School is special to Ronda Schabes because she was once a student at the school, as were her daughters. "I would have never dreamed when I was a student at Sunset that one day I would not only work here as an adult, but that I would also be presented with a $20,000 check during a school assembly for winning first place in a national contest," she says.

CHOCOLATE GANACHE PEANUT BUTTER CUPCAKES

I've been baking cakes for years, and I enjoy trying new combinations of flavors and textures. For these cupcakes, I blended two popular flavors: peanut butter and chocolate. As soon as I took my first bite, I knew I had created something divine! Most people who try them say they are the best thing they've ever eaten. They are definitely worth the time it takes to make them.

1st place

Ronda Schabes, Vicksburg, Michigan

2 cups sugar

1-3/4 cups all-purpose flour

3/4 cup baking cocoa

1/2 teaspoon salt

1/2 teaspoon baking soda

1/2 teaspoon baking powder

1 cup buttermilk

1 cup strong brewed coffee, room temperature

1/2 cup canola oil

2 eggs

1 teaspoon vanilla extract

FILLING:

1/2 cup creamy peanut butter

3 tablespoons unsalted butter, softened

1 cup confectioners' sugar

2 to 4 tablespoons 2% milk

GANACHE:

2 cups (12 ounces) semisweet chocolate chips

1/2 cup heavy whipping cream

PEANUT BUTTER FROSTING:

1 cup packed brown sugar

4 egg whites

1/4 teaspoon salt

1/4 teaspoon cream of tartar

1 teaspoon vanilla extract

2 cups unsalted butter, softened

1/3 cup creamy peanut butter

1. In a large bowl, combine the first six ingredients. Whisk the buttermilk, coffee, oil, eggs and vanilla until blended; add to the dry ingredients until combined. (Batter will be very thin.) Fill paper-lined muffin cups two-thirds full.

2. Bake at 350° for 18-20 minutes or until a toothpick inserted near the center comes out clean. Cool for 10 minutes before removing from pans to wire racks to cool completely.

3. In a small bowl, cream the peanut butter, butter, confectioners' sugar and enough milk to achieve piping consistency. Cut a small hole in the corner of a pastry or plastic bag; insert a small round tip. Fill with peanut butter filling. Insert tip into the top center of each cupcake; pipe about 1 tablespoon filling into each.

4. Place chocolate chips in a small bowl. In a small saucepan, bring cream just to a boil. Pour over chocolate; whisk until smooth. Dip the top of each cupcake into ganache; place on wire racks to set.

5. In a large heavy saucepan, combine the brown sugar, egg whites, salt and cream of tartar over low heat. With a hand mixer, beat on low speed for 1 minute. Continue beating on low over low heat until frosting reaches 160°, about 8-10 minutes. Pour into a large bowl; add vanilla. Beat on high until stiff peaks form, about 5 minutes.

6. Add butter, 1 tablespoon at a time, beating well after each addition. If mixture begins to look curdled, place frosting bowl in another bowl filled with hot water for a few seconds. Continue adding butter and beating until smooth. Beat in peanut butter for 1-2 minutes or until smooth.

7. Place frosting in a pastry or plastic bag with large star tip; pipe onto each cupcake. Store in an airtight container in the refrigerator. Let stand at room temperature before serving.

YIELD: 2 DOZEN.

NUTRITION FACTS: 1 cupcake equals 498 calories, 33 g fat (16 g saturated fat), 69 mg cholesterol, 196 mg sodium, 50 g carbohydrate, 2 g fiber, 6 g protein.

CRANBERRY BARS WITH CREAM CHEESE FROSTING

When I place a pan of these bars in the teachers lounge and come back after the last bell, the pan is always empty. You'll have the same results at potlucks and other gatherings. The white chips and cranberries make the bars seem extra special.

Teacher, San Marcos Elementary School, Chandler, Arizona

Mirella Hackett, Chandler, Arizona

3/4 cup butter, softened

1 cup sugar

3/4 cup sour cream

2 eggs

1/2 teaspoon almond extract

1/2 teaspoon vanilla extract

1-1/2 cups all-purpose flour

1 teaspoon baking powder

1/8 teaspoon salt

1 cup white baking chips

1 cup dried cranberries

1/2 cup chopped walnuts

FROSTING:

2 packages (8 ounces each) cream cheese, softened

1/4 cup butter, softened

2 cups confectioners' sugar

1 teaspoon vanilla extract

1/2 cup dried cranberries, chopped

1. In a large bowl, cream butter and sugar until light and fluffy. Beat in the sour cream, eggs and extracts. Combine the flour, baking powder and salt; gradually add to creamed mixture and mix well. Fold in the chips, cranberries and walnuts. Spread into a greased 15-in. x 10-in. x 1-in. baking pan.

2. Bake at 350° for 25-30 minutes or until a toothpick inserted near center comes out clean. Cool completely on a wire rack.

3. For frosting, in a small bowl, beat cream cheese and butter until fluffy. Add confectioners' sugar and vanilla; beat until smooth. Fold in cranberries. Spread over the top. Cut into bars. Refrigerate leftovers.

YIELD: 4 DOZEN.

NUTRITION FACTS: 1 bar equals 166 calories, 10 g fat (6 g saturated fat), 32 mg cholesterol, 77 mg sodium, 18 g carbohydrate, trace fiber, 2 g protein.

DOUBLE CHERRY PIE

The combination of tart, canned cherries and dried cherries make this so yummy. This is the best cherry pie I have ever raised to my lips!

Teacher, Kahoa Elementary, Lincoln, Nebraska

Jerri Gradert, Lincoln, Nebraska

3 cans (14-1/2 ounces each) pitted tart cherries, undrained

1 cup dried cherries

1/2 teaspoon almond extract

1 cup sugar

1/4 cup cornstarch

1/4 teaspoon salt

1/4 teaspoon ground nutmeg

Pastry for double-crust pie (9 inches)

1 tablespoon butter

1. Drain cherries, reserving 1 cup juice. Set cherries aside. In a small saucepan, combine dried cherries and reserved juice. Bring to a boil; let stand for 5 minutes. Drain and set aside to cool.

2. In a large bowl, combine the tart cherries, dried cherries and extract. In a small bowl, combine the sugar, cornstarch, salt and nutmeg. Add to cherry mixture; toss to coat.

3. Divide dough in half so that one portion is slightly larger than the other. Roll out larger portion to fit a 9-in. pie plate. Transfer pastry to pie plate. Trim pastry even with edges. Pour filling into crust. Dot with butter.

4. Roll out remaining pastry to fit top of pie. Place over filling. Trim, seal and flute edges. Cut slits in pastry. Bake at 375° for 40-45 minutes or until crust is golden brown and filling is bubbly. Cover edges with foil during the last 30 minutes to prevent overbrowning if necessary. Cool on a wire rack.

YIELD: 8 SERVINGS.

NUTRITION FACTS: 1 piece equals 473 calories, 16 g fat (7 g saturated fat), 14 mg cholesterol, 296 mg sodium, 81 g carbohydrate, 2 g fiber, 4 g protein.

ORANGE SANDWICH COOKIES

These cookies taste just like the orange Creamsicle treats you had as a kid. Soft orange cookies are filled with a buttery, smooth filling.

Teacher, Lewisburg Middle School, Lewisburg, Tennessee

Benita Villines, Spring Hill, Tennessee

---

1 cup butter, softened

4 ounces cream cheese, softened

1-3/4 cups confectioners' sugar

1/2 cup thawed orange juice concentrate

4 teaspoons grated orange peel

1/2 teaspoon vanilla extract

2-1/2 cups all-purpose flour

1/2 teaspoon baking soda

1/4 teaspoon salt

10 drops yellow plus 2 drops red food coloring

Additional confectioners' sugar

FILLING:

1/2 cup butter, softened

4 ounces cream cheese, softened

1/4 teaspoon vanilla extract

2 cups confectioners' sugar

1 tablespoon orange juice concentrate

1/8 teaspoon grated orange peel

1. In a large bowl, cream butter and cream cheese until light and fluffy. Gradually beat in confectioners' sugar. Beat in the orange juice concentrate, peel and vanilla. Combine the flour, baking soda and salt; gradually add to creamed mixture and mix well. Stir in food coloring. (Dough will be soft.)

2. Drop by rounded tablespoonfuls 3 in. apart onto ungreased baking sheets. Flatten slightly with a glass dipped in the confectioners' sugar.

3. Bake at 400° for 6-9 minutes or until edges begin to brown. Remove to wire racks to cool completely.

4. For filling, in a small bowl, cream butter, cream cheese and vanilla until light and fluffy. Gradually beat in confectioners' sugar. Add orange juice concentrate and peel.

5. Spread filling on the bottoms of half of the cookies; top with remaining cookies. Store in the refrigerator.

YIELD: 28 COOKIES.

NUTRITION FACTS: 1 cookie equals 227 calories, 13 g fat (8 g saturated fat), 35 mg cholesterol, 137 mg sodium, 27 g carbohydrate, trace fiber, 2 g protein.

Teacher
St. Paul Lutheran

Grafton, Wisconsin

Not only does Diane Schumann teach at St. Paul Lutheran School, she's a graduate—as are her four children. As the math teacher for the sixth through eighth grades, she started celebrating Pi Day (March 14, or 3.14) by baking a "mystery pie" for her students. "I bake a pie every year and the kids get to guess what type I've made," she says. "Whoever guesses correctly gets his or her name put in a hat. The lucky winner gets to take home the pie."

RASPBERRY ALMOND CHEESECAKE

My son requests this cheesecake for his birthday cake every year, and our school auction committee asks me to make it for their annual auction. It's definitely one of the best cheesecakes I make.

Diane Schumann, Fredonia, Wisconsin

2 cups vanilla wafers (about 60 wafers)
1/2 cup butter, melted
1/4 cup sugar
FILLING:
4 packages (8 ounces each) cream cheese, softened
1-1/4 cups sugar
1 tablespoon Triple Sec
1 teaspoon almond extract
1/8 teaspoon salt
4 eggs, lightly beaten
1/3 cup seedless raspberry spreadable fruit
1/2 teaspoon raspberry extract
TOPPING:
2 cups (16 ounces) sour cream
1/4 cup sugar
1/2 teaspoon almond extract

1. Place a greased 10-in. springform pan on a double thickness of heavy-duty foil (about 18 in. square). Securely wrap foil around pan. In a small bowl, combine wafer crumbs, butter and sugar. Press onto the bottom and 1 in. up the sides of prepared pan.

2. In a large bowl, beat cream cheese and sugar until smooth. Beat in the Triple Sec, extract and salt. Add the eggs; beat on low speed just until combined.

3. Remove 1 cup batter to a small bowl; stir in spreadable fruit and extract until well blended. Pour plain batter over crust. Drop the raspberry batter by tablespoons over plain batter; spread evenly. Place springform pan in a large baking pan; add 1 in. of hot water to larger pan.

4. Bake at 325° for 50-60 minutes or until almost set and top appears dull. Remove springform pan from the water bath. Let stand for 5 minutes.

5. For topping, combine all ingredients; spread over the top of cheesecake. Bake 5 minutes longer. Cool on a wire rack for 10 minutes. Carefully run a knife around edge of the pan to loosen; cool 1 hour longer. Refrigerate overnight. Remove sides of pan.

YIELD: 14 SERVINGS.

NUTRITION FACTS: 1 slice equals 558 calories, 38 g fat (23 g saturated fat), 173 mg cholesterol, 340 mg sodium, 44 g carbohydrate, 1 g fiber, 8 g protein.

Teacher
Chinn Elementary

Kansas City, Missouri

Cara Langer has been a first grade teacher for 10 years. "I love teaching kids to read, to have successful relationships and to become lifelong learners," she says.

MOCHA CHOCOLATE CHIP CHEESECAKE

Childhood food memories always bring me back to special times. This is one of the outstanding desserts my mom often served.

Cara Langer, Overland Park, Kansas

1-1/2 cups chocolate wafer crumbs

1/3 cup sugar

6 tablespoons butter, melted

FILLING:

1/2 cup heavy whipping cream

1 tablespoon instant coffee granules

3 packages (8 ounces each) cream cheese, softened

1 cup sugar

1 teaspoon vanilla extract

3 eggs, lightly beaten

1 cup (6 ounces) miniature semisweet chocolate chips, divided

1. Place a greased 9-in. springform pan on a double thickness of heavy-duty foil (about 18 in. square). Securely wrap foil around pan.

2. In a large bowl, combine the wafer crumbs, sugar and butter. Press onto the bottom of prepared pan.

3. In a small saucepan, combine the cream and coffee granules. Cook and stir until granules are dissolved; set aside to cool.

4. In a large bowl, beat cream cheese and sugar until smooth. Beat in coffee mixture and vanilla. Add the eggs; beat on low speed just until combined. Fold in 3/4 cup chocolate chips; pour into crust. Sprinkle with remaining chips. Place springform pan in a large baking pan; add 1 in. of hot water to larger pan.

5. Bake at 325° for 60-70 minutes or until center is just set and top appears dull. Remove springform pan from water bath. Cool on a wire rack for 10 minutes. Carefully run a knife around edge of pan to loosen; cool 1 hour longer. Refrigerate overnight. Remove sides of pan.

YIELD: 16 SERVINGS.

NUTRITION FACTS: 1 slice equals 388 calories, 28 g fat (16 g saturated fat), 108 mg cholesterol, 234 mg sodium, 33 g carbohydrate, 1 g fiber, 6 g protein.

PEACHES & CREAM JELLY ROLL

Cake rolls make a lovely presentation for a party, and they are simple to cut into even slices. My father taught me how to make them, and sometimes we get together and make them for family and friends.

Staff, Southwest Parke, Montezuma, Indiana

Malena Coleman, Rockville, Indiana

3 eggs

1/4 teaspoon vanilla extract

1/8 teaspoon salt

3/4 cup sugar

3/4 cup biscuit/baking mix

1 cup heavy whipping cream

1/4 cup confectioners' sugar, divided

3 cups chopped peeled fresh peaches

1. Line a greased 15-in. x 10-in. x 1-in. baking pan with waxed paper and grease the paper; sprinkle with flour and set aside.

2. In a large bowl, beat eggs on high speed for 3 minutes. Beat in vanilla and salt. Gradually add sugar, beating until mixture becomes thick and lemon-colored. Fold in biscuit mix. Spread in prepared pan.

3. Bake at 375° for 8-10 minutes or until cake springs back when lightly touched. Cool for 5 minutes. Invert onto a kitchen towel dusted with confectioners' sugar. Gently peel off waxed paper. Roll up cake in the towel jelly-roll style, starting with a short side. Cool completely on a wire rack.

4. For filling, in a small bowl, beat cream until it begins to thicken. Add 3 tablespoons confectioners' sugar; beat until stiff peaks form.

5. Unroll cake; spread half of whipped cream over cake to within 1/2 in. of edges. Top with peaches and remaining whipped cream. Roll up again. Place seam side down on a serving platter. Dust with remaining confectioners' sugar. Refrigerate for 2 hours.

YIELD: 12 SERVINGS.

NUTRITION FACTS: 1 slice equals 192 calories, 10 g fat (5 g saturated fat), 80 mg cholesterol, 144 mg sodium, 24 g carbohydrate, 1 g fiber, 3 g protein.

Teacher
Pendergast Elementary School

Phoenix, Arizona

As a fourth grade teacher at Pendergast Elementary School, Jenny Weaver finds fulfillment in knowing she's helping her students reach their greatest potential. Jenny also enjoys baking for her colleagues and she says, "If I was not a teacher, I would own my own bakery."

FRENCH TOAST CUPCAKES

Baking is like therapy to me! Whenever I feel down or stressed, I know I can go into the kitchen and whip up a batch of these delicious cupcakes that I created. I share my baked items with my family and friends. I sometimes crumble a few slices of bacon and sprinkle them over the top of freshly iced cupcakes. This delicious combination tastes like Sunday brunch in a cupcake.

Jenny Weaver, Glendale, Arizona

1/2 cup butter, softened

1-1/2 cups sugar

2 eggs

2 teaspoons vanilla extract

2 cups all-purpose flour

2 teaspoons ground cinnamon

1/2 teaspoon baking powder

1/2 teaspoon baking soda

1/4 teaspoon salt

1/4 teaspoon ground nutmeg

1-1/3 cups buttermilk

MAPLE BUTTERCREAM FROSTING:

1/2 cup butter, softened

1/4 cup shortening

1/2 cup maple syrup

Dash salt

2-1/2 cups confectioners' sugar

6 bacon strips, cooked and crumbled, optional

1. In a large bowl, cream butter and sugar until light and fluffy. Add eggs, one at a time, beating well after each addition. Beat in vanilla. Combine the flour, cinnamon, baking powder, baking soda, salt and nutmeg; add to the creamed mixture alternately with buttermilk, beating well after each addition.

2. Fill paper-lined muffin cups two-thirds full. Bake at 350° for 17-22 minutes or until a toothpick inserted near the center comes out clean. Cool for 10 minutes before removing from pans to wire racks to cool completely.

3. For frosting, in a small bowl, beat butter and shortening until fluffy. Beat in the maple syrup and salt. Add the confectioners' sugar; beat until smooth. Frost the cupcakes. Sprinkle with bacon if desired.

YIELD: 1-1/2 DOZEN.

NUTRITION FACTS: 1 cupcake (calculated without bacon) equals 334 calories, 14 g fat (7 g saturated fat), 51 mg cholesterol, 187 mg sodium, 51 g carbohydrate, 1 g fiber, 3 g protein.

Teacher
L.D. Batchelder School

**North Reading
Massachusetts**

During the school year, Nicole Jackson teaches third grade. But in the summer, she works as a crew member of a replica privateer schooner. One fall, as she and her new students were getting to know one another, she told the class she worked on a ship, the kind of ship you see in pirate movies. "I jokingly told them that I actually was a pirate. It wasn't until parent-teacher conferences when a parent said, 'So, Ms. Jackson, you're a pirate too? How do you find the time?' that I realized the students had believed me," she says.

BRANDY PEAR PIE

I tapped into my French heritage for this recipe by incorporating Calvados, an apple brandy from the Normandy region of France. The sweet filling is balanced out by a buttery crust, making for an indulgent treat.

Nicole Jackson, Beverly, Massachusetts

2-1/2 cups all-purpose flour
1/2 teaspoon salt
1 cup cold butter
1/2 cup ice water

FILLING:

1 cup raisins
1/2 cup apple brandy
1/2 cup sugar
1/4 cup all-purpose flour
1/2 teaspoon ground cinnamon
1/4 teaspoon salt
1/4 teaspoon ground nutmeg
4 cups cubed peeled fresh pears
2 tablespoons lemon juice
2 tablespoons butter

1. In a large bowl, combine the flour and salt; cut in butter until crumbly. Gradually add water, tossing with a fork until a ball forms. Divide the dough in half so that one portion is slightly larger than the other; wrap each in plastic wrap. Refrigerate for at least 1 hour or until easy to handle.

2. Meanwhile, in a small saucepan over low heat, cook raisins in brandy for 13-15 minutes or until raisins are plump. Strain, reserving liquid. Set raisins aside.

3. In a large bowl, combine the sugar, flour, cinnamon, salt and nutmeg. Add the pears, lemon juice, reserved raisins and 1/2 teaspoon of reserved liquid.

4. On a lightly floured surface, roll out larger portion of dough to fit a 9-in. pie plate. Transfer pastry to pie plate. Trim the pastry even with edges. Add pear filling; dot with butter.

5. Roll out remaining pastry to fit top of pie. Place over filling. Trim, seal and flute edges. Cut slits in pastry. Cover edges loosely with foil.

6. Bake at 400° for 45-55 minutes or until bubbly. Cool on a wire rack for at least 30 minutes.

YIELD: 8 SERVINGS.

NUTRITION FACTS: 1 slice equals 542 calories, 26 g fat (16 g saturated fat), 68 mg cholesterol, 406 mg sodium, 73 g carbohydrate, 4 g fiber, 6 g protein.

STRAWBERRY JAM CAKE

When I need a special-occasion cake, this is my go-to recipe. Everyone is crazy about it! Every year, I make it for a cake raffle at work for Relay for Life. It has done more than its part to raise a lot of money for a wonderful cause.

Teacher, Miller Elementary, Warner Robins, Georgia

Tammy Urbina, Warner Robins, Georgia

---

1 cup butter, softened

1-3/4 cups sugar

5 egg whites

2 cups pureed strawberries

1/2 cup sour cream

1 teaspoon strawberry extract

3 cups cake flour

2-1/2 teaspoons baking powder

1/4 teaspoon baking soda

1/4 teaspoon salt

FROSTING:

1 package (8 ounces) cream cheese, softened

1/4 cup butter, softened

3-1/4 cups confectioners' sugar

1/4 cup pureed strawberries

1/2 teaspoon strawberry extract

1 cup seedless strawberry jam, divided

Sliced fresh strawberries, optional

1. Grease and flour three 9-in. round baking pans; set aside.

2. In a large bowl, cream butter and sugar until light and fluffy. Add the egg whites, one at a time, beating well after each addition. Beat in the strawberries, sour cream and extract. Combine the flour, baking powder, baking soda and salt; add to the creamed mixture. Transfer batter to prepared pans.

3. Bake at 350° for 22-26 minutes or until a toothpick inserted near the center comes out clean. Cool for 10 minutes before removing from pans to wire racks to cool completely.

4. For frosting, in a large bowl, beat cream cheese and butter until fluffy. Add the confectioners' sugar, strawberries and extract; beat until smooth.

5. Place bottom cake layer on a serving plate; top with 1/2 cup jam and 1/2 cup frosting. Repeat layers. Top with remaining cake layer. Spread remaining frosting over top and sides of cake. Garnish with sliced strawberries if desired.

YIELD: 12 SERVINGS.

NUTRITION FACTS: 1 slice (calculated without sliced strawberries) equals 706 calories, 28 g fat (17 g saturated fat), 78 mg cholesterol, 377 mg sodium, 110 g carbohydrate, 1 g fiber, 7 g protein.

Teacher
Gorham Middle School

Gorham, Maine

Tracy Wheeler teaches music and chorus at Gorham Middle School. "The best part of my position is the subject that I teach," Tracy says. "It is always different, interesting and fun. I love helping students understand and create music, whether it is through singing harmonies in chorus, playing a riff on the guitar or creating a soundtrack for a movie."

TOFFEE CHEESECAKE TIRAMISU

I accidentally discovered this recipe when making a tiramisu for my friend's rehearsal dinner a couple of years ago. I did not have enough Mascarpone, so I decided to substitute cream cheese and the result was a huge success. It tastes like cheesecake and tiramisu mixed together.

Tracy Wheeler, Bridgton, Maine

1-1/4 cups brewed espresso

4 tablespoons rum, divided

4 tablespoons coffee liqueur, divided

1 package (7 ounces) crisp ladyfinger cookies, divided

1 carton (8 ounces) whipped cream cheese

1 carton (8 ounces) Mascarpone cheese

1/2 cup sugar

1 cup heavy whipping cream, whipped

2 teaspoons baking cocoa, divided

3/4 cup toffee bits

1. Cool espresso to room temperature. In a shallow bowl, combine the espresso, 2 tablespoons rum and 2 tablespoons liqueur. Quickly dip 12 cookies in half of the espresso mixture. Arrange in an ungreased 11-in. x 7-in. dish.

2. In a large bowl, combine the cream cheese, Mascarpone cheese, sugar, remaining rum and liqueur. Fold a fourth of whipped cream into the cream cheese mixture, then fold in remaining whipped cream.

3. Spoon half of cream cheese mixture over ladyfingers; spread evenly. Dust with 1 teaspoon cocoa. Repeat layers. Sprinkle with toffee bits. Cover and refrigerate for at least 4 hours or overnight.

YIELD: 12 SERVINGS.

EDITOR'S NOTE: This recipe was prepared with Alessi brand ladyfinger cookies.

NUTRITION FACTS: 1 piece equals 418 calories, 28 g fat (15 g saturated fat), 96 mg cholesterol, 208 mg sodium, 35 g carbohydrate, trace fiber, 4 g protein.

Staff
Washington Traditional School

Prescott, Arizona

Some of the first friends a child makes are at school. Laura Moore, the attendance and office clerk at Washington Traditional School, never forgot her best childhood friend, Jody, although they lost touch over the years. So you can imagine Laura's surprise when, on her first day at WTS, she learned Jody taught one of the school's fifth grade classes. "We screamed and cried and hugged each other," Laura says. "We had lost contact over 35 years ago and couldn't believe we had been working for the same school district for the last seven years."

CHOCOLATE GANACHE CAKE WITH RASPBERRY SAUCE

Divine and heavenly are the words that come to mind when I take a bite of this fudgy, scrumptious cake. Nothing soothes the soul like dark chocolate.

Laura Moore, Prescott, Arizona

2 pounds semisweet chocolate, chopped

1-1/4 cups butter, cubed

8 eggs

1/4 cup all-purpose flour

GANACHE:

2 cups (12 ounces) semisweet chocolate chips

3/4 cup heavy whipping cream

ORANGE-RASPBERRY SAUCE:

2 packages (12 ounces each) frozen unsweetened raspberries, thawed

1 cup sugar

2 tablespoons cornstarch

2 tablespoons cold water

1 teaspoon orange extract

CHOCOLATE WHIPPED CREAM:

1 cup heavy whipping cream

3 tablespoons sugar

2 tablespoons baking cocoa

1/2 teaspoon vanilla extract

1. Grease a 10-in. springform pan and dust with baking cocoa; set aside.

2. In a saucepan, melt the chocolate and butter over medium heat; stir until smooth. Set aside to cool. In a bowl, beat the eggs on medium-high speed for 5 minutes. Using low speed, add the flour, 1 tablespoon at a time. Gradually add the chocolate mixture; beat on medium for 2 minutes. Pour into prepared pan.

3. Bake at 350° for 25-28 minutes or just until set. Cool on a wire rack to room temperature. Remove sides of pan and invert onto a serving plate; invert again, so top side is up.

4. For ganache, in a small saucepan over low heat, melt the chocolate chips with cream; stir until smooth. Cool until slightly thickened, stirring occasionally. Spread ganache over top of cake, allowing some to drape over the sides.

5. For sauce, in a large saucepan, heat raspberries. Transfer raspberries to a fine mesh strainer over a large bowl. Mash and strain the raspberries, reserving juice. Discard seeds.

6. In another saucepan, combine the sugar, cornstarch, water and reserved raspberry juice until smooth. Bring to a boil. Reduce heat to medium; cook and stir for 2-3 minutes or until mixture reaches desired consistency. Stir in orange extract.

7. For whipped cream, in a small bowl, beat the cream until it begins to thicken. Add sugar, cocoa and vanilla; beat until soft peaks form. Garnish the cake with chocolate whipped cream and sauce.

YIELD: 16 SERVINGS.

NUTRITION FACTS: 1 slice equals 777 calories, 56 g fat (33 g saturated fat), 199 mg cholesterol, 154 mg sodium, 69 g carbohydrate, 7 g fiber, 10 g protein.

CHOCOLATE-HAZELNUT CREAM PIE

We've all seen peanut butter pies, so why not kick it up a notch and try a Nutella pie? This luscious dessert is such a treat. I sometimes add sliced bananas on top of the crust and then spoon the Nutella mixture over them for a banana hazelnut cream pie.

Teacher, Central Davis Junior High, Layton, Utah

Anna Smith, North Salt Lake, Utah

16 cream-filled chocolate sandwich cookies
1/4 cup butter, melted

FILLING:

1 package (8 ounces) cream cheese, softened
3/4 cup chocolate hazelnut spread
1/2 cup confectioners' sugar
1 teaspoon vanilla extract
1 cup heavy whipping cream

TOPPING:

1/4 cup heavy whipping cream
1 tablespoon light corn syrup
2 teaspoons butter
1/8 teaspoon salt
2 ounces semisweet chocolate, finely chopped
2 tablespoons chopped hazelnuts, toasted

1. Place the cookies in a food processor; cover and pulse for 1-2 minutes or until mixture resembles fine crumbs. Add butter; process until blended. Press crumb mixture onto the bottom and up the sides of a greased 9-in. pie plate.

2. Bake at 350° for 13-15 minutes. Cool on a wire rack for 30 minutes.

3. Meanwhile, in a large bowl, beat the cream cheese, hazelnut spread, confectioners' sugar and vanilla until smooth.

4. In a small bowl, beat whipping cream until stiff peaks form; fold into hazelnut mixture. Pour into pie crust. Refrigerate for 30 minutes.

5. In a small saucepan over medium heat, bring the cream, corn syrup, butter and salt to a boil. Remove from the heat; add chocolate. Cover and let stand for 5 minutes; stir until smooth. Set aside to cool to room temperature. Spread over pie. Garnish with hazelnuts. Chill for 1 hour.

YIELD: 8 SERVINGS.

EDITOR'S NOTE: Look for chocolate hazelnut spread in the peanut butter section.

NUTRITION FACTS: 1 piece equals 615 calories, 46 g fat (23 g saturated fat), 100 mg cholesterol, 315 mg sodium, 49 g carbohydrate, 2 g fiber, 6 g protein.

Teacher
James W. Lilley School

Sicklerville, New Jersey

Dawn Conte knew she wanted to be a teacher from the time she was a student herself. "Ever since I was in first grade, I have wanted to teach," says the first grade teacher. "Even after 23 years, I still get great joy from watching my students learn." Next to being in the classroom, Dawn loves being in the kitchen, and she often uses baking and cooking as a teaching method. "Whether I make Groundhog Day brownies, magical St. Patrick's Day bars, monkey mix, cinnamon buns or cupcakes, my students love to learn and celebrate with yummy, seasonal treats."

PETER PETER PUMPKIN WHOOPIES

When autumn rolls around and it's time for a bake sale, this is the recipe to which I turn. The whoopie pies are a fall favorite. Cream cheese filling is perked up with cinnamon and nutmeg and is perfect with its cake-like outside.

Dawn Conte, Sicklerville, New Jersey

1 package (18-1/4 ounces) spice cake mix
1-1/4 cups canned pumpkin
2 eggs
1/2 cup 2% milk
1/3 cup butter, softened
FILLING:
2 packages (3 ounces each) cream cheese, softened
1/2 cup marshmallow creme

1/3 cup butter, softened
1-1/2 cups confectioners' sugar
3/4 teaspoon vanilla extract
1/2 teaspoon ground cinnamon
1/8 teaspoon ground nutmeg

1. In a large bowl, combine the first five ingredients; beat until well blended. Drop by 1/4 cupfuls 3 in. apart onto lightly greased baking sheets. Bake at 375° for 7-10 minutes or until set and edges are lightly browned. Remove to wire racks to cool completely.

2. For filling, in a small bowl, beat cream cheese, marshmallow creme and butter. Beat in the remaining ingredients. Spread on the bottoms of half of the cookies; top with the remaining cookies. Store in the refrigerator.

YIELD: 10 WHOOPIE PIES.

NUTRITION FACTS: 1 whoopie pie equals 504 calories, 26 g fat (14 g saturated fat), 107 mg cholesterol, 557 mg sodium, 64 g carbohydrate, 2 g fiber, 7 g protein.

WHITE CHOCOLATE-COCONUT LAYER CAKE

This cake is special to me because I took a recipe I had been making for years and added my own touches. I incorporated fresh peaches and macadamia nuts into the batter and switched from dark to white chocolate. My family gave the results a big "thumbs-up!"

Teacher, Blackford High School, Hartford City, Indiana

Darl Collins, Markleville, Indiana

8 ounces white baking chocolate, chopped

3/4 cup butter, softened

1-1/2 cups sugar

1/8 teaspoon salt

4 eggs

1 teaspoon coconut extract

2-1/2 cups cake flour

6 teaspoons baking powder

1-1/4 cups 2% milk

1 cup frozen unsweetened sliced peaches, thawed and finely chopped

1/2 cup macadamia nuts, chopped, toasted

FROSTING:

6 ounces white baking chocolate, chopped

1/4 cup heavy whipping cream

1 cup butter, softened

1/2 teaspoon coconut extract

4 cups confectioners' sugar

1 cup flaked coconut, toasted

1/4 cup macadamia nuts, chopped, toasted

1. Line three 8-in. round baking pans with parchment paper; coat paper with cooking spray and set aside.

2. In a small bowl, melt chocolate; set aside.

3. In a large bowl, cream butter, sugar and salt until light and fluffy. Add eggs, one at a time, beating well after each addition. Beat in extract. In a small bowl, sift flour and baking powder; add to the creamed mixture alternately with milk, beating well after each addition.

4. Pat peaches dry with paper towels. Fold in peaches, chocolate and macadamia nuts. Divide among prepared pans.

5. Bake at 350° for 35-40 minutes or until a toothpick inserted near the center comes out clean. Cool for 15 minutes before removing from pans to wire racks to cool completely.

6. For frosting, in a microwave, melt chocolate with cream; cool to room temperature. In a large bowl, cream butter and extract until light and fluffy; add cooled chocolate mixture. Gradually beat in confectioners' sugar.

7. Spread between layers and over top and sides of cake. Sprinkle with coconut and macadamia nuts.

YIELD: 12 SERVINGS.

NUTRITION FACTS: 1 slice equals 937 calories, 52 g fat (29 g saturated fat), 156 mg cholesterol, 529 mg sodium, 113 g carbohydrate, 2 g fiber, 9 g protein.

Staff
Bloomfield Elementary School

Bloomfield, New York

This recipe began as a writing assignment between Sharon Balestra and fifth grade student Joey Johnson. "Joey likes to cook," Sharon says. "He and I enjoy talking about recipes and critiquing goodies that I bring in to share from home. So when I got the email about the opportunity to submit a recipe for the Taste of Home contest, I challenged Joey to write up a recipe that we could send in."

FULL-OF-GOODNESS OATMEAL COOKIES

I love to bake and bring in treats to leave in the faculty lounge for my colleagues. To avoid being blamed for ruining their healthy diets, I came up with this healthier version of the classic oatmeal cookie to make snacking on these a good choice instead of a guilty indulgence.

Sharon Balestra, Bloomfield, New York

2 tablespoons hot water
1 tablespoon ground flaxseed
1 cup pitted dried plums, chopped
1 cup chopped dates
1/2 cup raisins
1/3 cup butter, softened
3/4 cup packed brown sugar
1 egg
2 teaspoons vanilla extract
1/2 cup unsweetened applesauce
1/4 cup maple syrup
1 tablespoon grated orange peel

3 cups quick-cooking oats
1 cup all-purpose flour
1/2 cup whole wheat flour
1 teaspoon baking soda
1 teaspoon ground cinnamon
1/2 teaspoon salt
1/4 teaspoon ground nutmeg
1/4 teaspoon ground cloves

1. In a small bowl, combine water and flaxseed. In a large bowl, combine the plums, dates and raisins. Cover with boiling water. Let flaxseed and plum mixtures stand for 10 minutes.

2. Meanwhile, in a large bowl, cream butter and brown sugar until light and fluffy. Beat in egg and vanilla. Beat in the applesauce, maple syrup and orange peel. Combine the oats, flours, baking soda, cinnamon, salt, nutmeg and cloves; gradually add to creamed mixture and mix well. Drain plum mixture; stir plum mixture and flaxseed into dough.

3. Drop by rounded teaspoonfuls 2 in. apart onto lightly greased baking sheets. Bake at 350° for 8-11 minutes or until set. Cool for 2 minutes before removing from pans to wire racks.

YIELD: 6 DOZEN.

NUTRITION FACTS: 1 cookie equals 56 calories, 1 g fat (1 g saturated fat), 5 mg cholesterol, 40 mg sodium, 11 g carbohydrate, 1 g fiber, 1 g protein. DIABETIC EXCHANGE: 1 starch.

Staff, Susquenita High School

Duncannon, Pennsylvania

Lynn Merendino is an instructional aide with the Susquenita School District in Duncannon, Pennsylvania. Susquenita received its name from its two neighboring rivers, the Susquehanna and the Juniata. Working with the students is rewarding, and the staff makes her feel like she has a second family. "That's why I enjoy bringing baked goods in for my friends at school," she says.

ANY HOLIDAY SPRINKLE COOKIES

You can roll this cookie dough in any colored sugar to suit any holiday. I use red and green for Christmas, pastel colors for Easter and green for St. Patrick's Day. I always include these on cookie trays for school. After rolling dough in sugar, the logs can be frozen for up to 2 months. Let them thaw out slightly before slicing. They're easier to slice if very firm.

Lynn Merendino, Marysville, Pennsylvania

1/2 cup butter, softened

1 cup sugar

1 egg

1 tablespoon lemon juice

2 teaspoons vanilla extract

1-3/4 cups all-purpose flour

3/4 teaspoon salt

1/2 teaspoon baking soda

1 cup flaked coconut, finely chopped

6 tablespoons colored sugar

1. In a small bowl, cream butter and sugar until light and fluffy. Beat in the egg, lemon juice and vanilla. Combine the flour, salt and baking soda; gradually add to creamed mixture and mix well. Beat in coconut.

2. Shape into two 6-in. logs; roll each in colored sugar and wrap in plastic wrap. Refrigerate for 3 hours or until firm.

3. Unwrap and cut into 1/4-in. slices. Place 1 in. apart on ungreased baking sheets. Bake at 375° for 10-12 minutes or until set. Cool for 2 minutes before removing from pans to wire racks.

YIELD: 3 DOZEN.

NUTRITION FACTS: 1 cookie equals 86 calories, 4 g fat (2 g saturated fat), 13 mg cholesterol, 93 mg sodium, 13 g carbohydrate, trace fiber, 1 g protein.

BLUEBERRY CORNMEAL MUFFINS

When I bring treats for the staff, I try to keep them healthy, like this recipe. The cornmeal adds an interesting taste and texture.

Teacher, Gust Elementary School, Denver, Colorado

Elizabeth Bergeron, Denver, Colorado

1 cup yellow cornmeal

1/2 cup all-purpose flour

1/2 cup whole wheat flour

1/2 cup plus 1-1/2 teaspoons sugar, divided

4 teaspoons baking powder

1/2 teaspoon salt

2 eggs

3/4 cup fat-free milk

1/4 cup canola oil

1 teaspoon vanilla extract

2 cups fresh or frozen blueberries

1. In a small bowl, combine the cornmeal, flours, 1/2 cup sugar, baking powder and salt. In another bowl, combine the eggs, milk, oil and vanilla. Stir into the dry ingredients just until moistened. Fold in blueberries.

2. Fill greased muffin cups three-fourths full; sprinkle with remaining sugar. Bake at 350° for 18-22 minutes or until a toothpick inserted in the muffin comes out clean. Cool for 5 minutes before removing from the pan to a wire rack. Serve warm.

YIELD: 1 DOZEN.

EDITOR'S NOTE: If using frozen blueberries, use without thawing to avoid discoloring the batter.

NUTRITION FACTS: 1 muffin equals 185 calories, 6 g fat (1 g saturated fat), 36 mg cholesterol, 251 mg sodium, 30 g carbohydrate, 2 g fiber, 4 g protein. Diabetic Exchanges: 2 starch, 1 fat.

Teacher
DeFranco Elementary School

Bangor, Pennsylvania

Deb Lyon teaches Reading Intervention to fifth and sixth grade students at DeFranco Elementary School. "The best part of my position is that I work with small groups of students, and I am able to see the incredible progress they make over the year," she says. Deb often bakes for her students. One time, a student told her, "Mrs. Lyon, these cupcakes are way better than my mom's—but please don't tell her I said that!"

APRICOT-FILLED SANDWICH COOKIES

I bake these delightful cookies every year for Christmas. When I share a tray of my homemade treats with the faculty at school, these are always the first to disappear! I've even had requests to make them for wedding receptions.

Deb Lyon, Bangor, Pennsylvania

1 cup butter, softened
1 cup sugar
2 eggs
3 cups all-purpose flour
2/3 cup finely chopped walnuts

FILLING:

2 cups dried apricots
3/4 cup water
1/4 cup sugar
1/2 teaspoon ground cinnamon

TOPPING:

1/2 cup semisweet chocolate chips
1/2 teaspoon shortening
4 teaspoons confectioners' sugar

1. In a large bowl, cream butter and sugar until light and fluffy. Beat in eggs. Combine flour and walnuts; gradually add to creamed mixture and mix well.

2. Shape into 1-1/2-in.-thick logs. Cut into 1/4-in. slices. Place 2 in. apart on ungreased baking sheets.

3. Bake at 350° for 10-12 minutes or until bottoms begin to brown. Cool completely on pans on wire racks.

4. Meanwhile, in a large saucepan, combine apricots and water. Bring to a boil. Cook and stir for 10 minutes or until apricots are tender. Drain and cool to room temperature.

5. In a blender or food processor, combine the sugar, cinnamon and apricots. Cover and process until smooth. Spread over bottoms of half of the cookies; top with remaining cookies.

6. For topping, melt the chocolate chips and shortening; stir until smooth. Drizzle over the cookies. Sprinkle with the confectioners' sugar.

YIELD: 4 DOZEN.

NUTRITION FACTS: 1 cookie equals 122 calories, 6 g fat (3 g saturated fat), 19 mg cholesterol, 30 mg sodium, 17 g carbohydrate, 1 g fiber, 2 g protein.

CHOCOLATE MALT BALL COOKIES

I like malt ball candies, so I decided to create a cookie that others would like, too. These chewy cookies have fantastic flavor thanks to the malt powder.

Teacher, Country High School, Vacaville, California

Lynne Weddell, Vacaville, California

1 cup butter, softened

1 cup packed brown sugar

1 egg

1-1/4 cups old-fashioned oats

1 cup all-purpose flour

1/2 cup whole wheat flour

1/4 cup malted milk powder

1-1/2 teaspoons baking powder

1/4 teaspoon salt

2 cups coarsely chopped malted milk balls

1. In a large bowl, cream butter and brown sugar until light and fluffy. Beat in egg. Combine the oats, flours, milk powder, baking powder and salt; gradually add to creamed mixture and mix well. Stir in malted milk balls.

2. Drop by heaping tablespoonfuls 3 in. apart onto ungreased baking sheets. Bake at 350° for 10-14 minutes or until set and edges begin to brown. Cool cookies for 2 minutes before removing from pans to wire racks.

YIELD: 2-1/2 DOZEN.

NUTRITION FACTS: 1 cookie equals 158 calories, 8 g fat (5 g saturated fat), 24 mg cholesterol, 103 mg sodium, 20 g carbohydrate, 1 g fiber, 2 g protein.

A+ Recipes from SCHOOLS Across America

Teacher
Taylorville High School

Taylorville, Illinois

As a teacher and chair of the family & consumer sciences department at Taylorville High School, Melissa Williams loves to share her passion for cooking with her students. "I enjoy teaching them hands-on skills they can use in real life, whether in a professional or personal setting," she says. Taylorville High School has a lengthy list of notable graduates, including Pat Perry (1977), who became a Major League Baseball pitcher and pitched in the World Series.

BANANA MOCHA-CHIP MUFFINS

These moist muffins combine two incredible flavors—bananas and chocolate! The addition of coffee makes the muffins even more special.

Melissa Williams, Taylorville, Illinois

5 teaspoons instant coffee granules

5 teaspoons hot water

3/4 cup butter, softened

1-1/4 cups sugar

1 egg

1-1/3 cups mashed ripe bananas

1 teaspoon vanilla extract

2-1/4 cups all-purpose flour

1-1/2 teaspoons baking powder

1/2 teaspoon baking soda

1/2 teaspoon salt

1-1/2 cups semisweet chocolate chips

1. In a small bowl, dissolve coffee granules in hot water. In a large bowl, cream butter and sugar until light and fluffy. Add egg; beat well. Beat in the bananas, vanilla and coffee mixture. Combine the flour, baking powder, baking soda and salt; add to creamed mixture just until moistened. Fold in chocolate chips.

2. Fill paper-lined muffin cups two-thirds full. Bake at 350° for 18-20 minutes or until a toothpick inserted in muffin comes out clean. Cool for 5 minutes before removing from pans to wire racks. Serve warm.

YIELD: 2 DOZEN.

NUTRITION FACTS: 1 muffin equals 198 calories, 9 g fat (6 g saturated fat), 24 mg cholesterol, 145 mg sodium, 29 g carbohydrate, 1 g fiber, 2 g protein.

Teacher
Metcalfe School

Chicago, Illinois

Ellen Woodham-Johnson has been a school social worker for 28 years. She's spent the past 12 years of her career at the Ralph H. Metcalfe School on the far southside of Chicago. "As the school social worker, I have the pleasure of working with all of the school's children and offer counseling services for a variety of problems," she says.

CRAN-ORANGE OATMEAL COOKIES

Dried cranberries, coconut and orange make these crisp, chewy oatmeal cookies a real standout.

Ellen Woodham-Johnson, Matteson, Illinois

1 cup butter, softened

1 cup packed brown sugar

1/2 cup sugar

1 egg

1 tablespoon grated orange peel

1-1/2 teaspoons orange extract

1-3/4 cups all-purpose flour

1 teaspoon baking powder

1/4 teaspoon baking soda

2 cups old-fashioned oats

1 cup dried cranberries

1 cup flaked coconut

1. In a large bowl, cream butter and sugars until light and fluffy. Beat in the egg, orange peel and extract.

2. Combine the flour, baking powder and baking soda; gradually add to creamed mixture and mix well. Stir in the oats, cranberries and coconut. Shape into 1-in. balls; place 2 in. apart on ungreased baking sheets.

3. Bake at 375° for 11-13 minutes or until bottoms are browned. Remove to wire racks.

YIELD: 4 DOZEN.

NUTRITION FACTS: 1 cookie equals 107 calories, 5 g fat (3 g saturated fat), 14 mg cholesterol, 50 mg sodium, 15 g carbohydrate, 1 g fiber, 1 g protein.

DIPPED BROWNIE POPS

I had to have a quick fundraiser for a student organization, so I made these pretty brownie pops. The kids loved them and I sold more than 200 in one afternoon! For s'mores brownie pops, add crushed graham crackers to the dipped chocolate.

Teacher, Minico High School, Rupert, Idaho

Jamie Franklin, Murtaugh, Idaho

---

1 package fudge brownie mix (13-inch x 9-inch pan size)

16 Popsicle sticks

2/3 cup semisweet chocolate chips

3 teaspoons shortening, divided

2/3 cup white baking chips

Assorted sprinkles or chopped pecans

1. Line an 8- or 9-in. square baking pan with foil; grease the foil and set aside. Prepare and bake brownie mix according to the package directions for the size baking pan you used. Cool completely on a wire rack.

2. Using foil, lift brownie out of pan; remove foil. Cut brownie into sixteen squares. Gently insert a Popsicle stick into the side of each square. Cover and freeze for 30 minutes.

3. In a microwave, melt chocolate chips and 1-1/2 teaspoons shortening; stir until smooth. Repeat with white baking chips and remaining shortening.

4. Dip eight brownies halfway into chocolate mixture; allow excess to drip off. Dip remaining brownies halfway into white chip mixture; allow excess to drip off. Sprinkle with toppings of your choice. Place on waxed paper; let stand until set. Place in bags and fasten with twist ties or ribbon if desired.

YIELD: 16 BROWNIE POPS.

NUTRITION FACTS: 1 brownie pop equals 293 calories, 17 g fat (4 g saturated fat), 28 mg cholesterol, 150 mg sodium, 36 g carbohydrate, 1 g fiber, 3 g protein.

OLD-FASHIONED BUTTERSCOTCH CAKE WITH PENUCHE FROSTING

This recipe was passed down to me from my aunt, who was born in the 1920s. That was a time when things were made from scratch from start to finish. The penuche frosting nicely complements the cake.

Teacher, Cory-Rawson, Rawson, Ohio

Beth Vorst, Columbus Grove, Ohio

1-1/2 cups packed brown sugar

1/2 cup shortening

2 eggs

1 teaspoon vanilla extract

2-1/4 cups all-purpose flour

2-1/2 teaspoons baking powder

1 teaspoon salt

1 cup 2% milk

1 cup chopped pecans

PENUCHE FROSTING:

1/2 cup butter, cubed

2 cups packed brown sugar

1/2 cup 2% milk

1/2 teaspoon salt

1 teaspoon vanilla extract

3 cups confectioners' sugar

1. In a large bowl, cream brown sugar and shortening until light and fluffy. Add eggs, one at a time, beating well after each addition. Beat in vanilla. Combine the flour, baking powder and salt; add to the creamed mixture alternately with milk, beating well after each addition. Stir in pecans.

2. Transfer to a greased 13-in. x 9-in. baking pan. Bake at 350° for 25-30 minutes or until a toothpick inserted near the center comes out clean. Cool completely on a wire rack.

3. For frosting, in a small saucepan, melt butter. Stir in the brown sugar, milk and salt. Bring to a boil; cook and stir for 3 minutes. Remove from heat and stir in vanilla. Cool to room temperature, about 20 minutes. Gradually beat in the confectioners' sugar. Frost cake.

YIELD: 18 SERVINGS.

NUTRITION FACTS: 1 piece equals 455 calories, 16 g fat (5 g saturated fat), 38 mg cholesterol, 323 mg sodium, 76 g carbohydrate, 1 g fiber, 4 g protein.

Teacher
Ainsworth Community Schools

Ainsworth, Nebraska

Helping students think beyond themselves, bring beauty to the world and foster teamwork through music is Kim Bejot's goal as a music educator. She currently teaches instrumental music, music appreciation and African drumming. When she isn't teaching, playing music or baking, she's usually volunteering. "I am a longtime volunteer for Destination ImagiNation®, a worldwide creative problem-solving organization. Teaching teamwork, creativity and problem solving to kids is a great way to stay active in mind, body and spirit," she says.

CHOCOLATE RASPBERRY CUPCAKES

These cupcakes are so amazing that people have been known to inhale them in two bites. But most prefer to savor each decadent morsel. The cupcakes can be kept in the fridge for about a week and in the freezer for a month.

Kim Bejot, Ainsworth, Nebraska

1 cup baking cocoa

2 cups boiling water

1 cup butter, softened

2-1/2 cups sugar

4 eggs

2 tablespoons cold strong brewed coffee

2 teaspoons vanilla extract

2-3/4 cups all-purpose flour

2 teaspoons baking soda

1/2 teaspoon baking powder

1/2 teaspoon salt

1 cup seedless raspberry jam

FROSTING:

1 can (13.66 ounces) coconut milk

1 package (12 ounces) dark chocolate chips

1/2 cup butter, cubed

1/3 cup confectioners' sugar

2 tablespoons coffee liqueur

Toasted coconut

1. In a small bowl, combine cocoa and water; set aside to cool.

2. In a large bowl, cream butter and sugar until light and fluffy. Add eggs, one at a time, beating well after each addition. Beat in coffee and vanilla. Combine the flour, baking soda, baking powder and salt; add to creamed mixture alternately with cocoa mixture, beating well after each addition.

3. Fill paper-lined muffin cups two-thirds full. Drop jam by teaspoonfuls into center of each cupcake. Bake at 350° for 18-23 minutes or until a toothpick inserted in the cake portion comes out clean.

4. Cool for 10 minutes before removing from the pans to wire racks to cool completely. Spread 1/2 teaspoon of jam over each cupcake.

5. For frosting, spoon 1 cup cream from top of coconut milk and place in a small saucepan. Bring just to a boil; remove from the heat. Add chocolate chips; whisk until smooth. Stir in butter, confectioners' sugar and coffee liqueur. Refrigerate for 1-1/2 hours or until chilled.

6. In a small bowl, beat chocolate mixture until soft peaks form, about 15 seconds. Frost cupcakes. Garnish with coconut.

YIELD: 2-1/2 DOZEN.

NUTRITION FACTS: 1 cupcake (calculated without toasted coconut) equals 327 calories, 17 g fat (11 g saturated fat), 52 mg cholesterol, 206 mg sodium, 43 g carbohydrate, 1 g fiber, 4 g protein.

Staff, Talala Elementary School

Park Forest, Illinois

Julie Beckwith has been a speech-language pathologist for 15 years. "I love working with the students at Talala Elementary," she says. "They have a clear thirst for learning. It is wonderful to see them take pride in their accomplishments." The school's claim to fame came in the 1960s when the it was used by Coronet Films as a set for the movie, "Courtesy for Beginners." Talala students were used in the movie, and in return, the school received a copy of the film, a new screen and projector.

CARAMEL NUT-CHOCOLATE POPCORN CONES

These adorable treats were inspired by the chocolate-covered ice cream cones I used to eat when I was little. These are even better since there is no melting or dripping! They'll go fast at bake sales.

Julie Beckwith, Crete, Illinois

ICE CREAM CONES:
1 cup (6 ounces) semisweet chocolate chips
1/4 cup heavy whipping cream
12 ice cream sugar cones

CARAMEL CORN:
7 cups air-popped popcorn
1/2 cup semisweet chocolate chips
1/4 cup chopped pecans
25 caramels
2 tablespoons heavy whipping cream
1/8 teaspoon salt

TOPPING:
5 caramels
2 teaspoons heavy whipping cream, divided
1/4 cup semisweet chocolate chips
1/4 cup chopped pecans

1. Tightly cover a large roasting pan that is at least 3-in. deep with two layers of heavy-duty foil. Poke 12 holes, about 2 in. apart, in the foil to hold ice cream cones; set aside.

2. In a microwave-safe bowl, melt chocolate chips and cream; stir until smooth. Spoon about 2 teaspoons inside each cone, turning to coat. Dip rims of cones into chocolate, allowing excess chocolate to drip into bowl. Place cones in prepared pan. Let stand until chocolate is set.

3. Meanwhile, place the popcorn, chocolate chips and pecans in a large bowl; set aside.

4. In a microwave, melt the caramels, cream and salt on high for 2 minutes, stirring occasionally until smooth. Pour over popcorn mixture and toss to coat.

5. Using lightly greased hands, fill cones with popcorn mixture. Shape popcorn into a 2-in.-diameter ball on top of cones, pressing down until popcorn mixture is firmly attached to the cones.

6. For topping, place caramels and 1 teaspoon cream in a small microwave-safe bowl. Microwave on high at 20-second intervals until caramels are melted; stir until smooth. Drizzle over cones.

7. Microwave chocolate chips and remaining cream until smooth. Drizzle over cones. Immediately sprinkle with pecans. Let stand until set. Place in bags and fasten with twist ties or ribbon if desired.

YIELD: 1 DOZEN.

NUTRITION FACTS: 1 cone with about 1/2 cup popcorn mixture equals 335 calories, 17 g fat (7 g saturated fat), 13 mg cholesterol, 125 mg sodium, 48 g carbohydrate, 3 g fiber, 4 g protein.

GET UP & GO MUFFINS

I created this recipe by trial and error. I've only had one outstanding bran muffin at a restaurant and wanted to come up with an awesome one to make myself. These are moist, healthy, not too sweet, and full of grains and fruits. Best of all, they're tasty!

Staff, PUSD#1-Discovery Gardens, Prescott, Arizona

Nancy Rens, Prescott, Arizona

1-1/2 cups bran flakes

1/3 cup boiling water

1 cup whole wheat flour

1 cup all-purpose flour

3/4 cup packed brown sugar

1/3 cup quick-cooking oats

3/4 teaspoon baking powder

1/2 teaspoon baking soda

1/2 teaspoon salt

1 cup buttermilk

1/2 cup unsweetened applesauce

1 egg, beaten

2 tablespoons molasses

3/4 cup fresh or frozen blueberries

3/4 cup pitted dried plums, coarsely chopped

1/4 cup slivered almonds

2 tablespoons honey

1. Place the bran flakes and water in a small bowl. Cover and set aside.

2. In a large bowl, combine the flours, brown sugar, oats, baking powder, baking soda and salt.

3. In a small bowl, combine the buttermilk, applesauce, egg, molasses and bran mixture. Stir into dry ingredients just until moistened. Fold in the blueberries, plums and almonds. Fill greased muffin cups three-fourths full. Drizzle with honey.

4. Bake at 375° for 18-20 minutes or until a toothpick inserted near the center comes out clean. Cool for 5 minutes before removing from pans to wire racks. Serve warm.

YIELD: 1-1/2 DOZEN.

EDITOR'S NOTE: If using frozen blueberries, use without thawing to avoid discoloring the batter.

NUTRITION FACTS: 1 muffin equals 155 calories, 2 g fat (trace saturated fat), 12 mg cholesterol, 166 mg sodium, 33 g carbohydrate, 2 g fiber, 3 g protein. DIABETIC EXCHANGE: 2 starch.

ITALIAN RAINBOW COOKIES

My family has made these classic Italian cookies for generations. This homemade version is so much better than the bakery version. They are a special treat during the holidays or any time of year!

Teacher, JP Case Middle School, Flemington, New Jersey

Cindy Casazza, Hopewell, New Jersey

4 eggs

1 cup sugar

3-1/2 ounces almond paste, cut into small pieces

1 cup all-purpose flour

1 cup butter, melted and cooled

1/2 teaspoon salt

1/2 teaspoon almond extract

6 to 8 drops red food coloring

6 to 8 drops green food coloring

1/4 cup seedless raspberry jam

GLAZE:

1 cup (6 ounces) semisweet chocolate chips

1 teaspoon shortening

1. In a large bowl, beat eggs and sugar for 2 to 3 minutes or until thick and lemon-colored. Gradually add almond paste; mix well. Gradually add the flour, butter, salt and extract.

2. Divide batter into thirds. Tint one portion red and one portion green; leave the remaining portion plain. Spread one portion into each of three well-greased 11-in. x 7-in. baking dishes.

3. Bake at 375° for 7-11 minutes or until a toothpick inserted near the center comes out clean and edges begins to brown. Cool for 10 minutes before removing from pans to wire racks to cool completely.

4. Place red layer on waxed paper; spread with 2 tablespoons jam. Top with plain layer and remaining jam. Add green layer; press down gently.

5. For glaze, in a microwave, melt the chocolate chips and shortening; stir until smooth. Spread half over green layer. Refrigerate for 20 minutes or until set. Turn over; spread remaining glaze over red layer. Refrigerate for 20 minutes or until set.

6. With a sharp knife, trim edges. Cut rectangle lengthwise into fourths. Cut each portion into 1/4-in. slices.

YIELD: 11 DOZEN.

NUTRITION FACTS: 1 cookie equals 35 calories, 2 g fat (1 g saturated fat), 10 mg cholesterol, 21 mg sodium, 4 g carbohydrate, trace fiber, trace protein.

Teacher
Boyertown Area School District

Boyertown, Pennsylvania

Crystal Strick has been teaching family and consumer sciences at the Boyertown Area Senior High School for five years. "The best part of my position is knowing that I am teaching my students skills they will use for the rest of their lives," she says. "I feel privileged to be able to teach the cooking and nutrition classes, as well as the parenting and child development courses."

FROSTED WALNUT BROWNIE CUPS

Have a little taste of heaven with these mini brownie cups. They are always a huge hit and are simple to make.

Crystal Strick, Boyertown, Pennsylvania

2 cups (12 ounces) semisweet chocolate chips

1 cup butter, cubed

1-1/3 cups sugar

4 eggs

2 teaspoons vanilla extract

1 cup all-purpose flour

1 cup chopped walnuts

GANACHE:

2 cups (12 ounces) semisweet chocolate chips

3/4 cup heavy whipping cream

1. In a microwave, melt chocolate chips and butter; whisk until smooth. Cool slightly.

2. In a large bowl, beat sugar and eggs. Stir in the vanilla and chocolate mixture. Gradually add flour; stir in walnuts. Fill paper-lined miniature muffin cups almost full.

3. Bake at 350° for 20-23 minutes or until a toothpick inserted in the center comes out clean. Cool for 5 minutes before removing from pans to wire racks to cool completely.

4. Place chocolate chips in a small bowl. In a small saucepan, bring cream just to a boil. Pour over chocolate; whisk until smooth. Cool for 30 minutes or until ganache reaches a spreading consistency, stirring occasionally. Spread over the brownies.

YIELD: 32 BROWNIE CUPS.

NUTRITION FACTS: 1 brownie cup equals 353 calories, 24 g fat (13 g saturated fat), 49 mg cholesterol, 56 mg sodium, 39 g carbohydrate, 3 g fiber, 4 g protein.

Teacher
High Point School

Orland Park, Illinois

Cindy Beberman is a substitute teacher, primarily at High Point Elementary School in Orland Park, Illinois. For Cindy Beberman, substitute teaching is the perfect job because she gets to enjoy teaching a variety of students at all different learning stages. "I especially love working at High Point School because they make me feel I am a valued member of their team and they are always so helpful," she says. To thank them, she often bakes a batch of these cookies for the staff at the end of the year.

HAZELNUT ESPRESSO FINGERS IN CHOCOLATE

I make these cookies for teachers and staff at Christmas and at the end of the school year. Plus they are very popular at school bake sales. They sell for $6 a dozen and oftentimes, someone asks that I set some aside for later purchase in case we sell out!

Cindy Beberman, Orland Park, Illinois

1-1/2 cups hazelnuts, toasted

1 cup butter, softened

2/3 cup sugar

1 tablespoon instant espresso powder

2 teaspoons vanilla extract

2 cups all-purpose flour

1/2 teaspoon salt

3/4 cup milk chocolate chips

3/4 cup semisweet chocolate chips

2 teaspoons shortening

1. Place hazelnuts in a food processor; cover and process until ground. Set aside. In a large bowl, cream butter and sugar until light and fluffy. Beat in espresso powder and vanilla. Combine flour and salt; gradually add to creamed mixture and mix well.

2. Shape scant tablespoonfuls of dough into 2-in. logs. Place 2 in. apart on ungreased baking sheets. Bake at 350° for 9-11 minutes or until edges are lightly browned. Remove to wire racks to cool completely.

3. In a microwave, melt chocolate chips and shortening; stir until smooth. Dip each cookie halfway, allowing excess to drip off. Place on waxed paper; let stand until set.

YIELD: 5 DOZEN.

NUTRITION FACTS: 1 cookie equals 100 calories, 7 g fat (3 g saturated fat), 9 mg cholesterol, 43 mg sodium, 9 g carbohydrate, 1 g fiber, 1 g protein.

RASPBERRY PECAN SQUARES

The combination of shortbread and raspberry is one of my favorites. And this pair is topped with a pecan pie-like filling. Yum!

Teacher, Walter Johnson Middle School, Morganton, North Carolina

Donna Lindecamp, Morganton, North Carolina

1-1/4 cups all-purpose flour

1/2 cup sugar

1/2 cup cold butter

1/3 cup seedless raspberry jam

TOPPING:

2 eggs

1/2 cup packed brown sugar

2 tablespoons all-purpose flour

1 teaspoon vanilla extract

1/8 teaspoon salt

1/8 teaspoon baking soda

1 cup chopped pecans

1. In a small bowl, combine flour and sugar; cut in butter until crumbly. Press into a greased 9-in. square baking pan. Bake at 350° for 15-20 minutes or until lightly browned. Spread with jam.

2. In a small bowl, whisk the eggs, brown sugar, flour, vanilla, salt and baking soda; stir in pecans. Pour over jam. Bake about 20-25 minutes longer or until set. Cool on a wire rack. Cut into squares.

YIELD: 16 SQUARES.

NUTRITION FACTS: 1 square equals 217 calories, 12 g fat (4 g saturated fat), 41 mg cholesterol, 80 mg sodium, 27 g carbohydrate, 1 g fiber, 3 g protein.

RASPBERRY-ALMOND THUMBPRINT COOKIES

These crisp, buttery thumbprints have a hint of almond and a touch of sweetness from the raspberry jam and a light drizzle of almond glaze.

Staff, Weyerhaeuser Elementary School, Eatonville, Washington

Lana White, Roy, Washington

1 cup butter, softened

2/3 cup sugar

1/2 teaspoon almond extract

2 cups all-purpose flour

1/2 cup seedless raspberry jam

GLAZE:

1/3 cup confectioners' sugar

1/2 teaspoon almond extract

1 teaspoon water

1. In a large bowl, cream butter, sugar and extract until light and fluffy. Add flour and mix well. Chill for 1 hour.

2. Roll into 1-in. balls. Place 2 in. apart on greased baking sheets. Using the end of a wooden spoon handle, make an indentation in the center of each; fill each with 1/4 teaspoon jam. Bake at 350° for 13-16 minutes or until the edges are lightly browned. Remove to wire racks to cool completely.

3. For glaze, in a small bowl, combine the confectioners' sugar, extract and water. Drizzle over cookies.

YIELD: 3-1/2 DOZEN.

NUTRITION FACTS: 1 cookie equals 94 calories, 4 g fat (3 g saturated fat), 11 mg cholesterol, 31 mg sodium, 13 g carbohydrate, trace fiber, 1 g protein.

Teacher
Greenfield School District #75

Fairfield, Montana

Teaching at Greenfield School was Lisa Bedord's first full-time teaching position after living and working in two other locations in Montana with her husband, who also teaches. Lisa's mother attended Greenfield School as a child, and Lisa got to teach the children of four of her cousins. Cooking and good nutrition plays an important role at Greenfield School. The school has participated in the "Farm to School" program, which has students involved in the growing and harvesting of the school's garden produce.

HONEY & OAT YEAST BREAD

This recipe meets the three most important requirements I have for a recipe: easy, healthy, and kid approved! A woman my husband knows shared the directions for this moist, multi-grain bread.

Lisa Bedord, Power, Montana

1/2 cup water

6-1/2 teaspoons butter, divided

1/2 cup old-fashioned oats

1/2 cup unsweetened applesauce

1/4 cup honey

1 teaspoon salt

2 teaspoons active dry yeast

2 tablespoons warm water (110° to 115°)

1 egg

1-1/2 cups whole wheat flour

1-1/4 to 1-3/4 cups all-purpose flour

1. In a small saucepan, bring water and 4-1/2 teaspoons butter just to a boil. In a small bowl, pour boiling liquid over oats. Add the applesauce, honey and salt. Let stand until mixture cools to 110°-115°, stirring occasionally.

2. In a large bowl, dissolve yeast in warm water. Add oatmeal mixture, egg, whole wheat flour and 1 cup all-purpose flour. Beat until smooth. Stir in enough remaining all-purpose flour to form a soft dough (dough will be sticky).

3. Turn onto a floured surface; knead until smooth and elastic, about 6-8 minutes. Place in a greased bowl, turning once to grease the top. Cover and let rise in a warm place until doubled, about 1 hour.

4. Punch dough down. Shape into an 8-in. round loaf on a greased baking sheet. Cover and let rise in a warm place until doubled, about 30 minutes.

5. Melt remaining butter; brush over loaf. Bake at 375° for 25-30 minutes or until golden brown. Cool on wire rack.

YIELD: 1 LOAF (12 WEDGES).

NUTRITION FACTS: 1 wedge equals 162 calories, 3 g fat (2 g saturated fat), 23 mg cholesterol, 219 mg sodium, 30 g carbohydrate, 3 g fiber, 5 g protein. DIABETIC EXCHANGE: 2 starch.

Staff
St. Mary's Catholic School

Sault St. Marie, Michigan

Theresa Miller has been the secretary at St. Mary's Catholic School for 7 years. Prior to that, she worked with her family for nearly 30 years in the restaurant business. In addition to her passion for cooking, she loves music and shares that enthusiasm with the children of St. Mary's during the school week and the annual Christmas program. "The best part of my job is the daily interaction with students, parents, staff and volunteers," she says. "There are milestones I have passed and will never forget, such as the first time a child gave me a card and thanked me for being the best 'principal' ever."

LEMON CORNMEAL COOKIES

Anything lemon makes my day brighter. These soft cookies have a fabulous lemon aroma and a subtle lemon flavor.

Theresa Miller, Sault St. Marie, Michigan

3/4 cup butter, softened

1 package (8 ounces) cream cheese, softened

1 cup sugar

1 cup packed brown sugar

1 egg

3 tablespoons lemon juice

4 teaspoons grated lemon peel

1 tablespoon poppy seeds

3-1/3 cups all-purpose flour

3/4 cup cornmeal

1 teaspoon baking soda

1 teaspoon ground ginger

3/4 teaspoon salt

1 package (10 to 12 ounces) white baking chips

1. In a large bowl, cream the butter, cream cheese and sugars until light and fluffy. Beat in the egg, lemon juice, peel and poppy seeds. Combine the flour, cornmeal, baking soda, ginger and salt; gradually add to creamed mixture and mix well. Stir in chips.

2. Drop by heaping tablespoonfuls 2 in. apart onto parchment paper-lined baking sheets; flatten slightly with a glass. Bake at 350° for 12-15 minutes or until golden brown. Remove to wire racks. Store in an airtight container.

YIELD: 3 DOZEN.

NUTRITION FACTS: 1 cookie equals 199 calories, 9 g fat (5 g saturated fat), 24 mg cholesterol, 141 mg sodium, 28 g carbohydrate, 1 g fiber, 3 g protein.

For someone who loves to bake, Anna Ginsberg's favorite way to volunteer at her daughter's elementary school is by baking special treats for the staff during Teacher Appreciation Week. She also got to showcase her baking skills when her daughter's class celebrated "Culture Day" and students were asked to share foods from different countries. "I brought in homemade scones and talked about Wales," she says. "The fourth graders loved them!"

SWEET & SALTY CANDY

I've been making this candy for the past few years, serving it at Teacher Appreciation lunches and bake sales. It's special because it never fails to win praise from everyone who tries it. For bake sales, I break the candy up and package it in little cellophane bags, which I buy at a craft store.

Volunteer, Clayton Elementary School, Austin, Texas

Anna Ginsberg , Austin, Texas

---

2 cups miniature pretzels, coarsely crushed

1/2 cup corn chips, coarsely crushed

1/2 cup salted peanuts

1/2 cup butter, cubed

1/2 cup packed brown sugar

1-1/2 cups semisweet chocolate chips

1. Line a 13-in. x 9-in. baking pan with foil and grease the foil; set aside. In a large bowl, combine the pretzels, corn chips and peanuts.

2. In a small saucepan, melt butter. Stir in brown sugar until melted. Bring to a boil, stirring frequently. Boil for 1 minute, stirring twice. Pour over the pretzel mixture; toss to coat. Transfer to prepared pan.

3. Bake at 350° for 7 minutes. Sprinkle with chocolate chips. Bake 1-2 minutes longer or until chips are softened. Spread over top. Cool on a wire rack for 1 hour. Break into pieces.

YIELD: ABOUT 1-1/2 POUNDS.

NUTRITION FACTS: 1 ounce equals 136 calories, 9 g fat (4 g saturated fat), 10 mg cholesterol, 99 mg sodium, 15 g carbohydrate, 1 g fiber, 2 g protein.

WHITE CHOCOLATE CRANBERRY BISCOTTI

Over the years, I've adapted my most-requested biscotti recipe to add some of my favorite ingredients: cranberries, white chocolate and pistachios. This biscotti keeps and freezes well.

Teacher, Elmhurst Elementary, Ventura, California

Susan Nelson, Newbury Park, California

3/4 cup sugar

1/2 cup canola oil

2 eggs

1 teaspoon vanilla extract

1-3/4 cups all-purpose flour

1-1/2 teaspoons baking powder

1/2 teaspoon salt

3/4 cup white baking chips

3/4 cup dried cranberries

3/4 cup pistachios

1. In a small bowl, beat sugar and oil until blended. Beat in eggs and vanilla. Combine the flour, baking powder and salt; gradually add to sugar mixture and mix well. Stir in the chips, cranberries and pistachios.

2. Divide dough in half. On a parchment paper-lined baking sheet, shape each half into a 10-in. x 1-1/2-in. rectangle with lightly floured hands. Bake at 325° for 30-35 minutes or until lightly browned.

3. Place pans on wire racks. When cool enough to handle, transfer to a cutting board; cut diagonally with a serrated knife into 1/2-in. slices. Place cut side down on baking sheets. Bake for 6-7 minutes on each side or until golden brown. Remove to wire racks to cool completely.

YIELD: 2-1/2 DOZEN.

NUTRITION FACTS: 1 cookie equals 134 calories, 7 g fat (1 g saturated fat), 15 mg cholesterol, 81 mg sodium, 16 g carbohydrate, 1 g fiber, 2 g protein.

Volunteer
Southside Elementary School

Fernandina Beach, Florida

Susan Scarborough is an artist and photographer, but still finds time to volunteer at the school of her 7-year-old granddaughter, Amiera. She and Amiera often bake and donate goodies like Marshmallow Monkey Business to school functions. "I love to develop new recipes, and the awesome office staff at Southside Elementary School is always willing to do their part with taste testing," she says.

MARSHMALLOW MONKEY BUSINESS

Just like kids, I love fun treats, and these really fit the bill. Plus, they are so easy to make and package! I wrap them in cellophane bags with twist ties. As a variation, make the crispy treat with 3 tablespoons of peanut butter and reduce the butter to 2 tablespoons plus 1-1/2 teaspoons.

Susan Scarborough, Fernandina Beach, Florida

1 package (10 ounces) large marshmallows

3 tablespoons butter

6 cups Rice Krispies

1/2 cup chopped dried banana chips

20 Popsicle sticks

TOPPING:

2 cups (12 ounces) semisweet chocolate chips

2 tablespoons shortening

1/2 cup chopped salted peanuts

1/2 cup chopped dried banana chips

1. In a large saucepan, heat marshmallows and butter until melted. Remove from the heat. Stir in cereal and banana chips; mix well. Cool for 3 minutes.

2. Transfer mixture to waxed paper; divide into 20 portions. With buttered hands, shape each portion around a Popsicle stick to resemble a small banana.

3. In a microwave, melt the chocolate chips and shortening; stir until smooth. Dip the ends of "bananas" in chocolate; allow excess to drip off. Sprinkle with the peanuts and banana chips. Place on waxed paper; let stand until set. Store in an airtight container.

YIELD: 20 SERVINGS.

NUTRITION FACTS: 1 serving equals 235 calories, 12 g fat (6 g saturated fat), 5 mg cholesterol, 111 mg sodium, 33 g carbohydrate, 2 g fiber, 3 g protein.

Staff, Colton High School

Colton, Oregon

Char Ouellette has been the librarian para professional at Colton High School since September 1998. "I think the best part of my job is the connection I have established with the students," she says, adding that it's not uncommon for former students to stop by and pay her a visit. She is very proud to be a member of the Colton High School staff, which has been recognized at the national and state level for its educational programs. Most recently, it was named as a National Model School.

RASPBERRY-CREAM CHEESE LADDER LOAVES

Created by my dear friend Debbie, this is a delicious way to start your day. The bread may be sprinkled with granulated sugar before baking if desired.

Char Ouellette and Debbie Schwindt, Colton, Oregon

3-3/4 to 4-1/4 cups all-purpose flour

1/4 cup sugar

1 package (1/4 ounce) quick-rise yeast

1-1/4 teaspoons salt

1 teaspoon baking powder

1/2 cup buttermilk

1/2 cup sour cream

1/4 cup butter, cubed

1/4 cup water

1 egg

1/2 teaspoon almond extract

FILLING:

1 package (8 ounces) cream cheese, softened

1/4 cup sugar

3 tablespoons all-purpose flour

1 egg yolk

1/3 cup seedless raspberry jam

1. In a large bowl, combine 2 cups flour, sugar, yeast, salt and baking powder. In a small saucepan, heat the buttermilk, sour cream, butter and water to 120°-130°; add to dry ingredients. Beat on medium speed for 2 minutes. Add the egg, extract and 1/2 cup flour; beat 2 minutes longer. Stir in enough remaining flour to form a soft dough.

2. Turn dough onto a floured surface; knead until smooth and elastic, about 6-8 minutes. Cover and let rest for 10 minutes.

3. Meanwhile, in a small bowl, beat the cream cheese, sugar, flour and egg yolk until smooth; set aside.

4. Divide dough in half. Roll each piece into a 12-in. x 10-in. rectangle; place on greased baking sheets. Spread cheese mixture down the center of each rectangle. Stir jam; spoon over cheese mixture.

5. On each long side, cut 3/4-in.-wide strips about 2-1/2 in. into center. Starting at one end, fold alternating strips at an angle across filling; pinch ends to seal. Cover and let rise until doubled, about 1 hour.

6. Bake at 350° for 15-19 minutes or until golden brown. Cool on wire racks. Store leftovers in refrigerator.

YIELD: 2 LOAVES (8 SLICES EACH).

NUTRITION FACTS: 1 slice equals 262 calories, 10 g fat (6 g saturated fat), 54 mg cholesterol, 288 mg sodium, 37 g carbohydrate, 1 g fiber, 6 g protein.

S'MORES ON A STICK

My kids love to take these for treats everywhere. That's lucky for me since they are so easy to make. Beside the sprinkles, try mini candies for toppings.

Staff, Plains Elementary School USD #483, Plains, Kansas

Ronda Weirich, Plains, Kansas

---

1 can (14 ounces) sweetened condensed milk, divided

1 cup miniature marshmallows

1-1/2 cups miniature semisweet chocolate chips, divided

24 whole graham crackers, broken in half

Assorted sprinkles

24 Popsicle sticks

1. In a small microwave-safe bowl, microwave 2/3 cup milk on high for 1-1/2 minutes. Add marshmallows and 1 cup chips; stir until smooth. Drop by tablespoonfuls onto 24 graham cracker halves; spread evenly. Top with remaining graham cracker halves; press down gently.

2. Microwave remaining milk for 1-1/2 minutes. Add remaining chips; stir until smooth. Drizzle over cookies; decorate with sprinkles. Let stand for 2 hours before inserting a Popsicle stick into the center of each.

YIELD: 2 DOZEN.

NUTRITION FACTS: 1 serving equals 177 calories, 6 g fat (3 g saturated fat), 6 mg cholesterol, 118 mg sodium, 30 g carbohydrate, 1 g fiber, 3 g protein.

PEANUT BUTTER OATMEAL-CHIP COOKIES

This is a favorite of mine, my husband's, my classes' and my colleagues'. These cookies are just plain yummy! It also makes about 11 dozen...bake sale, here we come!

Teacher, Bearden Elementary, Okemah, Oklahoma

Dana Chew, Okemah, Oklahoma

2-1/2 cups butter, softened

2 cups sugar

2 cups packed brown sugar

1/2 cup creamy peanut butter

4 eggs

2 teaspoons vanilla extract

6 cups all-purpose flour

2 teaspoons salt

2 teaspoons baking soda

1/2 teaspoon baking powder

1 package (12 ounces) semisweet chocolate chips

1 package (11 ounces) peanut butter and milk chocolate chips

1 cup quick-cooking oats

1. In a large bowl, cream the butter, sugars and peanut butter until light and fluffy. Beat in eggs and vanilla. Combine the flour, salt, baking soda and baking powder; gradually add to creamed mixture and mix well.

2. Stir in the chips and oats. Drop by rounded tablespoonfuls 2 in. apart onto ungreased baking sheets. Bake at 375° for 9-12 minutes or until golden brown.

3. Cool for 2 minutes before removing from pans to wire racks.

YIELD: 11 DOZEN.

NUTRITION FACTS: 1 cookie equals 109 calories, 6 g fat (3 g saturated fat), 16 mg cholesterol, 93 mg sodium, 14 g carbohydrate, trace fiber, 1 g protein.

ASIAN STEAK SKEWERS

I'm always on the lookout for light meals that will satisfy my family, and these stuffed kabobs fit the bill. Served with a creamy mustard sauce, the colorful bundles are special enough for company.

Gina Hatchell, Mickleton, New Jersey

1 pound beef sirloin tip roast
1/3 cup reduced-sodium soy sauce
1/4 cup sugar
1/2 teaspoon ground ginger
1 cup water
4 medium carrots, julienned
1/2 pound fresh green beans, trimmed
1 large sweet red pepper, julienned
1/2 cup reduced-fat sour cream
2 tablespoons Dijon mustard
1-1/4 teaspoons prepared horseradish

1. Cut beef widthwise into 16 slices, 1/4 in. thick. In a large resealable plastic bag, combine soy sauce, sugar and ginger; add beef. Seal bag and turn to coat; refrigerate for 4 hours.

2. In a large saucepan, bring water and carrots to a boil. Reduce heat; cover and simmer for 3 minutes. Add the beans and red pepper; cover and simmer for 3-5 minutes or until vegetables are crisp-tender. Drain and immediately place vegetables in ice water. Drain and pat dry.

3. Drain and discard marinade. Arrange three beans, one carrot strip and one pepper strip down the center of each beef slice; roll up. For each kabob, use metal or soaked wooden skewers and thread two bundles on two parallel skewers.

4. Using long-handled tongs, moisten a paper towel with cooking oil and lightly coat grill rack. Grill kabobs, covered, over medium heat or broil 4 in. from the heat for 3-5 minutes on each side or until beef reaches desired doneness.

5. In a small bowl, combine sour cream, Dijon mustard and horseradish. Serve with kabobs.

YIELD: 4 SERVINGS.

NUTRITION FACTS: 4 rolls equals 304 calories, 10 g fat (5 g saturated fat), 87 mg cholesterol, 542 mg sodium, 21 g carbohydrate, 5 g fiber, 31 g protein. DIABETIC EXCHANGES: 4 lean meat, 3 vegetable, 1/2 fat.

CRUNCHY ROMAINE STRAWBERRY SALAD

This pretty salad is a hit at every event we've attended. It's a cinch to fix, and the combination of tastes and textures pleases every palate.

Leslie Lancaster, Zachary, Louisiana

1 package (3 ounces) ramen noodles

1 cup chopped walnuts

1/4 cup butter

1/4 cup sugar

1/4 cup canola oil

2 tablespoons red wine vinegar

1/2 teaspoon soy sauce

8 cups torn romaine

1/2 cup chopped green onions

2 cups fresh strawberries, sliced

1. Discard seasoning packet from ramen noodles or save for another use. Break noodles into small pieces. In a large skillet, cook noodles and walnuts in butter over medium heat for 8-10 minutes or until golden; cool.

2. For dressing, in a small bowl, whisk the sugar, oil, vinegar and soy sauce. Just before serving, combine the romaine, onions, strawberries and noodle mixture in a large bowl. Drizzle with dressing and toss gently.

YIELD: 12 SERVINGS.

NUTRITION FACTS: 1 cup equals 200 calories, 16 g fat (4 g saturated fat), 10 mg cholesterol, 81 mg sodium, 13 g carbohydrate, 2 g fiber, 4 g protein.

COLORFUL CHICKEN 'N' SQUASH SOUP

When I turned 40, I decided to live a healthier lifestyle, which included cooking better foods for my family. I make this soup every week, and everyone loves it.

Trina Bigham, Fairhaven, Massachusetts

1 broiler/fryer chicken (4 pounds), cut up

13 cups water

5 pounds butternut squash, peeled and cubed (about 10 cups)

1 bunch kale, trimmed and chopped

6 medium carrots, chopped

2 large onions, chopped

3 teaspoons salt

1. Place chicken and water in a stockpot. Bring to a boil. Reduce heat; cover and simmer for 1 hour or until chicken is tender.

2. Remove chicken from broth. Strain broth and skim fat. Return broth to the pan; add the squash, kale, carrots and onions. Bring to a boil. Reduce heat; cover and simmer for 25-30 minutes or until vegetables are tender.

3. When chicken is cool enough to handle, remove meat from bones and cut into bite-size pieces. Discard bones and skin. Add chicken and salt to soup; heat through.

YIELD: 14 SERVINGS (5-1/2 QUARTS).

NUTRITION FACTS: 1-1/2 cups equals 228 calories, 8 g fat (2 g saturated fat), 50 mg cholesterol, 579 mg sodium, 22 g carbohydrate, 6 g fiber, 18 g protein. DIABETIC EXCHANGES: 2 lean meat, 1 starch, 1 vegetable, 1/2 fat.

ONION BEEF AU JUS

Garlic, onions, soy sauce and onion soup mix flavor the tender beef in these savory, hot sandwiches served with a tasty, rich broth for dipping. The seasoned beef makes delicious cold sandwiches, too.

Marilyn Brown, West Union, Iowa

1 beef rump roast bottom round roast (4 pounds)
2 tablespoons canola oil
2 large sweet onions, cut into 1/4-inch slices
6 tablespoons butter, softened
5 cups water
1/2 cup soy sauce
1 envelope onion soup mix
1 garlic clove, minced
1 teaspoon browning sauce, optional
1 loaf (1 pound) French bread
1 cup (4 ounces) shredded Swiss cheese

1. In a Dutch oven over medium-high heat, brown roast on all sides in oil; drain. In a large skillet, saute onions in 2 tablespoons of butter until tender. Add the water, soy sauce, soup mix, garlic and browning sauce if desired. Pour over roast. Cover and bake at 325° for 2-1/2 hours or until meat is tender.

2. Let stand for 10 minutes before slicing. Return meat to pan juices. Slice bread in half lengthwise; cut into 3-in. sections. Spread remaining butter over bread.

3. Place bread on a baking sheet. Broil 4-6 in. from the heat for 2-3 minutes or until golden brown. Top bread with beef and onions; sprinkle with cheese. Broil 4-6 in. from the heat for 1-2 minutes or until cheese is melted. Serve with pan juices.

YIELD: 12 SERVINGS.

NUTRITION FACTS: 1 piece equals 422 calories, 19 g fat (8 g saturated fat), 114 mg cholesterol, 1,179 mg sodium, 24 g carbohydrate, 2 g fiber, 38 g protein.

FOUR-CHEESE BAKED ZITI

This pasta dish, made with Alfredo sauce, is deliciously different from typical tomato-based recipes. Extra cheesy, it goes together quickly and is always popular at potlucks.

Lisa Varner, Charleston, South Carolina

1 package (16 ounces) ziti small tube pasta

2 cartons (10 ounces) refrigerated Alfredo sauce

1 cup (8 ounces) sour cream

2 eggs, lightly beaten

1 carton (15 ounces) ricotta cheese

1/2 cup grated Parmesan cheese, divided

1/4 cup grated Romano cheese

1/4 cup minced fresh parsley

1-3/4 cups shredded part-skim mozzarella cheese

1. Cook pasta according to package directions; drain and return to the pan. Stir in Alfredo sauce and sour cream. Spoon half into a lightly greased 3-qt. baking dish.

2. Combine the eggs, ricotta cheese, 1/4 cup Parmesan cheese, Romano cheese and parsley; spread over pasta. Top with remaining pasta mixture; sprinkle with mozzarella and remaining Parmesan.

3. Cover and bake at 350° for 25 minutes or until a thermometer reads 160°. Uncover; bake 5-10 minutes longer or until bubbly.

YIELD: 12 SERVINGS.

NUTRITION FACTS: 1-1/3 cups equals 667 calories, 39 g fat (20 g saturated fat), 145 mg cholesterol, 1,037 mg sodium, 50 g carbohydrate, 2 g fiber, 29 g protein.

OATMEAL SURPRISE COOKIES

Chocolate-covered raisins and the warm, autumn flavor of pumpkin-pie spice turn these oatmeal cookies into prize-winning gourmet treats! Kids of all ages will down them by the dozen.

Rebecca Clark, Warrior, Alabama

1 cup butter, softened

3/4 cup packed brown sugar

1/2 cup sugar

2 eggs

1-1/2 cups all-purpose flour

1 teaspoon baking soda

1 teaspoon pumpkin pie spice

2-3/4 cups quick-cooking oats

1-1/2 cups chocolate-covered raisins

1. In a large bowl, cream butter and sugars until light and fluffy. Beat in eggs. Combine the flour, baking soda and pumpkin pie spice; gradually add to creamed mixture and mix well. Stir in oats and raisins.

2. Drop by tablespoonfuls 2 in. apart onto greased baking sheets. Flatten slightly. Bake at 350° for 13-15 minutes or until golden brown. Cool for 5 minutes before removing to wire racks. Store in an airtight container.

YIELD: 3 DOZEN.

NUTRITION FACTS: 1 cookie equals 149 calories, 7 g fat (4 g saturated fat), 25 mg cholesterol, 80 mg sodium, 21 g carbohydrate, 1 g fiber, 2 g protein. DIABETIC EXCHANGES: 1-1/2 starch, 1 fat.

WHITE CHOCOLATE MOUSSE CHERRY PIE

A cookie crust is topped with a cherry-almond filling and light-as-air mousse in this delectable dessert. It makes any dinner extra special.

Bernice Janowski, Stevens Point, Wisconsin

14 cream-filled chocolate sandwich cookies

3/4 cup chopped macadamia nuts

2 tablespoons butter, melted

FILLING:

1 tablespoon cornstarch

2 tablespoons water

1 can (21 ounces) cherry pie filling

1/2 teaspoon almond extract

WHITE CHOCOLATE MOUSSE:

1 cup cold 2% milk

1 package (3.3 ounces) instant white chocolate
  pudding mix

1 envelope unflavored gelatin

3 cups heavy whipping cream, divided

1/4 cup sugar

1/4 teaspoon almond extract

Chocolate curls, optional

1. In a food processor, combine cookies and nuts; cover and process until cookies are finely chopped. Add butter; cover and pulse until mixture resembles coarse crumbs.

2. Press onto the bottom and up the sides of an ungreased 9-in. deep-dish pie plate. Bake at 350° for 8-10 minutes or until set. Cool on a wire rack.

3. For filling, combine cornstarch and water in a small saucepan until smooth. Stir in pie filling. Bring to a boil; cook and stir for 1 minute or until slightly thickened. Remove from the heat; stir in extract. Cool completely.

4. For mousse, in a large bowl, whisk milk and pudding mix for 2 minutes; set aside. In a small saucepan, sprinkle gelatin over 1/2 cup cream; let stand for 1 minute. Heat over low heat, stirring until gelatin is completely dissolved. Remove from the heat.

5. In a large bowl, beat remaining cream until it begins to thicken. Add sugar and almond extract; beat until soft peaks form. Gradually beat in gelatin mixture. Fold into pudding. Refrigerate until slightly firm, about 30 minutes.

6. Spread cooled filling into crust; top with mousse. Refrigerate for 2 hours or until firm. Garnish with chocolate curls if desired.

YIELD: 8-10 SERVINGS.

NUTRITION FACTS: 1 piece equals 556 calories, 40 g fat (20 g saturated fat), 107 mg cholesterol, 338 mg sodium, 46 g carbohydrate, 2 g fiber, 5 g protein.

TERRIFIC TOMATO TART

This recipe is fabulous! Fresh colorful tomatoes, feta cheese and prepared pesto perfectly complement the crispy phyllo dough crust.

Diane Halferty, Corpus Christi, Texas

12 sheets phyllo dough (14 inches x 9 inches)

2 tablespoons olive oil

2 tablespoons dry bread crumbs

2 tablespoons prepared pesto

3/4 cup crumbled feta cheese, divided

1 medium tomato, cut into 1/4-inch slices

1 large yellow tomato, cut into 1/4-inch slices

1/4 teaspoon pepper

5 to 6 fresh basil leaves, thinly sliced

1. Place one sheet of phyllo dough on a baking sheet lined with parchment paper; brush with 1/2 teaspoon oil and sprinkle with 1/2 teaspoon bread crumbs. (Keep remaining phyllo covered with plastic wrap and a damp towel to prevent it from drying out.) Repeat layers, being careful to brush oil all the way to edges.

2. Fold each side 3/4 in. toward center to form a rim. Spread with the pesto and sprinkle with half of the feta cheese. Alternately arrange the red and yellow tomato slices over cheese. Sprinkle with pepper and remaining feta.

3. Bake at 400° for 20-25 minutes or until crust is golden brown and crispy. Cool on a wire rack for 5 minutes. Remove the parchment paper before cutting. Garnish with basil.

YIELD: 8 SERVINGS.

NUTRITION FACTS: 1 piece equals 135 calories, 7 g fat (2 g saturated fat), 7 mg cholesterol, 221 mg sodium, 13 g carbohydrate, 1 g fiber, 5 g protein. DIABETIC EXCHANGES: 1-1/2 fat, 1 starch.

SWEET PEPPER SANDWICHES

We love this recipe because it's easy and vegetarian. Family members assemble their own sandwiches to their liking.

Cara Neth, Fort Collins, Colorado

1 each small green, sweet red and yellow pepper, thinly sliced

1 small onion, thinly sliced

1 tablespoon olive oil

1 garlic clove, minced

1 tablespoon balsamic vinegar

2 ounces fresh mozzarella cheese

1/4 cup fat-free mayonnaise

1/2 teaspoon prepared horseradish

4 hard rolls, split and toasted

8 fresh basil leaves

1 plum tomato, thinly sliced

1. In a large nonstick skillet, saute peppers and onion in oil until crisp-tender. Add garlic; cook 1 minute longer. Drizzle with vinegar; toss to coat.

2. Cut mozzarella cheese into four slices. Combine mayonnaise and horseradish; spread over cut sides of rolls. Spoon the vegetable mixture onto bottom halves; top with cheese.

3. Broil 4-6 in. from the heat for 2-4 minutes or until cheese is melted. Top with basil leaves and tomato. Replace roll tops.

YIELD: 4 SERVINGS.

NUTRITION FACTS: 1 sandwich equals 278 calories, 10 g fat (3 g saturated fat), 13 mg cholesterol, 456 mg sodium, 39 g carbohydrate, 3 g fiber, 9 g protein. DIABETIC EXCHANGES: 2 starch, 1-1/2 fat, 1 vegetable.

PEPPERONI SPINACH QUICHE

Several years ago, I had to come up with a dish to serve at a pool party, and this colorful quiche was a hit.

Elynor Townsend, Summerfield, Florida

1 tube (8 ounces) refrigerated crescent rolls

1 large sweet red pepper, chopped

1 tablespoon olive oil

1 garlic clove, minced

5 eggs, lightly beaten

1/2 cup shredded part-skim mozzarella cheese

1/2 cup frozen chopped spinach, thawed and squeezed dry

1/4 cup sliced pepperoni, cut into strips

1/4 cup half-and-half cream

2 tablespoons grated Parmesan cheese

1 tablespoon minced fresh parsley

1 tablespoon minced fresh basil or 1 teaspoon dried basil

Dash pepper

1. Separate crescent dough into eight triangles; place in an ungreased 9-in. fluted tart pan with removable bottom with points toward the center. Press onto the bottom and up the sides to form a crust; seal seams. Set aside.

2. In a small skillet, saute red pepper in oil until tender. Add garlic; cook 1 minute longer. Remove from heat. In another small bowl, combine the remaining ingredients; stir in red pepper mixture. Pour into crust.

3. Bake at 375° for 25-30 minutes or until a knife inserted near the center comes out clean. Let stand for 5 minutes.

YIELD: 8 SERVINGS.

NUTRITION FACTS: 1 piece equals 235 calories, 15 g fat (5 g saturated fat), 145 mg cholesterol, 417 mg sodium, 14 g carbohydrate, 1 g fiber, 10 g protein.

SPICY PORK WITH GINGER-MAPLE SAUCE

My physical therapist shared this recipe with me and said it was completely foolproof. She was right. It's a real winner. I serve it with sauteed green beans.

Juanita Moore, Dana Point, California

2 teaspoons chili powder

1 teaspoon ground cinnamon

1 teaspoon pepper

1/2 teaspoon salt

1/4 teaspoon ground allspice

1 pork tenderloin (3/4 pound)

1/2 teaspoon olive oil

SAUCE:

1/2 cup chopped onion

1 tablespoon butter

1 teaspoon minced fresh gingerroot

1/2 cup chicken broth

1/4 cup maple syrup

1 tablespoon diced crystallized ginger

1. In a small bowl, combine chili powder, ground cinnamon, pepper, salt and ground allspice. Rub over pork. In a large skillet, brown the pork in oil on all sides. Transfer to an 11-in. x 7-in. baking dish coated with cooking spray. Bake, uncovered, at 375° for 15 minutes.

2. Meanwhile, in a small skillet, saute onion in butter until tender. Add fresh ginger; saute 1-2 minutes longer. Stir in broth, syrup and candied ginger. Bring to a boil; cook until sauce is reduced to about 1/2 cup. Pour over pork.

3. Bake 5-10 minutes longer or until a meat thermometer reads 160°. Let stand for 5 minutes before slicing.

YIELD: 2 SERVINGS.

NUTRITION FACTS: 1 serving equals 395 calories, 11 g fat (4 g saturated fat), 105 mg cholesterol, 883 mg sodium, 40 g carbohydrate, 3 g fiber, 36 g protein.

LEMONY VEGETABLES AND PASTA

The simplicity and flavor combination in this refreshing pasta dish are typical of authentic Italian cuisine. Buon appetito!

Erin Renouf Mylroie, Santa Clara, Utah

1 pound fresh asparagus, trimmed and cut into
  1-inch pieces
1 medium sweet red pepper, cut into 1-inch pieces
1 medium red onion, sliced
1 tablespoon olive oil
1/2 teaspoon salt
1/4 teaspoon pepper
4-1/2 cups uncooked bow tie pasta
1 tablespoon butter
1 tablespoon all-purpose flour
3 garlic cloves, minced
1/4 teaspoon crushed red pepper flakes
1 cup vegetable broth
1 cup shredded Parmesan cheese
1/2 cup sour cream
2 tablespoons lemon juice
1 tablespoon grated lemon peel
1/2 cup chopped pistachios
1/4 cup fresh basil leaves, thinly sliced
Additional shredded Parmesan cheese

1. In a large bowl, combine the first six ingredients. Transfer to a greased 15-in. x 10-in. x 1-in. baking pan. Bake at 450° for 10-15 minutes or until golden brown, stirring once.

2. Meanwhile, cook pasta according to package directions. In a large saucepan, melt butter over medium heat. Stir in flour, garlic and pepper flakes until blended. Whisk in broth until blended. Bring to a boil over medium-high heat; cook and stir for 2 minutes or until thickened and bubbly.

3. Reduce heat. Stir in cheese, sour cream, lemon juice and peel; heat through. Drain pasta and place in a large bowl. Add cheese sauce and asparagus mixture; toss to coat. Sprinkle with pistachios, basil and additional cheese.

YIELD: 7 SERVINGS.

NUTRITION FACTS: 1-1/2 cups equals 366 calories, 15 g fat (6 g saturated fat), 24 mg cholesterol, 559 mg sodium, 45 g carbohydrate, 4 g fiber, 15 g protein.

PEACHY SHRIMP TACOS

With three always-on-the-go teens, we often only have about 10 minutes to prepare dinner. This simple recipe has become a family favorite. You may use flour tortillas or even hard taco shells, but I like to use corn tortillas because of their slightly higher fiber content.

Veronica Callaghan, Glastonbury, Connecticut

1 cup salsa

1 cup frozen unsweetened sliced peaches, thawed and diced

1 pound cooked medium shrimp, peeled and deveined

1 tablespoon minced fresh cilantro

1-1/2 cups shredded Chinese napa cabbage

6 corn tortillas (6 inches), warmed

1. In a large skillet, combine salsa and peaches over medium heat until warmed. Add shrimp and cilantro; cook and stir until heated through.

2. Place 1/4 cupful cabbage down the center of each tortilla; top with a scant 1/2 cupful shrimp mixture.

YIELD: 6 SERVINGS.

NUTRITIONAL FACTS: 1 taco equals 165 calories, 2 g fat (trace saturated fat), 115 mg cholesterol, 308 mg sodium, 19 g carbohydrate, 2 g fiber, 17 g protein. DIABETIC EXCHANGES: 2 very lean meat, 1 starch.

BARBECUE PORK AND PENNE SKILLET

I'm the mother of four children and am an elementary school principal. Simple, delightful and quick meals are perfect for us.

Judy Armstrong, Prairieville, Louisiana

1 package (16 ounces) penne pasta

1 cup chopped sweet red pepper

3/4 cup chopped onion

1 tablespoon butter

1 tablespoon olive oil

3 garlic cloves, minced

1 carton (18 ounces) refrigerated fully cooked barbecued shredded pork

1 can (14-1/2 ounces) diced tomatoes with mild green chilies, undrained

1/2 cup beef broth

1 teaspoon ground cumin

1 teaspoon pepper

1/4 teaspoon salt

1-1/4 cups shredded cheddar cheese

1/4 cup chopped green onions

1. Cook pasta according to package directions. Meanwhile, in a large skillet, saute the red pepper and onion in butter and oil until tender. Add garlic; saute 1 minute longer. Stir in pork, tomatoes, broth, cumin, pepper and salt; heat through.

2. Drain the pasta. Add pasta and cheese to the pork mixture. Sprinkle with green onions.

YIELD: 8 SERVINGS.

NUTRITION FACTS: 1-1/4 cups equals 428 calories, 11 g fat (6 g saturated fat), 40 mg cholesterol, 903 mg sodium, 61 g carbohydrate, 4 g fiber, 20 g protein.

ITALIAN PEASANT SOUP

My father shared this quick soup with me. Loaded with sausage, chicken, and beans, it's nice for special occasions, too.

Kim Knight, Hamburg, Pennsylvania

1 pound Italian sausage links, casings removed and cut into 1-inch slices

2 medium onions, chopped

6 garlic cloves, chopped

1 pound boneless skinless chicken breasts, cut into 1-inch cubes

2 cans (15 ounces each) cannellini beans, rinsed and drained

2 cans (14-1/2 ounces) chicken broth

2 cans (14-1/2 ounces) diced tomatoes

1 teaspoon dried basil

1 teaspoon dried oregano

6 cups fresh spinach leaves, chopped

Shredded Parmesan cheese, optional

1. In a Dutch oven, cook sausage and onions over medium heat until no longer pink. Add garlic; cook 1 minute longer. Drain. Add chicken; cook and stir until no longer pink.

2. Stir in beans, broth, tomatoes, basil and oregano. Bring to a boil. Reduce heat; simmer, uncovered, for 10 minutes. Add spinach; heat just until wilted. Serve with cheese if desired.

YIELD: 11 SERVINGS (2-3/4 QUARTS).

NUTRITION FACTS: 1 cup equals 169 calories, 7 g fat (2 g saturated fat), 39 mg cholesterol, 471 mg sodium, 11 g carbohydrate, 3 g fiber, 16 g protein.

GRILLED VEGETABLE SANDWICH

Meat lovers won't even miss the meat, but they will rave about the flavor of this hearty grilled veggie sandwich!

Diana Tseperkas, Hamden, Connecticut

1 medium zucchini, thinly sliced lengthwise

1 medium sweet red pepper, quartered

1 small red onion, cut into 1/2-inch slices

1/4 cup prepared Italian salad dressing

1 loaf ciabatta bread (14 ounces), halved lengthwise

2 tablespoons olive oil

1/4 cup reduced-fat mayonnaise

1 tablespoon lemon juice

2 teaspoons grated lemon peel

1 teaspoon minced garlic

1/2 cup crumbled feta cheese

1. In a large resealable plastic bag, combine zucchini, pepper, onion and salad dressing. Seal the bag and turn to coat; refrigerate for at least 1 hour. Drain and discard marinade.

2. Brush cut sides of bread with oil; set aside. Place vegetables on grill rack. Grill the vegetables, covered, over medium heat for 4-5 minutes on each side or until crisp-tender. Remove and keep warm. Grill the bread, oil side down, over medium heat for 30-60 seconds or until toasted.

3. In a small bowl, combine mayonnaise, lemon juice, peel and garlic. Spread over bread bottom; sprinkle with cheese. Top with vegetables and remaining bread. Cut into four slices.

YIELD: 4 SERVINGS.

NUTRITION FACTS: 1 sandwich equals 484 calories, 20 g fat (4 g saturated fat), 13 mg cholesterol, 862 mg sodium, 69 g carbohydrate, 5 g fiber, 13 g protein.

CHICKEN VEGGIE CUPS

Frozen puff pastry makes these rich snacks a snap to prepare. Sometimes, I put a slice on top of each before baking.

Marty Kingery, Point Pleasant, West Virginia

2-1/2 cups diced cooked chicken breast

1 can (10-3/4 ounces) reduced-fat reduced-sodium condensed cream of chicken soup, undiluted

1 cup frozen chopped broccoli, thawed and drained

2 small plum tomatoes, seeded and chopped

1 small carrot, grated

1 tablespoon Dijon mustard

1 garlic clove, minced

1/4 teaspoon pepper

1 sheet frozen puff pastry, thawed

1/4 cup grated Parmesan cheese

1. In a large bowl, combine the first eight ingredients; set aside. On a lightly floured surface, roll pastry into a 12-in. x 9-in. rectangle. Cut lengthwise into four strips and widthwise into three strips. Gently press the puff pastry squares into muffin cups coated with cooking spray.

2. Spoon chicken mixture into pastry cups. Sprinkle with the Parmesan. Bake at 375° for 25-30 minutes or until golden brown. Serve warm.

YIELD: 1 DOZEN.

NUTRITION FACTS: 1 appetizer equals 182 calories, 10 g fat (3 g saturated fat), 23 mg cholesterol, 310 mg sodium, 13 g carbohydrate, 1 g fiber, 10 g protein.

CRANBERRY RICE WITH CARAMELIZED ONIONS

The sweet-tart flavor of cranberries accents this rice combination and gives a festive feel to everyday meals.

Tommi Roylance, Charlo, Montana

2-1/2 cups chicken vegetable broth

1/2 cup each uncooked wild rice and brown rice

3 medium onions, cut into wedges

2 teaspoons brown sugar

3 tablespoons butter

1 cup dried cranberries

1/2 teaspoon grated orange peel

1. In a large saucepan, bring broth to a boil. Add the wild rice. Reduce heat; cover and simmer for 10 minutes. Add brown rice. Cover; simmer for 45-50 minutes or until rice is tender and liquid is absorbed.

2. In a large skillet over medium heat, cook onions and brown sugar in butter until golden brown, stirring frequently. Add cranberries, orange peel and rice; heat through.

YIELD: 4 SERVINGS.

NUTRITION FACTS: 1 cup equals 400 calories, 10 g fat (5 g saturated fat), 23 mg cholesterol, 674 mg sodium, 74 g carbohydrate, 6 g fiber, 8 g protein.

A+ Recipes from SCHOOLS Across America

VEGGIE SHRIMP EGG ROLLS

These wonderful starters will be the hit of your next cocktail party. Try them with cooked crab, lobster or chicken instead. The apricot dipping sauce comes together in a pinch.

Carole Resnick, Cleveland, Ohio

2 teaspoons minced fresh gingerroot

1 garlic clove, minced

3 tablespoons olive oil, divided

1/2 pound uncooked medium shrimp, peeled, deveined and chopped

2 green onions, finely chopped

1 medium carrot, finely chopped

1 medium sweet red pepper, finely chopped

1 cup canned bean sprouts, rinsed and finely chopped

2 tablespoons water

2 tablespoons reduced-sodium soy sauce

38 wonton wrappers

APRICOT-MUSTARD DIPPING SAUCE:

3/4 cup apricot spreadable fruit

1 tablespoon water

1 tablespoon lime juice

1 tablespoon reduced-sodium soy sauce

1-1/2 teaspoons Dijon mustard

1/4 teaspoon minced fresh gingerroot

1. In a large skillet, saute ginger and garlic in 1 tablespoon oil over medium heat for 1 minute. Add the shrimp, onions, carrot, red pepper, bean sprouts, water and soy sauce; cook and stir for 2-3 minutes or until vegetables are crisp-tender and shrimp turn pink.

2. Reduce heat to low; cook for 4-5 minutes or the liquid has evaporated. Remove from the heat; let stand for 15 minutes.

3. Place a tablespoonful of shrimp mixture in the center of a wonton wrapper. (Keep wrappers covered with a damp paper towel until ready to use.) Fold bottom corner over filling. Fold sides toward center over filling. Moisten the remaining corner with water; roll up tightly to seal.

4. In a large skillet over medium heat, cook egg rolls, a few at a time, in remaining oil for 5-7 minutes on each side or until golden brown. Drain on paper towels.

5. In a blender, combine sauce ingredients; cover and process until smooth. Serve with egg rolls.

YIELD: 38 EGG ROLLS.

NUTRITIONAL FACTS: 2 egg rolls equals 108 calories, 3 g fat (trace saturated fat), 19 mg cholesterol, 222 mg sodium, 17 g carbohydrate, 1 g fiber, 4 g protein.
DIABETIC EXCHANGES: 1 starch, 1/2 fat.

ROASTED CHICKEN WITH GARLIC-SHERRY SAUCE

This garlic-kissed chicken is an elegant entree for guests. Leftovers are great in casseroles and open-face sandwiches.

Sheri Sidwell, Alton, Illinois

2 quarts water

1/2 cup salt

4 bone-in chicken breast halves (12 ounces)

3/4 teaspoon pepper, divided

2 teaspoons canola oil

8 garlic cloves, peeled and thinly sliced

1 cup reduced-sodium chicken broth

1/2 cup sherry or additional reduced-sodium chicken broth

3 fresh thyme sprigs

1/4 cup butter, cubed

1 teaspoon lemon juice

1. For brine, in a large saucepan, bring water and salt to a boil. Cook and stir until salt is dissolved. Remove from the heat; cool to room temperature.

2. Place a large heavy-duty resealable plastic bag inside a second large resealable plastic bag; add chicken. Carefully pour cooled brine into the bag. Squeeze out as much air as possible; seal bags and turn to coat. Refrigerate for 1-2 hours, turning several times.

3. Drain and discard brine. Rinse chicken with cold water; pat dry. Sprinkle with 1/2 teaspoon pepper. In a large ovenproof skillet, brown the chicken in canola oil over medium heat. Bake, uncovered, at 400° for 20-25 minutes or until a meat thermometer reads 170°. Remove chicken and keep warm. Drain drippings, reserving 1 tablespoon.

4. In drippings, saute garlic for 1 minute. Add broth, sherry and thyme. Bring to a boil; cook until liquid is reduced to 1 cup. Discard thyme. Stir in the butter, lemon juice and remaining pepper. Serve with chicken.

YIELD: 4 SERVINGS.

NUTRITION FACTS: 1 serving equals 534 calories, 29 g fat (12 g saturated fat), 197 mg cholesterol, 514 mg sodium, 3 g carbohydrate, trace fiber, 60 g protein.

A+ Recipes from SCHOOLS Across America

STEAK WITH CHIPOTLE-LIME CHIMICHURRI

Steak gets a flavor kick from chimichurri. This piquant, all-purpose herb sauce is so versatile, it complements most any grilled meat, poultry or fish.

Laureen Pittman, Riverside, California

2 cups chopped fresh parsley

1-1/2 cups chopped fresh cilantro

1 small red onion, quartered

5 garlic cloves, quartered

2 chipotle peppers in adobo sauce

1/2 cup plus 1 tablespoon olive oil, divided

1/4 cup white wine vinegar

1/4 cup lime juice

1 tablespoon dried oregano

1 teaspoon grated lime peel

1-1/4 teaspoons salt, divided

3/4 teaspoon pepper, divided

2 beef flat iron steaks

1. For chimichurri, place the parsley, cilantro, onion, garlic and chipotle peppers in a food processor; cover and pulse until minced. Add 1/2 cup oil, vinegar, lime juice, oregano, lime peel, 1/2 teaspoon salt and 1/4 teaspoon pepper; cover and process until blended. Cover and refrigerate until serving.

2. Drizzle steaks with remaining oil; sprinkle with remaining salt and pepper. Grill, covered, over medium heat for 8-10 minutes on each side or until meat reaches desired doneness (for medium-rare, a meat thermometer should read 145°; medium, 160°; well-done, 170°). Thinly slice across grain; serve with chimichurri.

YIELD: 8 SERVINGS.

NUTRITION FACTS: 1 serving equals 534 calories, 29 g fat (12 g saturated fat), 197 mg cholesterol, 514 mg sodium, 3 g carbohydrate, trace fiber, 60 g protein.

BARBECUED BURGERS

I can't take all the credit for these winning burgers. My husband's uncle passed down the special barbecue sauce recipe. We love it on everything...it was only natural to use it here.

Rhoda Troyer, Glenford, Ohio

SAUCE:
1 cup ketchup
1/2 cup packed brown sugar
1/3 cup sugar
1/4 cup honey
1/4 cup molasses
2 teaspoons prepared mustard
1-1/2 teaspoons Worcestershire sauce
1/4 teaspoon salt
1/4 teaspoon Liquid Smoke
1/8 teaspoon pepper

BURGERS:
1 egg, lightly beaten
1/3 cup quick-cooking oats
1/4 teaspoon onion salt
1/4 teaspoon garlic salt
1/4 teaspoon pepper
1/8 teaspoon salt
1-1/2 pounds ground beef
6 hamburger buns, split
Toppings of your choice

1. In a small saucepan, combine the first 10 ingredients. Bring to a boil. Remove from heat. Set aside 1 cup barbecue sauce to serve with burgers.

2. In a large bowl, combine the egg, oats, 1/4 cup of remaining barbecue sauce, onion salt, garlic salt, pepper and salt. Crumble beef over mixture; mix well. Shape into six patties.

3. Grill, covered, over medium heat for 6-8 minutes on each side or until a meat thermometer reads 160°, basting with 1/2 cup barbecue sauce during the last 5 minutes. Serve on buns with toppings of your choice and reserved sauce.

YIELD: 6 SERVINGS.

NUTRITION FACTS: 1 burger equals 626 calories, 19 g fat (7 g saturated fat), 121 mg cholesterol, 1,146 mg sodium, 86 g carbohydrate, 2 g fiber, 30 g protein.

BRIE CHERRY PASTRY CUPS

These yummy bites almost taste like dessert. They are always a big hit at parties.

Marilyn McSween, Mentor, Ohio

1 sheet frozen puff pastry, thawed

1/2 cup cherry preserves

4 ounces Brie cheese, cut into 1/2-inch cubes

1/4 cup chopped pecans walnuts

2 tablespoons minced chives

1. Unfold puff pastry; cut into 36 squares. Gently press squares onto the bottoms of 36 greased miniature muffin cups.

2. Bake at 375° for 10 minutes. Using the end of a wooden spoon handle, make a 1/2-in.-deep indentation in the center of each. Bake 6-8 minutes longer or until cups are golden brown. With spoon handle, press squares down again.

3. Spoon a rounded 1/2 teaspoonful of preserves into each cup. Top with the cheese; sprinkle with nuts and chives. Bake for 3-5 minutes or until cheese is melted.

YIELD: 3 DOZEN.

NUTRITIONAL FACTS: 1 each equals 61 calories, 3 g fat (1 g saturated fat), 3 mg cholesterol, 42 mg sodium, 7 g carbohydrate, 1 g fiber, 1 g protein. DIABETIC EXCHANGES: 1/2 starch, 1/2 fat.

CHUNKY APPLE CAKE

This tender, moist cake is full of old-fashioned comfort. For a festive occasion, top with a dollop of whipped cream.

Debi Benson, Bakersfield, California

1/2 cup butter, softened

2 cups sugar

2 eggs

1/2 teaspoon vanilla extract

2 cups all-purpose flour

1-1/2 teaspoons ground cinnamon

1 teaspoon ground nutmeg

1/2 teaspoon salt

1/2 teaspoon baking soda

6 cups chopped peeled tart apples

BUTTERSCOTCH SAUCE:

1/2 cup packed brown sugar

1/4 cup butter, cubed

1/2 cup heavy whipping cream

1. In a large bowl, cream butter and sugar until light and fluffy. Add eggs, one at a time, beating well after each addition. Beat in vanilla. Combine flour, cinnamon, nutmeg, salt and baking soda; gradually add to creamed mixture and mix well (batter will be stiff). Stir in apples.

2. Spread into a greased 13-in. x 9-in. baking dish. Bake at 350° for 40-45 minutes or until top is lightly browned and springs back when lightly touched. Cool for 30 minutes before serving.

3. Meanwhile, in a small saucepan, combine the brown sugar and butter. Cook over medium heat until butter is melted. Gradually add cream. Bring to a slow boil over medium heat, stirring constantly. Remove from the heat. Serve with cake.

YIELD: 12-14 SERVINGS.

NUTRITION FACTS: 1 piece equals 365 calories, 14 g fat (8 g saturated fat), 68 mg cholesterol, 244 mg sodium, 59 g carbohydrate, 2 g fiber, 3 g protein.

PECAN TOFFEE FUDGE

This quick fudge is always popular wherever it shows up. People love the creaminess and toffee bits. Plus, it's so easy to make.

Diane Willey, Bozman, Maryland

1 teaspoon butter

1 package (8 ounces) cream cheese, softened

3-3/4 cups confectioners' sugar

6 ounces unsweetened chocolate, melted and cooled

1/4 teaspoon almond extract

Dash salt

1/4 cup coarsely chopped pecans

1/4 cup English toffee bits

1. Line a 9-in. square pan with foil and grease the foil with butter; set aside. In a large bowl, beat cream cheese until fluffy. Gradually beat in confectioners' sugar. Beat in the melted chocolate, extract and salt until smooth. Stir in pecans and toffee bits.

2. Spread into prepared pan. Cover and refrigerate overnight or until firm. Using foil, lift fudge out of pan. Gently peel off foil; cut the fudge into 1-in. squares. Store in an airtight container in the refrigerator.

YIELD: 2-1/2 POUNDS.

NUTRITIONAL FACTS: 1 piece equals 49 calories, 3 g fat (1 g saturated fat), 3 mg cholesterol, 15 mg sodium, 7 g carbohydrate, trace fiber, 1 g protein. DIABETIC EXCHANGES: 1/2 starch, 1/2 fat.

PEACHES AND CREAM TORTE

Here is a dessert I make when I'm craving something cool and fruity. It's a lovely ending to any meal. The cream cheese adds zing to the fluffy filling.

Elva Roberts, Summerside, Prince Edward Island

2 cups graham cracker crumbs

1/3 cup packed brown sugar

1/2 cup butter, melted

FILLING:

1 can (29 ounces) sliced peaches

1-1/4 cups sugar, divided

2 tablespoons cornstarch

1 package (8 ounces) cream cheese, softened

2 cups heavy whipping cream

1. In a small bowl, combine graham cracker crumbs and brown sugar; stir in the butter. Set aside 1/4 cup for topping. Press remaining crumb mixture onto the bottom and 1 in. up the sides of a greased 9-in. springform pan. Place pan on a baking sheet. Bake at 350° for 10 minutes. Cool on a wire rack.

2. Drain peaches, reserving syrup in a 2-cup measuring cup. Add enough water to measure 1-1/2 cups. In a large saucepan, combine 1/4 cup sugar and cornstarch; stir in syrup mixture until smooth. Add peaches. Bring to a boil over medium heat; cook and stir for 2 minutes or until thickened. Cool to room temperature, stirring occasionally.

3. Meanwhile, in a large bowl, beat the cream cheese and the remaining sugar until smooth. In a small bowl, beat cream until stiff peaks form; fold into cream cheese mixture. Spread half of the cream cheese mixture over crust. Top with half of the peach mixture; repeat layers. Sprinkle with the reserved crumb mixture. Cover; refrigerate for 8 hours. Remove sides of pan before slicing.

YIELD: 12 SERVINGS.

NUTRITION FACTS: 1 piece equals 492 calories, 30 g fat (18 g saturated fat), 95 mg cholesterol, 217 mg sodium, 53 g carbohydrate, 1 g fiber, 3 g protein.

GRILLED JERK CHICKEN WINGS

I've been making this recipe ever since I can remember—and I always serve it at every party I give. It's so simple to fix, doesn't take a lot of ingredients or time, and is always a favorite with my guests. You can change it up for different crowds by varying the seasoning for a mild to extra-spicy kick.

Caren Adams, Fontana, California

1/2 cup Caribbean jerk seasoning

18 fresh chicken wingettes (2 to 3 pounds)

2 cups honey barbecue sauce

1/3 cup packed brown sugar

2 teaspoons prepared mustard

1 teaspoon ground ginger

1. Place jerk seasoning in a large resealable plastic bag; add chicken wings, a few at a time, and shake to coat. In a small bowl, combine the barbecue sauce, brown sugar, mustard and ginger; set aside.

2. Using long-handled tongs, moisten a paper towel with cooking oil and lightly coat the grill rack. Grill the chicken wings, covered, over medium heat or broil 4 in. from the heat for 12-16 minutes, turning occasionally.

3. Brush with sauce. Grill or broil, uncovered, 8-10 minutes longer, basting and turning several times.

YIELD: 6 SERVINGS.

EDITOR'S NOTE: Caribbean jerk seasoning may be found in the spice aisle of your grocery store.

NUTRITION FACTS: 3 pieces equals 548 calories, 24 g fat (6 g saturated fat), 113 mg cholesterol, 2,217 mg sodium, 47 g carbohydrate, trace fiber, 28 g protein.

INDEXES

General Index

This index lists the recipes by food category and major ingredients, so you can easily locate recipes that you need.

Appetizers

Bacon and Fontina Stuffed Mushrooms, 13
Bacon-Sausage Quiche Tarts, 15
Brie Cherry Pastry Cups, 245
Buffalo Wing Cheese Mold, 33
Canadian Meatballs, 9
Caramelized Onion Dip, 12
Chesapeake Crab Dip, 14
Chicken Veggie Cups, 239
Feta Cheese Balls, 8
Fruit Salsa with Cinnamon
    Tortilla Chips, 10
Gingered Cran-Orange
    Salsa over Cream Cheese, 16
Goat Cheese Spread in
    Roasted Pepper Cups, 11
Grilled Jerk Chicken Wings, 249
Grilled Sweet Potato Wedges, 39
Grilled Tandoori Chicken Kabobs, 155
Hot Bacon Cheddar Spread, 18
Huevos Diablos, 19
Jalapeno Hummus, 34
Jalapeno Popper Dip, 20
Layered Curried Cheese Spread, 30
Mango Salsa, 17
Mediterranean Artichoke and Red Pepper
    Roll-Ups, 22
Movie Theater Pretzel Rods, 25
Mozzarella Appetizer Tartlets, 27
Pear-Blue Cheese Tartlets, 24
Phyllo-Wrapped Brie with
    Sun-Dried Tomatoes, 28
Pork Canapes, 29
Pumpkin Mousse Dip, 21
Shrimp Salad Cocktails, 26
Smoky Chipotle Orange Dip, 31
Spanakopita Pinwheels, 35
Teacher's Caviar, 7
Terrific Tomato Tart, 230
Veggie Shrimp Egg Rolls, 241

Apples

California Chicken Salad, 150
Chipotle Butternut Squash Soup, 49
Chunky Apple Cake, 246
Cornucopia Salad, 75
Crunchy Apple Salad, 76
Curried Chicken Rice Salad, 104
French Apple Tart, 173
Fruit Salsa with Cinnamon
    Tortilla Chips, 10
Sausage Stuffing Muffins, 83

Apricots

Andouille-Stuffed Pork Loin, 139
Apricot-Filled Sandwich Cookies, 201
Spicy Apricot Chicken Thighs, 120
Veggie Shrimp Egg Rolls, 241

Artichokes

Artichoke & Spinach Enchiladas, 134
Mediterranean Artichoke and Red Pepper
    Roll-Ups, 22
Mushroom-Artichoke Brunch Bake, 126
Parmesan Artichoke Soup, 89

Bacon & Canadian Bacon

Bacon and Fontina Stuffed Mushrooms, 13
Bacon & Tomato-Topped Meat Loaf, 95
Bacon Cheeseburger Meatball Subs, 133
Bacon-Sausage Quiche Tarts, 15
Eggs Benedict Brunch Braid, 105
French Toast Cupcakes, 190
Hot Bacon Cheddar Spread, 18
Pasta Arrabbiata (Angry Pasta), 124

Bananas

Banana Mocha-Chip Muffins, 203
Grilled Bananas Foster, 175
I'm Stuffed French Toast, 138
Marshmallow Monkey Business, 219

Beans

Black-Eyed Pea Spinach Salad, 67
Chipotle-Black Bean Chili, 151
Cowboy Baked Beans, 60
Jalapeno Hummus, 34
N'Orleans Shrimp with Beans & Rice, 144
Quinoa and Black Bean Salad, 59
Teacher's Caviar, 7
White Bean Tuna Salad, 116
White Chicken Chili, 113

Beef (also see Ground Beef)

Asian Steak Skewers, 223
Bacon Cheeseburger Meatball Subs, 133
Beef Stew with Sesame Seed Biscuits, 102
Chipotle-Black Bean Chili, 151
French Beef Stew, 109
Maple-Glazed Corned Beef, 137
Onion Beef au Jus, 226
Reuben Pasta Salad, 77
Special Sauerbraten, 143
Steak with Chipotle-Lime Chimichurri, 243
Triple Pepper Steak Sandwiches, 101
Vegetable Beef Stew, 163

Blueberries

Blueberry Cornmeal Muffins, 200
Blueberry Spinach Salad, 38
Elegant Fresh Berry Tart, 180
I'm Stuffed French Toast, 138
Lemon Curd Chiffon Pie, 176

Breads

Banana Mocha-Chip Muffins, 203
Blueberry Cornmeal Muffins, 200
Dill and Chive Bread, 57
Garlic Asiago Bread, 62
Garlic Cheese Breadsticks, 68
Get Up & Go Muffins, 209
Ham and Cheddar Scones, 91
Honey & Oat Yeast Bread, 215
Movie Theater Pretzel Rods, 25
Raspberry-Cream Cheese
    Ladder Loaves, 220
Southwestern Corn Bread, 81

Breakfast & Brunch

Bacon-Sausage Quiche Tarts, 15
Banana Mocha-Chip Muffins, 203
Broccoli Quiche, 98
Caramel-Pecan French Toast Bake, 100
Eggs Benedict Brunch Braid, 105
Get Up & Go Muffins, 209
Ham and Cheddar Scones, 91
I'm Stuffed French Toast, 138
Mushroom-Artichoke Brunch Bake, 126
Peanut Butter Oatmeal-Chip Cookies, 222
Pepperoni Spinach Quiche, 232
Raspberry-Cream Cheese
    Ladder Loaves, 220

Broccoli

Chicken Tortellini in Cream Sauce, 96
Chicken Veggie Cups, 239
Cranberry Broccoli Slaw, 42

Cakes & Cupcakes

Almond Cake with Raspberry Sauce, 167
Carrot Cake Cupcakes, 181
Chocolate Ganache Cake with Raspberry
    Sauce, 194
Chocolate Ganache Peanut Butter
    Cupcakes, 183
Chocolate Raspberry Cupcakes, 207
Chunky Apple Cake, 246
Devil's Food Cake, 178
French Toast Cupcakes, 190
Frosted Walnut Brownie Cups, 211
Miniature Pumpkin Cake Towers, 170
Old-Fashioned Butterscotch Cake with
    Penuche Frosting, 206
Peaches & Cream Jelly Roll, 189
Pina Colada Cake, 172
Strawberry Jam Cake, 192
Strawberry-Lemon Crepe Cake, 177
White Chocolate-Coconut Layer Cake, 197

Candy

Caramel Nut-Chocolate Popcorn Cones, 208
Lime-in-the-Coconut Almond Bark, 36
Macadamia-Coconut Candy Clusters, 23
Pecan Toffee Fudge, 247
Sweet & Salty Candy, 217
Turtle Chips, 32

Carrots

Beef Stew with Sesame Seed Biscuits, 102
Carrot Cake Cupcakes, 181
Chipotle Butternut Squash Soup, 49

Colorful Chicken 'n' Squash Soup, 225
French Beef Stew, 109
Harvest Pumpkin Soup, 66
Veggie Shrimp Egg Rolls, 241

Cheese
Argentine Lasagna, 146
Artichoke & Spinach Enchiladas, 134
Au Gratin Potatoes with Green Chiles, 43
Bacon and Fontina Stuffed
    Mushrooms, 13
Bacon Cheeseburger Meatball Subs, 133
Bacon-Sausage Quiche Tarts, 15
Baked Greek Ratatouille, 37
Barbecue Pork and Penne Skillet, 236
BBQ Chicken Pizzas, 108
Blueberry Spinach Salad, 38
Brie Cherry Pastry Cups, 245
Broccoli Quiche, 98
Buffalo Wing Cheese Mold, 33
Butternut Squash Enchiladas, 149
Cheesy Mac & Cheese, 123
Chicken & Tortellini Spinach Salad, 156
Chicken Tortellini in Cream Sauce, 96
Crunchy Apple Salad, 76
Feta Cheese Balls, 8
Four-Cheese Baked Ziti, 227
Garlic Asiago Bread, 62
Garlic Cheese Breadsticks, 68
Goat Cheese Spread in Roasted
    Pepper Cups, 11
Greek Salad with Green Grapes, 56
Grilled Vegetable Sandwich, 238
Ham and Cheddar Scones, 91
Hot Bacon Cheddar Spread, 18
Mediterranean Artichoke and Red Pepper
    Roll-Ups, 22
Mozzarella Appetizer Tartlets, 27
Mushroom-Artichoke Brunch Bake, 126
Onion Beef Au Jus, 226
Orzo with Spinach and Pine Nuts, 80
Parmesan Artichoke Soup, 89
Parmesan Pork Cutlets, 97
Pear-Blue Cheese Tartlets, 24
Pepperoni Lasagna Roll-Ups, 129
Pepperoni Spinach Quiche, 232
Phyllo-Wrapped Brie with Sun-Dried
    Tomatoes, 28
Portobello Risotto with Mascarpone, 61
Reuben Pasta Salad, 77
Ricotta Gnocchi with Spinach &
    Gorgonzola, 127
Roasted Vegetable Pasta Salad, 44
Roasted Vegetable Quesadillas, 160
Shrimp Mac & Cheese Salad, 132
Shrimp-Stuffed Poblano Peppers, 125
Spanakopita Pinwheels, 35
Spinach Artichoke Pizza, 107
Spinach Souffle, 48
Sue's Cream of Baked Potato Soup, 46
Sweet Pepper Sandwiches, 231
Swiss Sweet Onion Casserole, 40
Terrific Tomato Tart, 230
Thai Chicken Pizza, 93

Turkey Cordon Bleu with
    Alfredo Sauce, 136
Tuscan Burgers with Pesto Mayo, 141

Cheesecakes
Mocha Chocolate Chip Cheesecake, 188
Peppermint Cheesecake, 179
Raspberry Almond Cheesecake, 187
Toffee Cheesecake Tiramisu, 193

Cherries
Black Forest Fudge Sauce, 182
Brie Cherry Pastry Cups, 245
Double Cherry Pie, 185
Pork Tenderloin with Dried Cherries, 94
White Chocolate Mousse Cherry Pie, 229

Chicken (also see Turkey)
BBQ Chicken Pizzas, 108
Buffalo Wing Cheese Mold, 33
California Chicken Salad, 150
Chicken & Tortellini Spinach Salad, 156
Chicken Marsala Lasagna, 106
Chicken Tortellini in Cream Sauce, 96
Chicken Veggie Cups, 239
Colorful Chicken 'n' Squash Soup, 225
Curried Chicken Rice Salad, 104
Curried Chicken Sloppy Joes, 153
Curried Chicken Soup, 50
Grilled Jerk Chicken Wings, 249
Grilled Rosemary Chicken, 114
Grilled Tandoori Chicken Kabobs, 155
Herbed Lemon Chicken, 118
Italian Peasant Soup, 237
Italian Wedding Soup, 135
Mango-Chutney Chicken Salad, 166
Mediterranean Chicken Soup, 70
Pesto Chicken Salad Sandwiches, 128
Roasted Chicken with Garlic-Sherry
    Sauce, 242
Savory Oven-Fried Chicken, 158
Spicy Apricot Chicken Thighs, 120
Spicy Coconut Chicken Strips, 122
Sunday Paella, 130
Thai Chicken Lettuce Wraps, 162
Thai Chicken Pizza, 93
White Chicken Chili, 113

Chili
Chipotle-Black Bean Chili, 151
White Chicken Chili, 113

Chocolate (also see White Chocolate)
Apricot-Filled Sandwich Cookies, 201
Banana Mocha-Chip Muffins, 203
Black Forest Fudge Sauce, 182
Caramel Nut-Chocolate Popcorn
    Cones, 208
Chocolate-Amaretto Mousse Pie, 168
Chocolate Ganache Cake with Raspberry
    Sauce, 194
Chocolate Ganache Peanut Butter
    Cupcakes, 183
Chocolate-Hazelnut Cream Pie, 195

Chocolate Raspberry Cupcakes, 207
Devil's Food Cake, 178
Dipped Brownie Pops, 205
Frosted Walnut Brownie Cups, 211
Hazelnut Espresso Fingers in
    Chocolate, 212
Italian Rainbow Cookies, 210
Marshmallow Monkey Business, 219
Peanut Butter Oatmeal-Chip Cookies, 222
Pecan Toffee Fudge, 247
Peppermint Cheesecake, 179
Sweet & Salty Candy, 217
Turtle Chips, 32

Coconut
Any Holiday Sprinkle Cookies, 199
Cran-Orange Oatmeal Cookies, 204
Macadamia-Coconut Candy Clusters, 23
White Chocolate-Coconut Layer Cake, 197

Coffee
Banana Mocha-Chip Muffins, 203
Chocolate Ganache Peanut Butter
    Cupcakes, 183
Chocolate Raspberry Cupcakes, 207
Hazelnut Espresso Fingers in Chocolate,
    212
Mocha Chocolate Chip Cheesecake, 188
Toffee Cheesecake Tiramisu, 193

Cookies & Bars
Any Holiday Sprinkle Cookies, 199
Apricot-Filled Sandwich Cookies, 201
Chocolate Malt Ball Cookies, 202
Cran-Orange Oatmeal Cookies, 204
Cranberry Bars with Cream Cheese
    Frosting, 184
Dipped Brownie Pops, 205
Full-of-Goodness Oatmeal Cookies, 198
Hazelnut Espresso Fingers in
    Chocolate, 212
Italian Rainbow Cookies, 210
Lemon Cornmeal Cookies, 216
Oatmeal Surprise Cookies, 228
Orange Sandwich Cookies, 186
Peanut Butter Oatmeal-Chip Cookies, 222
Raspberry-Almond Thumbprint
    Cookies, 214
Raspberry Pecan Squares, 213
White Chocolate Cranberry Biscotti, 218

Corn & Cornmeal
Blueberry Cornmeal Muffins, 200
Fiesta Corn Salad, 54
Lemon Cornmeal Cookies, 216
Southwestern Corn Bread, 81

Cranberries
Baked Cranberry Peach Sauce, 88
Chicken & Tortellini Spinach Salad, 156
Cran-Orange Oatmeal Cookies, 204
Cranberry Ambrosia Salad, 72

Cranberries (continued)

Cranberry Bars with Cream Cheese Frosting, 184
Cranberry Broccoli Slaw, 42
Cranberry Rice with Caramelized Onions, 240
Gingered Cran-Orange Salsa over Cream Cheese, 16
Sausage Stuffing Muffins, 83
White Chocolate Cranberry Biscotti, 218

Desserts (also see Cakes & Cupcakes; Candy; Cheesecakes; Cookies & Bars; Pies & Tarts)

Baked Cranberry Peach Sauce, 88
Black Forest Fudge Sauce, 182
Grilled Bananas Foster, 175
Marshmallow Monkey Business, 219
Peaches and Cream Torte, 248
Peter Peter Pumpkin Whoopies, 196
Pumpkin Mousse Dip, 21
Raspberries with White Chocolate Sauce and Sugared Almonds, 171
S'mores on a Stick, 221

Eggplant

Baked Greek Ratatouille, 37
Pasta with Eggplant Sauce, 154
Ricotta Gnocchi with Spinach & Gorgonzola, 127
Roasted Vegetable Pasta Salad, 44
Vegetable Beef Stew, 163

Eggs

Bacon-Sausage Quiche Tarts, 15
Broccoli Quiche, 98
Eggs Benedict Brunch Braid, 105
Huevos Diablos, 19
Mushroom-Artichoke Brunch Bake, 126
Pepperoni Spinach Quiche, 232
Spinach Souffle, 48

Fish (see Seafood)

Fruit (also see individual listings)

California Chicken Salad, 150
Elegant Fresh Berry Tart, 180
Fruit Salsa with Cinnamon Tortilla Chips, 10
Full-of-Goodness Oatmeal Cookies, 198
Get Up & Go Muffins, 209
Greek Salad with Green Grapes, 56
Layered Curried Cheese Spread, 30
Orange & Blackberry Panther Tart, 169

Ground Beef

Italian Peasant Soup, 237
Orzo with Spinach and Pine Nuts, 80
Spinach Artichoke Pizza, 107
Weeknight Pasta Supper, 165

Ham

Chicken Marsala Lasagna, 106
Ham and Cheddar Scones, 91

Lemon & Lime

Herbed Lemon Chicken, 118
Key Lime Pie with Shortbread Macadamia Crust, 174
Lemon Cornmeal Cookies, 216
Lemon Curd Chiffon Pie, 176
Lemony Vegetables and Pasta, 234
Pork Tenderloin with Cilantro-Lime Pesto, 131
Steak with Chipotle-Lime Chimichurri, 243
Strawberry-Lemon Crepe Cake, 177

Main Dishes

Andouille-Stuffed Pork Loin, 139
Argentine Lasagna, 146
Artichoke & Spinach Enchiladas, 134
Asian Steak Skewers, 223
Bacon & Tomato-Topped Meat Loaf, 95
Bacon Cheeseburger Meatball Subs, 133
Barbecue Pork and Penne Skillet, 236
Barbecued Burgers, 244
Bayou Okra Sausage Stew, 145
BBQ Chicken Pizzas, 108
BBQ Hoedown Tacos, 142
Beef Stew with Sesame Seed Biscuits, 102
Blackened Catfish with Mango Avocado Salsa, 147
Butternut Squash Enchiladas, 149
Cajun Shrimp, 140
Cheese Tortellini and Kale Soup, 148
Cheesy Mac & Cheese, 123
Chicken & Tortellini Spinach Salad, 156
Chicken Marsala Lasagna, 106
Chicken Tortellini in Cream Sauce, 96
Chipotle-Black Bean Chili, 151
Colorful Chicken 'n' Squash Soup, 225
Creamy Clam Linguine, 103
Creamy Pesto Shrimp Linguine, 110
Curried Chicken Rice Salad, 104
Four-Cheese Baked Ziti, 227
French Beef Stew, 109
Grilled Rosemary Chicken, 114
Grilled Salmon Kyoto, 111
Grilled Tandoori Chicken Kabobs, 155
Grilled Vegetable Sandwich, 238
Grilled Whiskey Chops, 112
Herbed Lemon Chicken, 118
Herbed Salmon Fillets, 152
Italian Peasant Soup, 237
Italian Wedding Soup, 135
Lemony Vegetables and Pasta, 234
Lime-Cilantro Marinade for Chicken, 164
Maple-Glazed Corned Beef, 137
Mushroom-Artichoke Brunch Bake, 126
N'Orleans Shrimp with Beans & Rice, 144
Onion Beef Au Jus, 226
Parmesan Pork Cutlets, 97
Pasta Arrabbiata (Angry Pasta), 124
Pasta with Eggplant Sauce, 154
Peachy Shrimp Tacos, 235
Pepperoni Lasagna Roll-ups, 129
Pepperoni Spinach Quiche, 232
Pesto Chicken Salad Sandwiches, 128
Pork Medallions with Squash & Greens, 157

Pork Tenderloin with Cilantro-Lime Pesto, 131
Pork Tenderloin with Dried Cherries, 94
Ricotta Gnocchi with Spinach & Gorgonzola, 127
Roasted Chicken with Garlic-Sherry Sauce, 242
Roasted Vegetable Quesadillas, 160
Savory Oven-Fried Chicken, 158
Shrimp-Stuffed Poblano Peppers, 125
Slow-Cooked Pulled Pork, 99
Southwestern Shrimp with Salsa, 119
Special Sauerbraten, 143
Spicy Apricot Chicken Thighs, 120
Spicy Chicken Sausage Lettuce Wraps, 159
Spicy Coconut Chicken Strips, 122
Spicy Pork with Ginger-Maple Sauce, 233
Spinach Artichoke Pizza, 107
Steak with Chipotle-Lime Chimichurri, 243
Sunday Paella, 130
Sweet & Sassy Baby Back Ribs, 115
Thai Chicken Lettuce Wraps, 162
Thai Chicken Pizza, 93
Triple Pepper Steak Sandwiches, 101
Turkey Cordon Bleu with Alfredo Sauce, 136
Tuscan Burgers with Pesto Mayo, 141
Tuscan Portobello Stew, 161
Tuscan Sausage and Potato Soup, 117
Vegetable Beef Stew, 163
Weeknight Pasta Supper, 165
White Chicken Chili, 113

Mango

Blackened Catfish with Mango Avocado Salsa, 147
Mango-Chutney Chicken Salad, 166
Mango Salsa, 17

Mushrooms

Bacon and Fontina Stuffed Mushrooms, 13
French Beef Stew, 109
Hungarian Mushroom Soup, 79
Portobello Risotto with Mascarpone, 61
Tuscan Portobello Stew, 161
Weeknight Pasta Supper, 165

Nuts

Almond Cake with Raspberry Sauce, 167
Caramel Nut-Chocolate Popcorn Cones, 208
Caramel-Pecan French Toast Bake, 100
Chocolate-Amaretto Mousse Pie, 168
Chocolate-Hazelnut Cream Pie, 195
Crunchy Apple Salad, 76
Frosted Walnut Brownie Cups, 211
Hazelnut Espresso Fingers in Chocolate, 212
Key Lime Pie with Shortbread Macadamia Crust, 174
Macadamia-Coconut Candy Clusters, 23
Marshmallow Monkey Business, 219
Orzo with Spinach and Pine Nuts, 80
Pecan Rice Pilaf, 55
Pecan Toffee Fudge, 247

Raspberries with White Chocolate Sauce and Sugared Almonds, 171
Raspberry Pecan Squares, 213
Sesame Spaghetti Salad with Peanuts, 82
Strawberry & Pecan Salad, 85

Oats
Barbecued Burgers, 244
Chocolate Malt Ball Cookies, 202
Cran-Orange Oatmeal Cookies, 204
Full-of-Goodness Oatmeal Cookies, 198
Get Up & Go Muffins, 209
Honey & Oat Yeast Bread, 215
Oatmeal Surprise Cookies, 228
Peanut Butter Oatmeal-Chip Cookies, 222

Onions
Caramelized Onion Dip, 12
Cranberry Rice with Caramelized Onions, 240
French Onion Soup, 58
Onion Beef Au Jus, 226
Swiss Sweet Onion Casserole, 40

Oranges
Cran-Orange Oatmeal Cookies, 204
Gingered Cran-Orange Salsa over Cream Cheese, 16
Orange & Blackberry Panther Tart, 169
Orange Sandwich Cookies, 186
Smoky Chipotle Orange Dip, 31

Pasta & Noodles
Argentine Lasagna, 146
Barbecue Pork and Penne Skillet, 236
Basil Tomato Soup with Orzo, 41
California Chicken Salad, 150
Cheese Tortellini and Kale Soup, 148
Cheesy Mac & Cheese, 123
Chicken & Tortellini Spinach Salad, 156
Chicken Marsala Lasagna, 106
Chicken Tortellini in Cream Sauce, 96
Creamy Clam Linguine, 103
Creamy Pesto Shrimp Linguine, 110
Four-Cheese Baked Ziti, 227
Italian Sausage Soup, 69
Italian Wedding Soup, 135
Lemony Vegetables and Pasta, 234
Mediterranean Chicken Soup, 70
Mediterranean Pasta Salad, 78
Orzo with Spinach and Pine Nuts, 80
Pasta Arrabbiata (Angry Pasta), 124
Pasta with Eggplant Sauce, 154
Pepperoni Lasagna Roll-Ups, 129
Reuben Pasta Salad, 77
Roasted Vegetable Pasta Salad, 44
Sesame Spaghetti Salad with Peanuts, 82
Shrimp Mac & Cheese Salad, 132
Spicy Couscous & Tomato Soup, 52
Weeknight Pasta Supper, 165

Peaches
Baked Cranberry Peach Sauce, 88
Peaches & Cream Jelly Roll, 189

Peaches and Cream Torte, 248
Peachy Shrimp Tacos, 235
White Chocolate-Coconut Layer Cake, 197

Peanut Butter
Chocolate Ganache Peanut Butter Cupcakes, 183
Peanut Butter Oatmeal-Chip Cookies, 222
Spicy Coconut Chicken Strips, 122
Thai Chicken Pizza, 93

Pears
Brandy Pear Pie, 191
Pear-Blue Cheese Tartlets, 24

Peppers
Chipotle-Black Bean Chili, 151
Chipotle Butternut Squash Soup, 49
Goat Cheese Spread in Roasted Pepper Cups, 11
Grilled Vegetable Sandwich, 238
Huevos Diablos, 19
Jalapeno Hummus, 34
Jalapeno Popper Dip, 20
Mediterranean Artichoke and Red Pepper Roll-Ups, 22
Roasted Vegetable Pasta Salad, 44
Roasted Vegetable Quesadillas, 160
Shrimp-Stuffed Poblano Peppers, 125
Steak with Chipotle-Lime Chimichurri, 243
Sweet Pepper Sandwiches, 231
Triple Pepper Steak Sandwiches, 101

Pies & Tarts
Brandy Pear Pie, 191
Chocolate-Amaretto Mousse Pie, 168
Chocolate-Hazelnut Cream Pie, 195
Double Cherry Pie, 185
Elegant Fresh Berry Tart, 180
French Apple Tart, 173
Key Lime Pie with Shortbread Macadamia Crust, 174
Lemon Curd Chiffon Pie, 176
Orange & Blackberry Panther Tart, 169
White Chocolate Mousse Cherry Pie, 229

Pineapple
Curried Fried Rice with Pineapple, 64
Pina Colada Cake, 172

Pork (also see Ham; Sausage)
Andouille-Stuffed Pork Loin, 139
Bacon Cheeseburger Meatball Subs, 133
Barbecue Pork and Penne Skillet, 236
Grilled Whiskey Chops, 112
Hot and Sour Soup, 45
Parmesan Pork Cutlets, 97
Pork Canapes, 29
Pork Medallions with Squash & Greens, 157
Pork Tenderloin with Cilantro-Lime Pesto, 131
Pork Tenderloin with Dried Cherries, 94
Slow-Cooked Pulled Pork, 99

Spicy Pork with Ginger-Maple Sauce, 233
Sweet & Sassy Baby Back Ribs, 115

Potatoes
Au Gratin Potatoes with Green Chiles, 43
Garden Fresh Potato Salad, 87
Garden Mashed Potatoes, 71
Halibut Chowder, 65
Ricotta Gnocchi with Spinach & Gorgonzola, 127
Roasted Vegetable Quesadillas, 160
Sue's Cream of Baked Potato Soup, 46
Three Potato Salad, 53
Tuscan Sausage and Potato Soup, 117

Pumpkin
Harvest Pumpkin Soup, 66
Miniature Pumpkin Cake Towers, 170
Peter Peter Pumpkin Whoopies, 196
Pumpkin Mousse Dip, 21

Raspberries
Almond Cake with Raspberry Sauce, 167
Chocolate Ganache Cake with Raspberry Sauce, 194
Chocolate Raspberry Cupcakes, 207
Elegant Fresh Berry Tart, 180
Fruit Salsa with Cinnamon Tortilla Chips, 10
Lemon Curd Chiffon Pie, 176
Raspberries with White Chocolate Sauce and Sugared Almonds, 171
Raspberry Almond Cheesecake, 187
Raspberry-Almond Thumbprint Cookies, 214
Raspberry-Cream Cheese Ladder Loaves, 220
Raspberry Pecan Squares, 213

Rice
Cranberry Rice with Caramelized Onions, 240
Curried Chicken Rice Salad, 104
Curried Fried Rice with Pineapple, 64
Deep-Fried Rice Balls, 84
N'Orleans Shrimp with Beans & Rice, 144
Pecan Rice Pilaf, 55
Portobello Risotto with Mascarpone, 61
Sunday Paella, 130
Swiss Sweet Onion Casserole, 40

Salads
Black-Eyed Pea Spinach Salad, 67
Blueberry Spinach Salad, 38
California Chicken Salad, 150
Chicken & Tortellini Spinach Salad, 156
Cilantro Couscous Salad, 47
Confetti Jicama Salad, 90
Cornucopia Salad, 75
Cranberry Ambrosia Salad, 72
Cranberry Broccoli Slaw, 42
Crunchy Apple Salad, 76
Crunchy Romaine Strawberry Salad, 224
Curried Chicken Rice Salad, 104

Salads (continued)
Fiesta Corn Salad, 54
Garden Fresh Potato Salad, 87
Greek Salad with Green Grapes, 56
Lime-Cilantro Marinade for Chicken, 164
Mango-Chutney Chicken Salad, 166
Mediterranean Pasta Salad, 78
Mozzarella Appetizer Tartlets, 27
Orzo with Spinach and Pine Nuts, 80
Quinoa and Black Bean Salad, 59
Reuben Pasta Salad, 77
Roasted Vegetable Pasta Salad, 44
Sesame Spaghetti Salad with Peanuts, 82
Shrimp Mac & Cheese Salad, 132
Spicy Cucumber Salad, 51
Strawberry & Pecan Salad, 85
Thai Chicken Lettuce Wraps, 162
Three Potato Salad, 53
Tossed Salad with Cilantro Vinaigrette, 86
White Bean Tuna Salad, 116

Sausage
Andouille-Stuffed Pork Loin, 139
Bacon & Tomato-Topped Meat Loaf, 95
Bacon-Sausage Quiche Tarts, 15
Bayou Okra Sausage Stew, 145
Canadian Meatballs, 9
Cheese Tortellini and Kale Soup, 148
Italian Peasant Soup, 237
Italian Sausage Soup, 69
Italian Wedding Soup, 135
Pepperoni Lasagna Roll-Ups, 129
Pepperoni Spinach Quiche, 232
Sausage Stuffing Muffins, 83
Spicy Chicken Sausage Lettuce Wraps, 159
Sunday Paella, 130
Tuscan Sausage and Potato Soup, 117

Seafood
Blackened Catfish with Mango Avocado
  Salsa, 147
Cajun Shrimp, 140
Chesapeake Crab Dip, 14
Crab Soup with Sherry, 63
Creamy Clam Linguine, 103
Creamy Pesto Shrimp Linguine, 110
Grilled Salmon Kyoto, 111
Halibut Chowder, 65
Herbed Salmon Fillets, 152
N'Orleans Shrimp with Beans & Rice, 144
Peachy Shrimp Tacos, 235
Shrimp Mac & Cheese Salad, 132
Shrimp Salad Cocktails, 26
Shrimp-Stuffed Poblano Peppers, 125
Southwestern Shrimp with Salsa, 119
Sunday Paella, 130
Veggie Shrimp Egg Rolls, 241
White Bean Tuna Salad, 116

Side Dishes
Au Gratin Potatoes with Green Chiles, 43
Baked Greek Ratatouille, 37
Cheesy Mac & Cheese, 123
Cowboy Baked Beans, 60

Garden Mashed Potatoes, 71
Grilled Sweet Potato Wedges, 39
Orzo with Spinach and Pine Nuts, 80
Spinach Souffle, 48
Swiss Sweet Onion Casserole, 40

Soups & Chili
Basil Tomato Soup with Orzo, 41
Cheese Tortellini and Kale Soup, 148
Chipotle Butternut Squash Soup, 49
Colorful Chicken 'n' Squash Soup, 225
Crab Soup with Sherry, 63
Curried Chicken Soup, 50
Easy Gazpacho, 73
French Onion Soup, 58
Halibut Chowder, 65
Harvest Pumpkin Soup, 66
Herbed Tomato Bisque, 74
Hot and Sour Soup, 45
Hungarian Mushroom Soup, 79
Italian Peasant Soup, 237
Italian Sausage Soup, 69
Italian Wedding Soup, 135
Mediterranean Chicken Soup, 70
Parmesan Artichoke Soup, 89
Spicy Couscous & Tomato Soup, 52
Sue's Cream of Baked Potato Soup, 46
Sweet Potato Soup, 92
Tuscan Sausage and Potato Soup, 117

Spinach
Argentine Lasagna, 146
Artichoke & Spinach Enchiladas, 134
Black-Eyed Pea Spinach Salad, 67
Blueberry Spinach Salad, 38
Chicken & Tortellini Spinach Salad, 156
Chicken Marsala Lasagna, 106
Italian Peasant Soup, 237
Orzo with Spinach and Pine Nuts, 80
Pepperoni Spinach Quiche, 232
Ricotta Gnocchi with Spinach &
  Gorgonzola, 127
Spanakopita Pinwheels, 35
Spinach Artichoke Pizza, 107
Spinach Souffle, 48
Weeknight Pasta Supper, 165

Strawberries
Elegant Fresh Berry Tart, 180
Fruit Salsa with Cinnamon Tortilla Chips, 10
I'm Stuffed French Toast, 138
Lemon Curd Chiffon Pie, 176
Strawberry & Pecan Salad, 85
Strawberry Jam Cake, 192
Strawberry-Lemon Crepe Cake, 177

Sweet Potatoes
Grilled Sweet Potato Wedges, 39
Sweet Potato Soup, 92
Three Potato Salad, 53

Tomatoes
Bacon & Tomato-Topped Meat Loaf, 95
Baked Greek Ratatouille, 37

Basil Tomato Soup with Orzo, 41
Easy Gazpacho, 73
Herbed Tomato Bisque, 74
Phyllo-Wrapped Brie with Sun-Dried
  Tomatoes, 28
Southwestern Shrimp with Salsa, 119
Terrific Tomato Tart, 230

Turkey
Turkey Cordon Bleu with Alfredo
  Sauce, 136
Weeknight Pasta Supper, 165

Vegetables
Bayou Okra Sausage Stew, 145
Confetti Jicama Salad, 90
Lemony Vegetables and Pasta, 234
Spicy Cucumber Salad, 51
Vegetable Beef Stew, 163

Vegetarian
Artichoke & Spinach Enchiladas, 134
Baked Greek Ratatouille, 37
Butternut Squash Enchiladas, 149
Easy Gazpacho, 73
Four-Cheese Baked Ziti, 227
Grilled Vegetable Sandwich, 238
Huevos Diablos, 19
Mediterranean Artichoke and Red Pepper
  Roll-Ups, 22
Mushroom-Artichoke Brunch Bake, 126
Pasta with Eggplant Sauce, 154
Ricotta Gnocchi with Spinach &
  Gorgonzola, 127
Roasted Vegetable Quesadillas, 160
Spicy Couscous & Tomato Soup, 52
Spinach Artichoke Pizza, 107
Spinach Souffle, 48
Sweet Pepper Sandwiches, 231
Terrific Tomato Tart, 230
Tuscan Portobello Stew, 161

White Chocolate
Cranberry Bars with Cream Cheese
  Frosting, 184
Dipped Brownie Pops, 205
Lemon Cornmeal Cookies, 216
Lime-in-the-Coconut Almond Bark, 36
Macadamia-Coconut Candy Clusters, 23
Raspberries with White Chocolate Sauce
  and Sugared Almonds, 171
White Chocolate-Coconut Layer Cake, 197
White Chocolate Cranberry Biscotti, 218
White Chocolate Mousse Cherry Pie, 229

Zucchini & Squash
Baked Greek Ratatouille, 37
Butternut Squash Enchiladas, 149
Chipotle Butternut Squash Soup, 49
Colorful Chicken 'n' Squash Soup, 225
Grilled Vegetable Sandwich, 238
Pork Medallions with Squash & Greens, 157
Roasted Vegetable Quesadillas, 160
Spicy Chicken Sausage Lettuce Wraps, 159

Alphabetical Index

This index lists every recipe in alphabetical order, so you can easily find your favorite recipes.

A

Almond Cake with Raspberry Sauce, 167
Andouille-Stuffed Pork Loin, 139
Any Holiday Sprinkle Cookies, 199
Apricot-Filled Sandwich Cookies, 201
Argentine Lasagna, 146
Artichoke & Spinach Enchiladas, 134
Asian Steak Skewers, 223
Au Gratin Potatoes with Green Chiles, 43

B

Bacon and Fontina Stuffed Mushrooms, 13
Bacon & Tomato-Topped Meat Loaf, 95
Bacon Cheeseburger Meatball Subs, 133
Bacon-Sausage Quiche Tarts, 15
Baked Cranberry Peach Sauce, 88
Baked Greek Ratatouille, 37
Banana Mocha-Chip Muffins, 203
Barbecue Pork and Penne Skillet, 236
Barbecued Burgers, 244
Basil Tomato Soup with Orzo, 41
Bayou Okra Sausage Stew, 145
BBQ Chicken Pizzas, 108
BBQ Hoedown Tacos, 142
Beef Stew with Sesame Seed Biscuits, 102
Black-Eyed Pea Spinach Salad, 67
Black Forest Fudge Sauce, 182
Blackened Catfish with Mango Avocado Salsa, 147
Blueberry Cornmeal Muffins, 200
Blueberry Spinach Salad, 38
Brandy Pear Pie, 191
Brie Cherry Pastry Cups, 245
Broccoli Quiche, 98
Buffalo Wing Cheese Mold, 33
Butternut Squash Enchiladas, 149

C

Cajun Shrimp, 140
California Chicken Salad, 150
Canadian Meatballs, 9
Caramel Nut-Chocolate Popcorn Cones, 208
Caramel-Pecan French Toast Bake, 100
Caramelized Onion Dip, 12
Carrot Cake Cupcakes, 181
Cheese Tortellini and Kale Soup, 148
Cheesy Mac & Cheese, 123
Chesapeake Crab Dip, 14
Chicken & Tortellini Spinach Salad, 156
Chicken Marsala Lasagna, 106

Chicken Tortellini in Cream Sauce, 96
Chicken Veggie Cups, 239
Chipotle-Black Bean Chili, 151
Chipotle Butternut Squash Soup, 49
Chocolate-Amaretto Mousse Pie, 168
Chocolate Ganache Cake with Raspberry Sauce, 194
Chocolate Ganache Peanut Butter Cupcakes, 183
Chocolate-Hazelnut Cream Pie, 195
Chocolate Malt Ball Cookies, 202
Chocolate Raspberry Cupcakes, 207
Chunky Apple Cake, 246
Cilantro Couscous Salad, 47
Colorful Chicken 'n' Squash Soup, 225
Confetti Jicama Salad, 90
Cornucopia Salad, 75
Cowboy Baked Beans, 60
Crab Soup with Sherry, 63
Cran-Orange Oatmeal Cookies, 204
Cranberry Ambrosia Salad, 72
Cranberry Bars with Cream Cheese Frosting, 184
Cranberry Broccoli Slaw, 42
Cranberry Rice with Caramelized Onions, 240
Creamy Clam Linguine, 103
Creamy Pesto Shrimp Linguine, 110
Crunchy Apple Salad, 76
Crunchy Romaine Strawberry Salad, 224
Curried Chicken Rice Salad, 104
Curried Chicken Sloppy Joes, 153
Curried Chicken Soup, 50
Curried Fried Rice with Pineapple, 64

D

Deep-Fried Rice Balls, 84
Devil's Food Cake, 178
Dill and Chive Bread, 57
Dipped Brownie Pops, 205
Double Cherry Pie, 185

E

Easy Gazpacho, 73
Eggs Benedict Brunch Braid, 105
Elegant Fresh Berry Tart, 180

F

Feta Cheese Balls, 8
Fiesta Corn Salad, 54
Four-Cheese Baked Ziti, 227
French Apple Tart, 173
French Beef Stew, 109
French Onion Soup, 58
French Toast Cupcakes, 190

Frosted Walnut Brownie Cups, 211
Fruit Salsa with Cinnamon Tortilla Chips, 10
Full-of-Goodness Oatmeal Cookies, 198

G

Garden Fresh Potato Salad, 87
Garden Mashed Potatoes, 71
Garlic Asiago Bread, 62
Garlic Cheese Breadsticks, 68
Get Up & Go Muffins, 209
Gingered Cran-Orange Salsa over Cream Cheese, 16
Goat Cheese Spread in Roasted Pepper Cups, 11
Greek Salad with Green Grapes, 56
Grilled Bananas Foster, 175
Grilled Jerk Chicken Wings, 249
Grilled Rosemary Chicken, 114
Grilled Salmon Kyoto, 111
Grilled Sweet Potato Wedges, 39
Grilled Tandoori Chicken Kabobs, 155
Grilled Vegetable Sandwich, 238
Grilled Whiskey Chops, 112

H

Halibut Chowder, 65
Ham and Cheddar Scones, 91
Harvest Pumpkin Soup, 66
Hazelnut Espresso Fingers in Chocolate, 212
Herbed Lemon Chicken, 118
Herbed Salmon Fillets, 152
Herbed Tomato Bisque, 74
Honey & Oat Yeast Bread, 215
Hot and Sour Soup, 45
Hot Bacon Cheddar Spread, 18
Huevos Diablos, 19
Hungarian Mushroom Soup, 79

I

I'm Stuffed French Toast, 138
Italian Peasant Soup, 237
Italian Rainbow Cookies, 210
Italian Sausage Soup, 69
Italian Wedding Soup, 135

J

Jalapeno Hummus, 34
Jalapeno Popper Dip, 20

K

Key Lime Pie with Shortbread Macadamia Crust, 174

L

Layered Curried Cheese Spread, 30
Lemon Cornmeal Cookies, 216
Lemon Curd Chiffon Pie, 176
Lemony Vegetables and Pasta, 234
Lime-Cilantro Marinade for Chicken, 164
Lime-in-the-Coconut Almond Bark, 36

M

Macadamia-Coconut Candy Clusters, 23
Mahogany-Glazed Mushroom
  Burgers, 121
Mango-Chutney Chicken Salad, 166
Mango Salsa, 17
Maple-Glazed Corned Beef, 137
Marshmallow Monkey Business, 219
Mediterranean Artichoke
  and Red Pepper Roll-Ups, 22
Mediterranean Chicken Soup, 70
Mediterranean Pasta Salad, 78
Miniature Pumpkin Cake Towers, 170
Mocha Chocolate Chip Cheesecake, 188
Movie Theater Pretzel Rods, 25
Mozzarella Appetizer Tartlets, 27
Mushroom-Artichoke Brunch Bake, 126

N

N'Orleans Shrimp with Beans & Rice, 144

O

Oatmeal Surprise Cookies, 228
Old-Fashioned Butterscotch
  Cake with Penuche Frosting, 206
Onion Beef Au Jus, 226
Orange & Blackberry Panther Tart, 169
Orange Sandwich Cookies, 186
Orzo with Spinach and Pine Nuts, 80

P

Parmesan Artichoke Soup, 89
Parmesan Pork Cutlets, 97
Pasta Arrabbiata (Angry Pasta), 124
Pasta with Eggplant Sauce, 154
Peaches & Cream Jelly Roll, 189
Peaches and Cream Torte, 248
Peachy Shrimp Tacos, 235
Peanut Butter Oatmeal-Chip Cookies, 222
Pear-Blue Cheese Tartlets, 24
Pecan Rice Pilaf, 55
Pecan Toffee Fudge, 247
Peppermint Cheesecake, 179
Pepperoni Lasagna Roll-Ups, 129
Pepperoni Spinach Quiche, 232
Pesto Chicken Salad Sandwiches, 128
Peter Peter Pumpkin Whoopies, 196

Phyllo-Wrapped Brie with Sun-Dried
  Tomatoes, 28
Pina Colada Cake, 172
Pork Canapes, 29
Pork Medallions with Squash & Greens, 157
Pork Tenderloin with Cilantro-Lime
  Pesto, 131
Pork Tenderloin with Dried Cherries, 94
Portobello Risotto with Mascarpone, 61
Pumpkin Mousse Dip, 21

Q

Quinoa and Black Bean Salad, 59

R

Raspberries with White Chocolate Sauce
  and Sugared Almonds, 171
Raspberry Almond Cheesecake, 187
Raspberry-Almond Thumbprint
  Cookies, 214
Raspberry-Cream Cheese Ladder
  Loaves, 220
Raspberry Pecan Squares, 213
Reuben Pasta Salad, 77
Ricotta Gnocchi with Spinach &
  Gorgonzola, 127
Roasted Chicken with Garlic-Sherry
  Sauce, 242
Roasted Vegetable Pasta Salad, 44
Roasted Vegetable Quesadillas, 160

S

Sausage Stuffing Muffins, 83
Savory Oven-Fried Chicken, 158
Sesame Spaghetti Salad with Peanuts, 82
Shrimp Mac & Cheese Salad, 132
Shrimp Salad Cocktails, 26
Shrimp-Stuffed Poblano Peppers, 125
Slow-Cooked Pulled Pork, 99
Smoky Chipotle Orange Dip, 31
S'mores on a Stick, 221
Southwestern Corn Bread, 81
Southwestern Shrimp with Salsa, 119
Spanakopita Pinwheels, 35
Special Sauerbraten, 143
Spicy Apricot Chicken Thighs, 120
Spicy Chicken Sausage Lettuce Wraps, 159
Spicy Coconut Chicken Strips, 122
Spicy Couscous & Tomato Soup, 52
Spicy Cucumber Salad, 51
Spicy Pork with Ginger-Maple Sauce, 233
Spinach Artichoke Pizza, 107
Spinach Souffle, 48
Steak with Chipotle-Lime Chimichurri, 243
Strawberry & Pecan Salad, 85
Strawberry Jam Cake, 192

Strawberry-Lemon Crepe Cake, 177
Sue's Cream of Baked Potato Soup, 46
Sunday Paella, 130
Sweet & Salty Candy, 217
Sweet & Sassy Baby Back Ribs, 115
Sweet Pepper Sandwiches, 231
Sweet Potato Soup, 92
Swiss Sweet Onion Casserole, 40

T

Teacher's Caviar, 7
Terrific Tomato Tart, 230
Thai Chicken Lettuce Wraps, 162
Thai Chicken Pizza, 93
Three Potato Salad, 53
Toffee Cheesecake Tiramisu, 193
Tossed Salad with Cilantro Vinaigrette, 86
Triple Pepper Steak Sandwiches, 101
Turkey Cordon Bleu with Alfredo
  Sauce, 136
Turtle Chips, 32
Tuscan Burgers with Pesto Mayo, 141
Tuscan Portobello Stew, 161
Tuscan Sausage and Potato Soup, 117

V

Vegetable Beef Stew, 163
Veggie Shrimp Egg Rolls, 241

W

Weeknight Pasta Supper, 165
White Bean Tuna Salad, 116
White Chicken Chili, 113
White Chocolate-Coconut Layer Cake, 197
White Chocolate Cranberry Biscotti, 218
White Chocolate Mousse Cherry Pie, 229